Metals in America's Historic Buildings

Uses and Preservation Treatments

Part I. A Historical Survey of Metals

by Margot Gayle and David W. Look, AIA

Part II. Deterioration and Methods of Preserving Metals

by John G. Waite, AIA

U.S. Department of the Interior
National Park Service
Cultural Resources
Preservation Assistance
Washington, D.C.
1992

Acknowledgements

(1992 Revision)

Appreciation is extended to the Open Space Institute for providing essential financial support for updating and publishing the second edition of **Metals in America's Historic Buildings.** Margot Gayle, President of the Friends of Cast Iron Architecture, receives special acknowledgement for her tireless efforts in helping to make the publication possible. The Friends of Cast Iron Architecture are also thanked for their long-term involvement in this publication.

Next, John G. Waite, Mesick-Cohen-Waite Architects, is credited with undertaking skillful revisions to the first edition of Metals so it once again reflects the most up-to-date technology possible for a broad audience. Martin Weaver, Director of the Center for Preservation Research, Graduate School of Architecture, Columbia University, provided valuable comments. Dennis Montagna, architectural historian in the National Park Service's Mid-Atlantic Regional Office, updated the section on the cleaning of bronze.

Staff members of the firm of Mesick-Cohen-Waite Architects, in Albany, New York provided energetic support during the review and revision process. Special thanks go to William G. Foulks, A. Patricia Hughes, and Clay S. Palazzo for their assistance with the project.

Charles Fisher, Preservation Assistance Division, National Park Service, was instrumental in initiating the revision of **Metals in America's Historic Buildings** and bringing it to a successful conclusion. Fisher was team leader for this cooperative publication project. Staff members Kay Weeks and Susan Lassale were responsible for editing the cumulative revisions; Weeks also served as liaison with graphic designer, Charles Beyl, Alexandria, Virginia, to achieve a new look for the now classic sourcebook. Finally, Dahlia Hernandez is credited with the arduous task of typing all of the Part II text, as well as the extensive changes required.

Library of Congress Cataloging in Publication Data
Metals in America's historic buildings : uses and
  preservation treatments
      p. cm.
   Includes bibliographical references.
   Contents: Pt. 1. A historical survey of metals /
by Margot Gayle and David W. Look — Pt. 2.
Deterioration and methods of preserving metals /
by John G. Waite.
   ISBN 0-16-038073-1 : $10.00
   1. Architectural metal-work—Deterioration.
2. Architectural metal-work—Conservation and
restoration. 3. Historic buildings—Conservation and
restoration. I. Gayle, Margot. Historical survey of
metals. 1992. II. Waite, John G. Deterioration and
methods of preserving. 1992.
NA3940.M47 1992
721'.0447—dc20
                                92-34883
                                   CIP

Acknowledgements

Many people have helped in a variety of ways to make this publication possible. Some have read the manuscript and made comments and suggestions. Others have given photographs or have gone out of their way to find or take desired views. Facts such as dates, names of architects and fabricators have been located or confirmed by people all over the country. Special thanks go to all the State Historic Preservation Officers and their staffs who have assisted our research. Numerous historical societies and local historians have contributed information. The Friends of Cast Iron Architecture have given exceptional cooperation and encouragement. Although space will not allow us to state how each person has helped, we would like to acknowledge the following:

Carolyn Adams
John Albers
Alden Aust, AIP
Bernard Averbuch
Steven T. Baird, AIA
Betty J. Berry
Penelope Hartshorne Batcheler
Douglas G. Bucher
William Edmund Booth
Jack E. Boucher
Fred Burdorf
Alan Burnham, FAIA
John Burns, AIA
Mario Campioli, FAIA
Elliott M. Carroll, FAIA
Orville W. Carroll
Giorgio Cavaglieri, FAIA
James A. Cohen
Deborah Cooney
Charles Cummings
H.W. Cummings
Eric Delony
Mary B. Dierickx
James L. Dillon
Cynthia Durko
George Eisenman

Eugene Ferguson
Perry Fisher
Beverly Fluty
Albeert France-Lanord
James Goode
Randy Gould
Anne Grimmer
Carol Grissom
Edward Hamilton
Margaret Hance
William J. Hawkins, III
Pamela Hawkes
Robert Haynes
Robert Hester
Thomas Hollaman, AIA
Nancy Holmes
Mary Ison
Nancy Jackson
Leslie Kenyon, AIA
Carlton Knight, III
Dr. Jerome Kruger
Elizabeth Leach
Dr. Antionette J. Lee
Ray Lindberg
Becket Logan
Kenneth Lynch

George McCue
Robert McKay
the late Harley J. McKee, FAIA
Ann Masson
Henry J. Magaziner, FAIA
Sarah A. Marusin
Sebastian Mazzola
Benjamin Mendel, Jr., AIA
John I. Mesick
Merritt K. Meyer
Earl Minton
Esther Mipaas
W. Brown Morton, III
Robert M. Organ
Nicholas Pappas, AIA
Carole Perrault
Ford Petross
Charles E. Peterson, FAIA
Veronica C. Pidala
Robert N. Pierpont
Carolyn Pitts
Dorothy Provine
Mayor Helen Putnam
Lee Roberts
Cervin Robinson
Tony Rossell
Rodris Roth
Earl Saunders

Mayor Donald Shaeffer
Stan Shaffer
Stewart Slocum
Walter Smalling, Jr.
Baird M. Smith, AIA
Cyril Stanley Smith
Jack Stokvis
Allan Stross
Sarah Sweetser
Florian Thayne
Milton Thompson
de Teel Patterson Tiller
Robert Tschaggeny
Clover Vail
Jan Van Trump
Robert M. Vogel
Judith Wagner
Diana S. Waite
Phoebe Dent Weil
Ben Whitmire
H. Weber Wilson
Herbert C. Wilson
Linda Wilson
Edmund Wittkamp
William Worthen
Karel Yasko
Arthur Ziegler

In daring to list and publicly thank the above mentioned people, we run the risk of omitting a few people; we apologize to those who have extended help which is sincerely appreciated.

Contents

Foreword

Metals in America's Historic Building was initially developed in 1980 under the direction of Lee H. Nelson, FAIA, to promote an awareness of metals in the buildings and monuments of the United States, and to make recommendations for the preservation and repair of such metals. It is intended for use by owners, architects, and building managers who are responsible for the preservation and maintenance of America's architectural heritage. When metal building components need rehabilitation or maintenance, information on proper preservation techniques for each metal and its alloys has not been readily available. What has been needed is a general reference on metals used in architecture: where they are used, how to identify them, and when to replace them. This is intended to be such a sourcebook on historic architectural metals.

Part I of this report is by Margot Gayle, President of the Friends of Cast-Iron Architecture, New York City, and by David W. Look, AIA, National Park Service historical architect. Reprinted in 1992, it presents short, illustrated surveys of the architectural metals most often used in American buildings and other architectural features such as sculpture, foundations, and "street furniture." The photographs document common uses of metals such as copper roofing, zinc statuary, cast-iron storefronts, and so forth.

Part II has been updated in 1992 by its original author, John G. Waite, partner, Mesick-Cohen-Waite, Architects, Albany, New York. It examines the questions of how architectural metals deteriorate and concentrates on the techniques available to architects and conservators in preserving and maintaining the metal components. The various metallic elements and their alloys illustrated in Part I are treated individually in Part II according to their deterioration patterns and appropriate preservation treatments.

Taken together, the two parts argue for a heightened awareness of the metals in our buildings and call for more investigation of proper installation, maintenance, and conservation practices. Comments and suggestions regarding this publication are encouraged and should be sent to Preservation Assistance Division, National Park Service, U.S. Department of the Interior, P.O. Box 37127, Washington, DC 20013-7127

E. Blaine Cliver
Chief, Preservation Assistance Division

Part I. A Historical Survey of Metals

by Margot Gayle and David W. Look, AIA

Chapter 1: Introduction

The metals in America's historic buildings, public monuments, and "street furniture" dotting the landscape comprise at least 15 distinctive metallic materials. They serve a wide range of uses, from nails to elaborate staircases, from streetlights and fire hydrants to fountains, from doorknobs to structural beams and trusses, and from domes to the statues on their pinnacles.

It is easy to take for granted the metals that make up the ordinary objects and structures of the everyday environment. The metals discovered by early civilizations—the bronze and iron of prehistory—are still in use. Trial and error brought refinements to the processing of older metals and produced new ones which machine power later made available in large quantities. Fabricators and designers put metals into a large array of domestic implements and building elements even before they knew the physical and chemical properties of the metals or the prospects of compatibility between one metal and another. The application of science to technology has brought a greater understanding of the optimum performance and limits of the numerous, indispensible metals in our surroundings. Metal elements add richness to the appearance of buildings and landscapes, often combining aesthetic appeal and utility. But it is the permanence and stability of metals, when properly cared for, which has led to their role as major building components of modern times.

Figure 1. Cast-iron Ornamentation, Carson Pirie Scott and Company Store, Madison and State streets, Chicago, Illinois, 1899-1906; Louis H. Sullivan, architect; Winslow Brothers, foundry. *The two lower floors of this building are embellished by Sullivan's extraordinarily complex designs executed in cast iron which enframe the windows and curved corner entrance. Cast iron was used in every conceivable form in the 19th century; it was the utilitarian metal. Cast-iron columns, storefronts, whole building facades, and stairs appeared, as did cast-iron doors, windows, clocks, fountains, and furniture. What could not be made of cast iron was made of wrought iron or steel. Beams were made of wrought iron or steel, and metal ceilings and roofs were made of sheet iron or steel. Often ironworkers combined cast iron and wrought iron in a design, using each metal for the elements for which it was best suited. (Becket Logan)*

The first part of this report is a survey of the metals in architecture, with historical notes on their development into modern forms and usages. The discussion concentrates on metals in American buildings, streetscapes, parks, and monuments. The metals most frequently found in our built environment include lead, tin, zinc, copper and its alloys, nickel and its alloys, iron and its alloys, and aluminum. Dominance of the ferrous metals, especially cast iron, will be discussed in relation to technological breakthroughs that made iron and later, steel, available in such variety and at so moderate a cost that their use affected almost every aspect of American life.

A high degree of craftsmanship went into fabrication of the metals in older American buildings. Often it was local artisans who designed and built fine staircases, exterior light standards, railings, or metal sculptures. Such craftsmanship, which is for the most part irreplaceable, deserves recognition and preservation. The decorative, and, lately, the structural metal components of American buildings should be appreciated as part of the nation's artistic heritage.

It is clear that metal components of all types are fundamental to the appearance and integrity of our historic buildings; metal elements greatly influence their character, their basic form, and their interior spaces. Only with more of an appreciation of the variety of architectural metals in domestic and public structures can steps be taken to identify and preserve them.

Figure 2. Bronze Entrance Door, Bowery Savings Bank, 110 East 42nd Street, New York City, 1923; York and Sawyer, architects; William H. Jackson, foundry. *Cast in the boom era after World War I, this main entrance door reflects the aura of success and stability bank officials sought. The color of polished bronze probably accounts for its use as much as its permanence and molding qualities. This is a good example of a building in which art, architecture, and sculpture were combined in an overall concept down to the smallest detail. (Courtesy of the Bowery Savings Bank)*

Figure 3. Monel Metal Gates, National Bank of Commerce (Guardian Building), 500 Griswald Street, Detroit, Michigan, 1929; Smith, Hinchman, and Grylls, architects; Gorham Co., foundry. *These geometric Art Deco style gates are fabricated from a nickel-copper alloy developed in the 20th century. Monel metal combined hardness and durability and was used for roofs and plumbing as well as decorative details in the 1920s and 1930s. It was one of the so called "white metals" popular during that period. The scarity of nickel during World War II accounts for its decline. In the 1950s, stainless steel, which is less expensive, supplanted Monel metal. (Alan Stross)*

Figure 4. Aluminum Lamp, U.S. Custom House, Chestnut, Second, and Third streets, Philadelphia, Pennsylvania, 1933; Ritter and Shay, architects; Edward Ardolino, sculptor. *Aluminum was first refined from bauxite in the 19th century and was considered a rare metal. Its light weight and corrosion resistance were recognized as qualities appropriate for a variety of uses, but many years passed before sufficient quantities were produced at a reasonable cost. By the 1930s aluminum was in wide use for exterior, weather-resistant architectural elements as well as interior decorative details. (Esther Mipaas)*

Chapter 2: Lead

Lead ores, often found with veins of silver and zinc, are widely distributed around the world. The discovery and early use of lead predates recorded history. Reduction of a high-grade, concentrated lead ore to a pure metal is relatively easy because of lead's low melting point; the process could have been discovered by any civilization that had learned to use fire and was near an outcropping of lead ore.

At the time of the European discovery of America, native Americans mined and used lead to make utensils and to ornament ceremonial objects. French explorers had identified lead mines in the upper Mississippi region by the late 17th century. Colonial Americans sought lead for making shot and pewter, an alloy of lead and tin; however, American manufacture of lead was limited by the British. More lead was imported than mined or processed in the United States until the mid-19th century.

Until the end of the 18th century, lead pipes were made by bending sheets into tubes joined by leadburning, a form of welding. In a January 1800 advertisement in *New-York Daily Advertiser*, George Youle announced that he "manufactures lead pipes to convey the water from the logs in the street into the house." By logs, he meant the buried, hollow log mains the Manhattan Water Company had laid to distribute water from their reservoir. Seamless pipes were later made by extruding molten lead. (To *extrude* is to form heated metal into a desired cross-sectional shape by forcing it through a shaped opening, or die.)

The use of lead pipes was common in the United States until the harmful effects of lead poisoning became widely known. It was not until the late 19th century that the medical profession alerted the population to the danger through published articles. Legislation against the use of lead, and precautions in the handling and manufacturing of lead, were slow to materialize. Lead is still used in plumbing today, but not for water pipes; molten lead is used to caulk cast-iron pipe joints. Since lead is soft and malleable, the lead caulking is capable of withstanding movements from vibrations, settlement, and temperature changes.

Roofing and Related Items

The primary use of lead in historic buildings was for roofing. Since the 16th century, lead has been used in England for roofing, flashing, gutters, downspouts, and conductor heads—the latter often with decorative details such as shields, initials, and dates. Until the late 17th century, lead was hand cast on sand beds, which gave the plates a stippled surface. Molds could be pressed into the wet sand to produce decorative details in the castings. Later, cast sheets of lead were rolled in mills to produce smooth, thinner sheets which reduced the weight of lead roofs, making some of them lighter than tile or slate roofs.

Historically, lead was a logical choice for roofs with low pitches or for flat areas, and for built-in gutters behind parapets, because it could provide a watertight surface when the edges of the sheets were fused by lead-burning. Steeper slopes were often unwisely reroofed with lead. Lead was better suited for low roofs, as steep roofs provided little support for the heavy metal sheets. The use of lead for roofing important buildings and for other building components spread to the English colonies in America, since England was the prime producer of lead in the world.

The plantation house "Rosewell," near Whitemarsh, Virginia, is believed to have had the first roof in the American colonies entirely covered with imported English lead. The house was built by Mann Page I and his son between 1726 and 1744. An insurance record dated 1802 documents existence of the lead roof, which was removed in 1838 when the house was extensively remodeled and a new tinplate roof installed.

By the time of the American Revolution, large quantities of imported lead were used for flashings, gutters, conductor heads, and downspouts on public buildings and the homes of wealthy people. During the Revolution, many of these leaden architectural elements were removed and melted to make shot for the war effort. In Philadelphia, preserved inventories of these donations give documentary evidence to the extent of the use of lead, especially for rain conductor heads and downspouts (figure 5).

In the early years of the New Republic, a few of the Federal buildings in Washington, D.C., had lead roofs, which were reported to have leaked frequently. Architect Benjamin H. Latrobe recognized that the temperature fluctuations of the mid-Atlantic states caused lead sheets to tear; this damage from constant expansion and contraction is called *fatigue*. Lead on steeper roofs is also subject to the slow flow by gravity, called *creep*. (see part II, chapter 10.) Soft lead roofs were more suited to the milder climate of England and France where lead roofs have survived for 200–300 years. But lead roof

Figure 5. Lead Rain Conductor Head, Library Hall, Philadelphia, Pennsylvania, 1789–1790; from designs of Dr. William Thornton. *When the library was razed in 1884, this conductor head was saved and became part of the collection of the Library Company of Philadelphia. Many early rain conductor heads were constructed of lead, and frequently included date flanges, as seen here. However, this is the only known example of a lead conductor head with an "open book" motif. (Jack E. Boucher)*

Figure 6. Lead Roofing, Saint Thomas Church, Fifth Avenue and 53rd Street, New York City, 1909–1914; Cram, Goodhue, and Ferguson, architects; Henry Hope and Sons, lead craftsman. *Ralph Adams Cram designed St. Thomas Church using the spirit and many of the techniques of medieval builders, including the use of small overlapping sheets of lead for roofing curved surfaces. The decorative grapevine frieze and panel borders, also of lead, show the versatility of this material, which can be cast with sharp detail. (Becket Logan)*

construction still exists. The National Cathedral in Washington, D.C., which is still under construction, has a hardened lead roof made from an alloy of 90% lead, 10% antimony, and a trace of tin.

American architects sometimes specified lead finials, crockets, cresting, spires, or turrets for 19th- or early-20th-century Romanesque or Gothic Revival churches, municipal buildings, or university buildings. A fine example is the small, rounded turret with its ball finial on the 53rd Street side of St. Thomas Church in New York City (figure 6).

Lead-Coated Metals

Another durable roofing material used during the 19th century in America and sometimes specified by modern architects for restoration projects, is *terne* or *terneplate*— sheet iron or sheet steel coated with a lead-tin alloy. Terneplate roofing was first produced by Joseph Truman in New York City in 1825. As reported in the August 1889 issue of *Carpentry and Building*, the first terneplate roof was still in good condition after 64 years of weathering. Unfortunately, the article did not name the building or give its address.

Lead

Lead alone does not alloy with iron, as do tin and iron to make tinplate. Early terneplate was tinplate hot dipped in lead. Later it was learned that lead alloys containing 7% to 25% tin would wet the surface of the sheet metal sufficiently to allow the terne to alloy with the iron or steel. The best terneplate has a 15% to 20% tin content, with the remainder lead.

Terneplate is often confused with tinplate because they look alike, especially when painted, and because early terne was actually tinplate dipped in molten lead. Most 19th-century catalogues referred to tinplate as "bright tin" and to terneplate as "leaded tin." However, builders commonly referred to all roofing plates as tinplates regardless of their composition. Like tinplate, terneplate roofs were installed with soldered flat seams on low-pitched roofs (figure 130) and standing steams for steeper roofs (see chapter 3). Metal shingles were made of terneplate (figure 7) as well as tinplate, and from galvanized iron and steel. Terneplate was also used for flashing and gutters.

Figure 7.   Terneplate Pantiles, Union Depot, foot of NW Sixth Avenue, Portland, Oregon, 1892–1894; Van Brunt and Howe, architects. *The pantiles are identical to the 1895 "Spanish Tile" advertised by Merchant and Company of Philadelphia and painted a terra-cotta color to imitate a real clay tile roof. (John G. Waite)*

Today terne-coated stainless steel is available. It was used to reroof the Jefferson Market Courthouse in Greenwich Village, New York City, when the building was adapted for use as a public library in the 1960s.

In the 1930s, Revere Copper and Brass Company introduced lead-coated copper. Reroofing of the main section of the Philip Schuyler Mansion in Albany, New York, in 1935 was an early application of it. Lead-coated copper combines the appearance and durability of lead with the workability and long-term economy of copper. The sheet copper is dipped twice—once in a lead-tin alloy and once in pure lead—then it is rolled. Since the copper is not exposed to the weather, it does not corrode or cause stains on other building materials. Lead-coated copper flashings and valleys are often used with slate roofs to provide extra protection against the erosive effect of broken-off slate particles. These flashings are

also used on shingle roofs where painting the flashings is impossible because the metal is mostly covered by shingles.

Window Cames

Cames, or lead rods with an H-shaped cross-section, have been used to hold small pieces of glass together for window panes since the 12th century. Since lead is soft and easily worked, it could be bent around irregularly shaped pieces of glass for domestic or church windows. The edges of the glass pieces could be fitted into the top and bottom slots of the H-shaped cames, which could then be soldered where two or more intersected. Some early buildings in colonial America had casement windows; many fragments of both diamond-shaped glass and of lead cames have been found in Virginia and New England. When sash windows were first introduced to America in the 18th century, lead served as weights to counterbalance the sash. Forty pounds was the average weight required for large single-hung windows. The weights for single- and double-hung windows were made of cast iron when it became more available.

The skillful application of lead and glass in doorway fanlights and sidelights appeared in some late Georgian and many Federal houses. Later, during the Victorian era, stained-glass windows, doors, and decorative skylights became fashionable for public buildings and residences as well as for churches. The stained-glass skylight in the Capital Hotel in Little Rock, Arkansas, is a good example of this (figure 8).

Figure 8.   Leaded Glass Skylight, Capital Hotel, 117 West Markham Street, Little Rock, Arkansas, 1873. *Lead has long been used to join pieces of glass into windows utilizing lead "cames", which are H-shaped sections grooved to fit glass into the top and bottom channels with soldered joints. (Earl Saunder)*

Half-timber revival-style buildings of the 1920s and 1930s frequently had steel casement windows with diamond-shaped panes of glass set in lead; sometimes the decorative spandrels above and/or below the windows were made of cast, beaten, or stamped thin sheets of lead. Louis Comfort Tiffany used lead in producing ornamental windows, skylights, and lamps.

Sculpture

Both the Egyptians and Greeks used lead for small pieces of sculpture; however, it was not until the end of the 17th century that lead garden urns, statues, borders, planters, and basins became popular for formal gardens in Europe. Lead statuary was favored for garden ornamentation, especially for fountains, since it does not rust or corrode where water flows over the figures and does not need painting. Some lead fountains were gilded with gold. "Rosewell" is reported to have had a lead aquarium, and the garden at the Governor's Palace in Williamsburg, Virginia, may have had a few small lead urns. Joseph Wilton erected a large lead equestrian statue of King George III of England in New York City in 1770. Patriots destroyed the statue during the American Revolution, melting down most of the fragments for shot.

Unfortunately, lead is so soft that statuary, fonts, and fountains cannot be very large, because without support the cantilevered parts may sag and become distorted. Lead sculptures and landscape accessories were popular in the 19th and early 20th centuries (figure 9), and are still produced in traditional and contemporary designs.

Paint

Both the Greeks and Romans were acquainted with lead pigments, which were generally classed as either red lead (*minium*) or white lead (*ceruse*). For two centuries, the dominant use of lead in American buildings was in lead-based paints. Red lead was used extensively as an anti-corrosive pigment for iron, while white lead was more important commercially because of its widespread use in paints for wooden houses. White lead was not used in paint for iron, however, because it had been observed that white lead increased corrosion, especially on wrought iron.

Lead-based paint was one of the most durable materials developed as a protective exterior coating. Until very recently it was also used to paint interiors. A wide variety of colors was achieved by mixing lead oxides, linseed oil, and pigments. But the use of lead-based paints has largely been discontinued due to federal restrictions based on the high incidence of lead poisoning when children chewed woodwork or toys covered with lead-based paints.

Concern over lead poisoning from paints and the high cost of lead roofing has reduced the common use of lead for certain architectural elements; however, lead is still used in modern construction. Some contemporary uses of lead in buildings include lead extruded in a continuous length as sheathing for cables, the use of sheet lead in partitions for noise reduction, as pads for vibrating machinery, and as shielding for X-ray and nuclear radiation.

Figure 9. Lead Flowerbox, Adrian van Sinderen House, 70 Willow Street, Brooklyn, New York, ca. 1839. *This is one of three large lead flowerboxes, supported by huge cast-iron brackets, which were added later in the 19th century to the facade of this Greek Revival house. The brackets were painted with sanded paint to look like brownstone. (David W. Look)*

Chapter 3: Tin

Tin is a silvery-white metal that has been known since prehistoric times. Because it is a soft metal, it is rarely used by itself. Thus the principal architectural uses of tin fall into two categories: the alloying of tin with other metals such as copper to form bronze, and the coating of tin on harder metals, such as tinplated iron or steel.

Bronzes usually contain about 90% copper and 10% tin; however, the content may vary widely, and some bronzes have a high tin content. Historically, bell metal of the finest tonal quality has been a bronze which was one-fourth tin. Before glass mirrors were invented, primitive mirrors were made of "speculum" or "white bronze," an alloy of more than one-third tin and the remainder copper. (For further information on bronze, see chapter 5.)

Pure Tin

The architectural use of pure tin was and is rare; it is usually limited to very small objects or very specialized uses. The shiny, nontarnishing nature of tin made it suitable for lighting devices such as perforated lanterns, candle shields, wall sconces, and mirror frames.

Tinplate

Sheets of iron were first coated with tin in Bohemia in the 14th or 15th century. Tin-plated iron sheets may have originally been used for armor, but later usage centered on roofing. Until the 20th century, tin-plating was achieved by hand dipping sheets of iron in molten tin. The size of the finished sheets was limited by the dimensions of the vats holding the molten tin and the amount of material workers could hand dip easily. It was a cumbersome process, not substantially improved until electroplating—the depositing of tin upon a base metal with an electric current—came into use in the 20th century.

Small deposits of tin have been mined along the border between North and South Carolina, in the Dakotas, in California, and in Alaska; however, there are no commercially important deposits of tin in the United States today. Attempts to establish a tinplate industry in the mid-1870s in Ohio and Pennsylvania, soon met with economic failure when the price of tinplate dropped in 1875. The tinplate industry was finally established in America as a result of the McKinley Bill of 1890, which put a tariff on imported tinplate. By 1896 America produced 98% of its own tinplate using, of course, imported tin. Although tin is an expensive metal, so little of it is used in the process that tinplate has been competitive with other roofing materials, about a third the cost of sheet copper.

Tinplate Roofing and Related Items

The prime use of tin in America has been as a coating on iron, and later sheet steel, for roofing. French Canada used tinplate roofing in the late 17th and 18th centuries, long before its southern neighbor.

Probably from his travels in Europe, Thomas Jefferson observed that tinplate roofs were lightweight and durable, some having lasted over 100 hundred years. About 1800, he chose tin for roofing his home "Monticello" near Charlottesville, Virginia. The Arch Street Meetinghouse in Philadelphia had tinplate shingles installed in a herringbone pattern on a "piazza" roof in 1804 and the Exchange Coffee House, built in Boston about 1808, had a tinplate roof. Tinplate roofs soon became popular for houses, especially in the cities, and gradually replaced wooden shingle roofs, which were considered fire hazards. Roofs of tinned sheet iron were often used on significant public buildings.

"Tin roofs," as they were commonly called, were noncombustible, lightweight, and durable. When kept well painted, tinplate roofs often lasted 50–100 years or longer. They were usually painted with "tinner's red," which had a red or reddish-brown color, although a few were painted light green, probably to simulate the appearance of more expensive copper roofs.

For the first third of the 19th century, tinned iron roofs were constructed from plates measuring a standard 10 inches by approximately 14 inches. In the 1830s, plates 20 inches by 14 inches became available. Most early tinplate roofs had flat seams and were soldered together to produce a continuous waterproof covering. These were used on both low-pitched roofs and steeper roofs. (figure 10a and b). Standing seam tinplate roofs did not come into common use until the Civil War era. Tinplates were soldered together with flat seams to form long strips, which were joined to other strips by standing seams. The pattern of the dominant standing seams gave the typical vertical pattern to these roofs. Standing seam roofs were not used on flat or on very low-pitched roofs where water might collect, since standing seam roofs are not watertight (figure 10c).

By the 1870s, technological improvements in production made possible plates 20 inches by 28 inches. Each time the size of the plates was increased, the number of

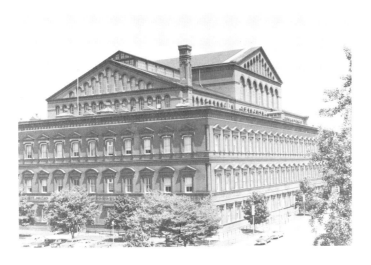

Figure 10. "Tinplate" Roofing, Old Pension Building, Fifth and G Streets, NW, Washington, DC, 1883; Montgomery C. Meigs, engineer. *(a) The building consists of offices around the perimeter of a large court. The roof over the offices has a very low pitch and is covered with flat-seam tinplate, while the steep-pitched roofs over the court have batten tinplate roofs. (b) Flat seam tinplate roofing was used on low-pitched roofs because the edges of the plates could be interlocked and soldered together to provide a continuous waterproof covering. Stamped on each plate of the Pension Building roof is "Holkinshee Forge Best Roofing, 40 lbs., Manion Process License." The metal is actually terneplate. Surviving examples of true tinplate iron or steel are rare.. (c) The batten tinplate roofs over the central court were typical of steep-pitched roofing of tin and other materials. They can be seen at a distance and provide a strong design element to the building. (David W. Look)*

seams was reduced, thus decreasing labor costs and the number of potential leaks. Eventually, rolls of tin-plated iron 28 inches wide and 96 inches long were manufactured. The first commercial electrolytic tinplate roofing line went into production at United States Steel Corporation in 1937. The electroplated rolls had a thinner layer of tin than hand-dipped tinplate. Today, continuous rolls of tinplate roofing are available. Continuous tin roofing has a slightly different appearance than roofs made of numerous tin plates or strips, and extremely long sheets may become wavy because of inadequate allowance for expansion and contraction.

In addition to plates and rolled strips, machine-pressed tinplate shingles became popular in the second half of the 19th century. Shingles pressed to form raised designs such as "Spanish Tile," "Merchant's Gothic shingles," "Diamond Tile," and "Gothic Tile" were used for Mansard and other roofs with sufficient pitch. Plates and rolled strips with flat and standing seams could be used on low-pitched roofs, but shingles depended on overlap and pitch to shed water (figure 11). Shingles were also used on vertical surfaces such as bulkheads on roofs, and as a covering for exterior walls. Tinplate was also used for flashings, valleys, ridges, hips, gutters, downspouts and dormers, as well as for fire-resistant coverings for wooden doors and shutters. Formed metal siding

was stamped to imitate pressed brick, rock-faced stone, and even ashlar quoins.

Decorative Uses

Ornamental window and door lintels, balusters, cresting, finials, and urns were also tinned. What is commonly known as the "tin ceiling" is a misnomer as these decorative sheets were never tinned; they were almost always painted sheet iron or steel (see section on sheet iron and steel).

Builders have long attempted to find corrosion-resistant metals and to make commonly available metals such as iron and steel more corrosion resistant. Tinplate, in a way, created a market for metal building components. Later, the market was partially taken over by terneplate, pure zinc architectural elements, and galvanized sheet iron and steel.

Although tinplate is still available today for roofing and flashing, it is generally considered expensive since the initial cost is more than that for common modern roofing types such as asphalt shingles or built-up roofs. However, since a well-maintained tinplate roof (maintenance consisting of inspection and periodic painting) will last several times longer than either of these types of roofing, it is more economical when the cost is prorated over the longer lifespan.

SAINT PAUL ROOFING, CORNICE AND ORNAMENT COMPANY

"ST. PAUL" METAL SHINGLES.
Made of Painted or Galvanized Steel, Tin or Copper.

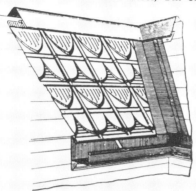

A special feature of the "St. Paul" Metal Shingles is the **embossing**, which is very high, sharp and distinct, and gives a very ornamental finish to any structure.

All nails are covered. Made with a lock joint that gives perfect security in rain or wind.

They are much superior to wood, slate or tin for steep roofs, being fire-proof, unbreakable and do not become loose by expansion. Can be used on roofs having 4 inches or more pitch per foot.

See instructions for laying on following page.

Showing Ridge, Valley and Gutter Finish with St. Paul Shingles.

Smaller sized shingles are best adapted to small roof surfaces and spires, and hip roofs where considerable cutting is required at hips, valleys, dormers, etc., as they can be cut to less waste than larger shingles. The larger sizes are best adapted to larger, unbroken surfaces where little cutting is required, as they are more quickly laid and have a smaller proportion of joints per square. We can furnish with these all ridge rolls, crestings, hips, caps or shingles, eaves, course plates, etc., to give the roof a neat and complete appearance.

No 1.

No. 1—Covering size 8x12 inches; 150 to a square (100 sq. ft.).

No. 2—Covering size 11x15 inches; 89 to a square (100 sq. ft.).

No. 2.

No. 4.

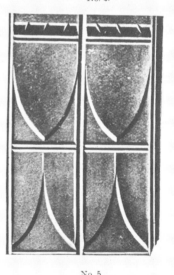

No. 5.

No. 3.

No. 3—Covering size 11x23 inches; 55 pieces to the square (100 sq. ft.).

No. 4—Covering size 11½x16½ inches; 75 pieces to the square (100 sq. ft.).

No. 5—Covering size 12x18 inches; 67 pieces to the square (100 sq. ft.).

Figure 11. Tinplated Steel Shingles. *"St. Paul" metal shingles ranged in size from 8 by 12 inches to 12 by 18 inches and were available in painted steel, galvanized steel, tin (plated steel), and sheet copper from the St. Paul, Minnesota, roofing company's 1905 catalog. Individual shingles were connected with interlocking joints to prevent uplift by the wind, a distinct advantage over strips of roofing made to resemble shingles (see figure 122). St. Paul was one of many companies producing metal shingles and roofing in the late 19th and early 20th centuries. (Library of Congress)*

Chapter 4: Zinc

Zinc is a bluish-white metal sometimes called "spelter." In refining copper-bearing ores, the Romans noticed that a white powder condensed on the flues of the furnaces. Now known as "zinc fume" or "zinc dust," this powder, a compound of zinc, was called *cadmira* by the Romans. They used it, probably accidently at first, to produce the first brass.

Pure metallic zinc was first produced in commercial quantities in 1738 by William Champion in Warmley, England. Although pure zinc is brittle at normal temperatures, it can be rolled when heated to temperatures between 212° and 300°F. because the hot rolling breaks down the crystalline structure. Sheet zinc was first hot rolled by Hobson and Sylvester of Sheffield, England, who patented the process in 1805. However, zinc production never became a big industry in England, nor was it used extensively there in construction, except for workers cottages.

Large deposits of calamine, a zinc ore, were discovered in Flanders in the 18th century; however, these deposits were not utilized until after the end of the century when that area came under French control. In 1807, a zinc-works was established by Abbe Daniel Dony at Liege (now in Belgium) and the first sheet zinc was rolled there in 1811. This was the beginning of the zinc industry, which experimented with sheet zinc as a roofing material. Soon there was a plentiful supply of high-quality zinc and new uses were sought. Although zinc deposits were abundant in the United States, no effort was made to develop the industry here until after 1838.

Pure Zinc Roofing and Related Items

The successful use of zinc roofing in Belgium led to its application in France and Germany, where it replaced more expensive copper and lead in roofing. Although the use of zinc roofing was popular on the continent, it never became popular in England. In the 1820s, Belgian sheet zinc was imported in America; and by the 1830s, builders in New York City and elsewhere had installed sheet zinc roofs. The St. Charles Hotel in New Orleans had a sheet zinc roof by 1837, and the dome and roof of St. Vincent de Paul Church in New York City was similarly covered by 1851. Although the popularity and use of zinc roofing in America varied greatly, its use was never as widespread as tinplate roofing.

Pure zinc is subject to creep at ordinary temperatures. After the corrugation process was patented in England in 1829 (see sheet iron and steel section), corrugated sheets of pure zinc were tried for roofing; but they sagged when placed on roof purlins and were therefore unsuitable.

Zinc-Coated Metal

I. M. Sorel, a French chemist, patented a galvanizing process in 1837, as did H. W. Crawford in England. Both methods employed a "hot dipping" process to coat sheet iron with zinc. By 1839 "galvanized" sheet iron roofing was being used in New York City. The Merchant's Exchange in Manhattan was one of the first buildings to have both a galvanized roof and galvanized gutters.

By the mid-1850s, galvanized sheets were available 24 inches wide by 72 inches long, much longer than any tinplate then on the market. Like tinplate, early galvanized iron was hand dipped. Early attempts at electroplate galvanizing were not successful; however, the process was eventually perfected and today almost all galvanized iron and steel is electroplated. Soon 50-foot rolls of galvanized sheet iron were produced.

Some galvanized sheet roofing was pressed with designs, a mode very popular in the Victorian era (figure 141). Galvanized iron and steel were used to make metal shingles (figure 11) and pantiles (figure 12) by forming them to imitate other roofing materials—wood shingles, slate, and terra-cotta tile. It was also used to make waterproof flashings and roof crestings and finials (figure 13).

By the 1850s, corrugated sheet iron was galvanized and was soon used on nearly every building type, from factories and train sheds to post offices and customhouses. Galvanized iron roofing apparently did not prove acceptable for public buildings, though it had widespread application for industrial structures, farms, and temporary buildings.

Decorative Uses

Zinc was cast for sculpture and decorative elements in Germany as early as 1832. Zinc cemetery monuments and tombstones were manufactured in America, especially in Connecticut, in the latter half of the 19th century (figure 14). Probably ordered from catalogs, they can still be found in cemeteries. Even after a century of weathering and exposure, most still look new since they are protected by the gray layer of zinc carbonate that has formed on the surface.

SAINT PAUL ROOFING, CORNICE AND ORNAMENT COMPANY

"SAINT PAUL" METAL TILES.

Made of Painted or Galvanized Steel, or Copper.

Showing Complete Roof.

Single.

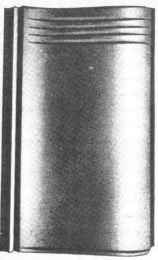

"Saint Paul" Metal tiles are suitable for any building—stone, brick or frame, where the pitch is more than 3 inches to a foot. For a roof to be satisfactory, it must at all times be absolutely weatherproof. "Saint Paul" tiles affords perfect protection against rain, snow, hail or sleet.

No. 1 Single—Covering size 11¼x16½ inches; 78 pieces to the square.

EAVES COURSE PLATE.

CLUSTER.

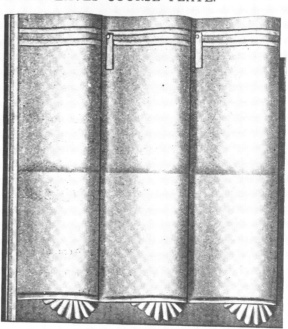

No. 6 Cluster—Covering size 17½x19 inches; 44 pieces to the square.

No. 7—This shows our "Saint Paul" eaves course plate or starter, used along the eaves for the first course of No. 6 metal tile. When ordering style No. 6, specify how many lineal feet of No. 7 you require. Covering size 19 inches wide by 20 inches long.

Figure 12. Sheet Metal Pantiles. *These pantiles, to look like terra-cotta tiles, could be installed one at a time or in clusters of six. A roof with these pantiles needed a pitch of at least 3 inches per foot. The special eaves course plates shown here had decorated edges. The pantiles were available in 1905 in painted or galvanized steel or copper. These are similar to the pantiles on Union Depot, Portland, Oregon (see figure 7). (Library of Congress)*

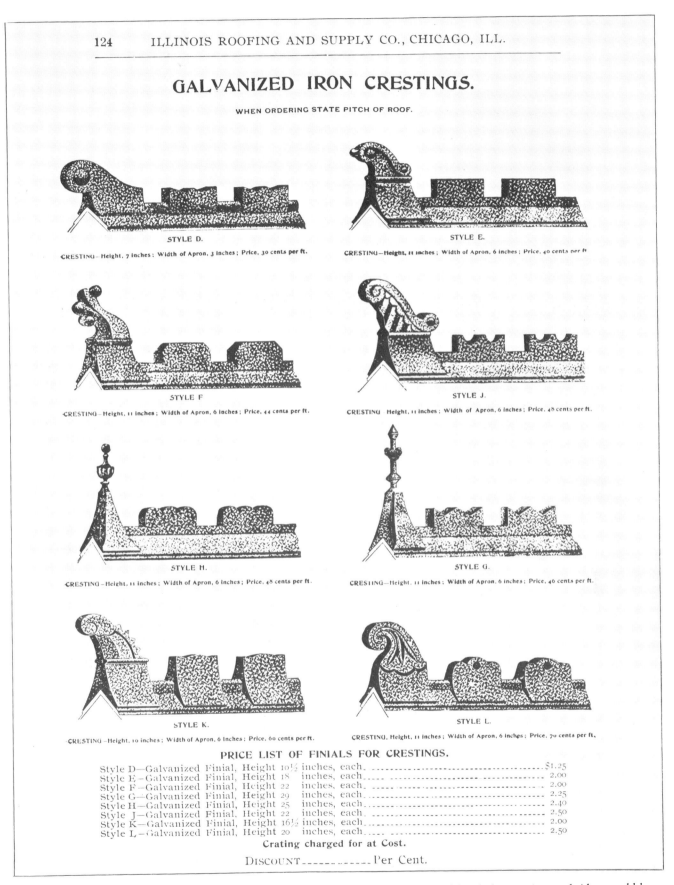

124   ILLINOIS ROOFING AND SUPPLY CO., CHICAGO, ILL.

GALVANIZED IRON CRESTINGS.

WHEN ORDERING STATE PITCH OF ROOF.

STYLE D.

CRESTING—Height, 7 inches; Width of Apron, 3 inches; Price, 30 cents per ft.

STYLE E.

CRESTING—Height, 11 inches; Width of Apron, 6 inches; Price, 40 cents per ft

STYLE F

CRESTING—Height, 11 inches; Width of Apron, 6 inches; Price, 44 cents per ft.

STYLE J.

CRESTING Height, 11 inches; Width of Apron, 6 inches; Price, 48 cents per ft.

STYLE H.

CRESTING—Height, 11 inches; Width of Apron, 6 inches; Price, 48 cents per ft.

STYLE G.

CRESTING—Height, 11 inches; Width of Apron, 6 inches; Price, 40 cents per ft.

STYLE K.

CRESTING—Height, 10 inches; Width of Apron, 6 inches; Price, 60 cents per ft.

STYLE L.

CRESTING, Height, 11 inches; Width of Apron, 6 inches; Price, 70 cents per ft.

PRICE LIST OF FINIALS FOR CRESTINGS.

Style D—Galvanized Finial, Height 10½ inches, each		$1.25
Style E—Galvanized Finial, Height 18 inches, each		2.00
Style F—Galvanized Finial, Height 22 inches, each		2.00
Style G—Galvanized Finial, Height 29 inches, each		2.25
Style H—Galvanized Finial, Height 25 inches, each		2.40
Style J—Galvanized Finial, Height 22 inches, each		2.50
Style K—Galvanized Finial, Height 16½ inches, each		2.00
Style L—Galvanized Finial, Height 20 inches, each		2.50

Crating charged for at Cost.

DISCOUNT _____ Per Cent.

Figure 13.   Galvanized Iron Crestings and Finials. *Galvanized sheet metal cresting and finials for capping roof ridges could be purchased in a variety of motifs and from a number of catalogs. Finials were sold in 1896 individually and as cresting by the linear foot from the Illinois Roofing and Supply Company of Chicago, Illinois. (Library of Congress)*

Figure 15. Zinc Statues, *Art and Architectural Metal Work Catalogue,* **W. H. Mullins, Salem, Ohio, 1896.** *Many of the statues of Freedom, Liberty, Justice, and the Muses that grace the tops of domes and cupolas were pressed in zinc and painted to match the stone of the courthouses, city halls, libraries, or other public or private monumental buildings on which they stood. A prime producer of these statues was W. H. Mullins whose employees posed for this group photograph with some 52 figures ready for shipment to the Cotton States and International Exposition in Atlanta, Georgia. In the foreground, note the four griffins, which are identical to those on the Waterworks in Peoria, Illinois. (Library of Congress)*

Figure 14. Zinc Grave Marker, Herkimer, New York, ca.1874; Monumental Bronze Co., Bridgeport, Connecticut. *The manufacturer's name is discreetly recorded in small letters along the edge of the plinth. This company's 1882 catalog used the phrase "pure cast zinc" while insisting that "unlike commercial zinc ours is a pure metal, like gold or silver." The embossed epitaph is still crisp and new looking. In some respects the zinc monuments have survived in better condition than their stone counterparts. These light gray markers were cast in many sections, sandblasted to produce a rough stone-like surface, then bolted together with the connections disguised. (Margot Gayle)*

Zinc statues adorn many city halls, county courthouses, and post offices. Some may have been custom designed, but many were purchased from zincworks catalogues such as that of W. H. Mullins of Salem, Ohio. During the last quarter of the 19th century, foundries hired artisans and sculptors to model figures in clay and make the molds. Zinc statues were then fabricated from pressed and cast sections, some of enormous size (figure 15). A zinc statue of a fireman holding a rescued child stands on a cast-iron base in both Owego and Middletown, New York.

Decorative architectural elements were frequently cast in zinc, since it molded readily, was relatively inexpensive compared to stone, and could be painted to imitate more expensive metals. Urns, balusters, and letters (for signs) were often cast in zinc. Architectural brackets for cornices and capitals for columns and pilasters were cast in zinc (figure 16).

Moldings on late-19th-century American buildings that appear to be carved wood or stone are often cast or pressed sheet zinc or a combination of both. Even the balusters and rails on many balconies were fabricated totally of zinc.

According to the sixtieth anniversary issue of *Sheet Metal Worker* (January 1934, page 32), the first sheet iron cornice was made as a result of an accident witnessed by a sheet metal worker. In 1834 a heavy cornice stone being hoisted to the top of a tall building fell, killing two workmen. The witness, whose name was not given, began experimenting with the fabrication of a hollow cornice made of folded and pressed sheet metal. The first machine for shaping cornices, called a "cornice brake," was designed by "the predecessors of the J. M. Robinson & Co." The first galvanized sheet iron cornice made on this machine was erected on the old National Theatre in Cincinnati, Ohio, ca. early 1840s.

Other architectural elements such as window and door lintels were fabricated with pressed or folded galvanized iron (figure 17). Many later cornices, lintels, and bay fronts were further embellished with cast zinc ornament applied to the galvanized sheet iron (figure 18). Eventually, whole facades were made of galvanized sheet iron

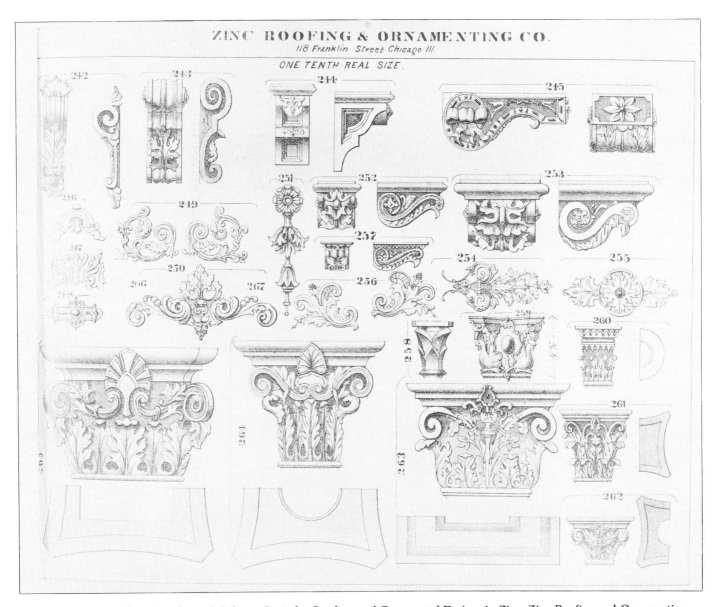

Figure 16. Zinc Brackets, Scrolls, and Column Capitals, Catalogue of Ornamental Designs in Zinc, Zinc Roofing and Ornamenting Co., Chicago, Illinois, 1871. *Although some of these pieces could have been stamped in one piece, most were cast or stamped in sections and applied to a pressed metal support. (Library of Congress)*

Figure 17.   Zinc Lintels, Catalogue of Ornamental Designs in Zinc, Zinc Roofing and Ornamenting Co., 1871. *Many window and door lintels that from a distance appear to be stone or wood are pressed sheet metal, often coated with zinc. Sheet metal was lighter and less expensive than cast iron or stone, was easier to install, and could be painted to imitate stone or more expensive metals such as bronze or copper. The lintel designs were probably made up of galvanized sheet iron sections; the bottom design has applied cast zinc ornaments. Notice that the brackets and rosettes have separate numbers; they were probably ordered for the lintel or for other locations on the facade. (Library of Congress)*

Figure 18.   Galvanized Sheet Iron Bay with Applied Zinc Ornament, 608 Indiana Avenue, NW, Washington D.C. *When sheet metal work is kept well painted, it is very difficult to identify it as sheet iron or steel, galvanized or tinplated. However, if the metal is not maintained, its composition becomes more obvious. Paint does not adhere well to pure zinc, or to galvanized iron or steel. When the paint peels, it usually comes off completely, including the primer, to reveal a clean metal surface. If the metal is galvanized, it will have a spangled appearance and may show some rust or rust stains from the iron base metal. If it is cast or pressed zinc, it will have a grayish-white appearance. This bay is covered with galvanized sheet iron with pure zinc ornaments on the surface. Even if well painted, a magnet test will reveal what is galvanized iron or steel (which is magnetic) and what is pure zinc (which is non-magnetic). (David W. Look)*

Pressed galvanized sheet iron and steel facades, cornices, lintels, and other components were in widespread demand from the 1880s to the 1910s. They were fabricated by many sheet metal companies; the two largest firms were George L. Mesker and Company of Evansville, Indiana, and Mesker Brothers of St. Louis, Missouri. These firms together sold over 12,000 storefronts and shipped them by railroad to practically every state. Each year the two firms and others sent out thousands of catalogues, one of which was reproduced in the *Bulletin of the Association for Preservation Technology* (vol. 9, no. 4, 1977).

These commercial facades generally imitated wood, stone, and cast-iron fronts at a fraction of the cost of the other materials. The pieces of sheet metal were riveted and/or soldered together and then nailed to wooden framing. They came complete with doors, windows, and glass—everything that was needed for a complete facade, including a set of instructions for erection. The first-floor columns and pilasters were usually cast iron to take the added wear and tear of street-level pedestrian traffic.

Although these mass-produced facades were not held in high esteem by architects, they brought ornament and "style" to countless business districts. In many small towns, especially in the West, the only buildings of any significance on Main Street may be the galvanized sheet iron storefronts purchased through a catalog. Like cast-iron facades, these storefronts were often painted stone colors and then dusted with sand to add a stone-like tex-ture. It is not unusual to find a loft building with three stone or brick walls and a pressed sheet metal facade that imitates stone or brick.

Paint

In the mid-18th century, a German chemist named Cramer produced zinc oxide by burning pure zinc in air. In France, Courtois made the first zinc oxide paint in 1781; it was nontoxic and resistant to pollution. Although zinc oxide paint had whiteness, fine texture, and opacity, it lacked body and required several coats to cover the surface. Zinc oxide paint became commercially successful and readily available in America about 1850 when this deficiency was corrected. By the 1870s, zinc oxide paint was widely used here. Since then, zinc-chromate paint and zinc-rich paint, which contains metallic zinc dust, have been developed. Both of these paints are good inhibitors against rust on iron and steel.

During the early decades of the 20th century, the use of pure zinc roofing and ornament decreased and now, pure zinc as a building material is rarely used. However, zinc is still used in alloys such as brass and nickel silver (see chapters 5 and 6 for further information on brass and nickel silver), and in the electroplating of steel. Today, galvanized steel, usually corrugated, is used for roofing industrial and agricultural buildings, but seldom used on public buildings or residences of any significance. Galvanized nails and sheet metal ducts are common in modern construction.

Chapter 5: Copper and Copper Alloys

The "cupric" metals include copper and its alloys: especially *bronze,* an alloy of copper and tin, and *brass,* an alloy of copper and zinc.

Copper

Copper is usually found combined with other elements in sulfide and oxide ores; however, it does exist in a relatively pure state in nature. Naturally pure copper is known as "native" copper. The Neolithic people first discovered such copper about 8000 B.C.

The French and English explorers learned of large native copper deposits in what is now Michigan from the Indians in the 17th and 18th centuries. Exploitation of these deposits began in 1844, resulting in the first "mining boom" in the United States. After the 1880s,

however, the center of copper mining moved west to Montana, Colorado, and Utah. Today, the United States is self-sufficient in its production of copper.

Copper is a very durable metal; it withstands corrosion to a remarkable degree. The characteristic green patina—actually copper sulfate that forms on its surface—acts as a protective coating against further reaction with the atmosphere. Pure copper is strong but ductile, which means it can be stretched or "drawn," as in making wire. It is also malleable and thus can be hammered, beaten, or rolled into sheets or shapes without breaking. Copper was first rolled in England in the late 17th century. Of the many utilitarian and decorative uses of copper, undoubtedly its use as sheathing for ships and as roofing and flashing material on buildings

Figure 19.   Copper Roof, Old Senate Chamber, United States Capitol, 1819; Benjamin H. Labrobe, architect. *After the British burned the Capitol in 1814, the entire structure was rebuilt, including a new copper roof. Little is known about the roofing installed in 1819 since it was removed in 1900. It was probably all flat seams because the machine for forming standing seam roofing was not invented until about the time of the Civil War. When the surfaces were reroofed in 1975, every effort was made to duplicate the 1900 roofing patterns, configuration, and size of sheets. Sheet copper can be shaped to cover many types of curved surfaces. The dome has standing seams while the cupola and the area around the dome, which is flatter, have flat seams. (Charles Parrott)*

has been most important, followed by its use in ornamental details. In the 20th century, piping systems and electrical wiring became important new uses of copper.

Roofing and Related Items

Sheet copper used as roofing is lighter than wooden shingles and much lighter than slate, tile, or lead. Roofing copper can be folded readily into waterproof seams, or shaped over curved frameworks for cupolas and domes (figure 19).

Some of America's most important buildings had copper roofs, and many lasted for nearly two centuries. In 1795 the First Bank of the United States in Philadelphia was covered with a roof of English copper sheets (24 by 48 inches), with standing seams held in place by copper clips and cast nails. The section over the front pediment is still in service, although the rest of the roof was drastically altered in 1902.

Roofing material for the dome of the Massachusetts State House (1795-1798) was ordered from Paul Revere's newly opened rolling mill. But there was still not enough American production, for instance, to supply the sheet copper for the New York City Hall (1803-1811); most sheet copper was imported through the early decades of the 19th century. Copper roofs on public and important private buildings were not so rare by the time Old Christ Church in Philadelphia was roofed in copper in the 1830s. The copper on Christ Church fulfilled the builders' objective to install roofing material of great durability and longevity; the roof served its purpose until 1967.

The initial cost of copper was traditionally high, but its length of service more than compensated for the price. Because of these high costs, copper in quantity was used only on major structures, mostly public buildings. However, copper in small quantities was widely used on more modest buildings for roof flashings, gutters, and downspouts (figure 20), and decorative elements. Copper was also commonly used for weather vanes and finials (figures 21 and 22). The resistance of

Figure 21. **Copper Grasshopper Weather Vane by Shem Drowne, 1742, Faneuil Hall, Dock Square, Boston, Massachusetts.** *The weather vane is wrought iron except for the grasshopper and the four points of the compass which are copper. The grasshopper, which is gilded and has glass eyes, measures 53 inches long, 6 1/4 inches wide, and weighs 38 pounds. The history of the weather vane is well documented. In 1755 it was damaged by an earthquake; it was later repaired by Thomas Drowne in 1768. On January 11, 1974, the weather vane disappeared only to be found a few days later wrapped in a blanket and hidden in the cupola. The weather vane had been damaged during the attempted theft, but it was repaired and reinstalled on February 15, 1974. (Index of American Design, Mass-Me-230, National Gallery of Art)*

Figure 20. **Copper Conductor Heads and Downspouts, former U.S. Post Office, Bounded by Hamilton, Clark, Ward streets and Lee Place, Paterson, New Jersey, 1899; William Martin Aiken, Architect of the Treasury.** *Rain conductor heads and downspouts are almost always made of metal, in some cases copper. The former post office, now an annex to the Paterson County Court House, includes copper conductor heads and downspouts as part of the rich Flemish architectural design. Twenty of these decorative devices are spaced on all four sides of the banded red brick and stone building. (Jack Stokvis)*

copper to corrosion was valuable for these purposes, as was its malleability. It could be shaped to the bends and angles around chimneys and at roof edges and dormers. All nails, screws, bolts, and cleats used with sheet copper had to be made of copper or a copper alloy; otherwise "galvanic" action between the dissimilar metals would occur, causing deterioration (see section on deterioration in chapter 10).

Decorative Uses

Copper was hammered or stamped into decorative details to ornament the cornice lines of many buildings (figure 23), and to sheath oriel and bay windows as well (figure 24). Copper was also fabricated into running moldings, masks, lion heads, rain conductor heads (figure 20), and Greek-inspired anthemions at roof edges.

Occasionally, statues used as architectural ornaments were made of copper. Sections of sheet copper can be hammered over wooden or other forms to create statues. Once the copper sheets have taken the shape of the form, they are removed and soldered together over a wooden or metal framework. The most famous example of this type of statue is the Statue of Liberty, which consists of copper sheathing over a steel framework. The 152-foot-tall statue, erected in New York Harbor, was a centennial gift from France (figure 25).

Another widely known sheet copper statue of great beauty is Augustus Saint-Gaudens' "Diana," which he designed as a weather vane to top the tower of the old Madison Square Garden in New York City. The 13-foot gilded statue, a huntress poised on one toe with bow and arrow ready, stood silhouetted 347 feet above the street

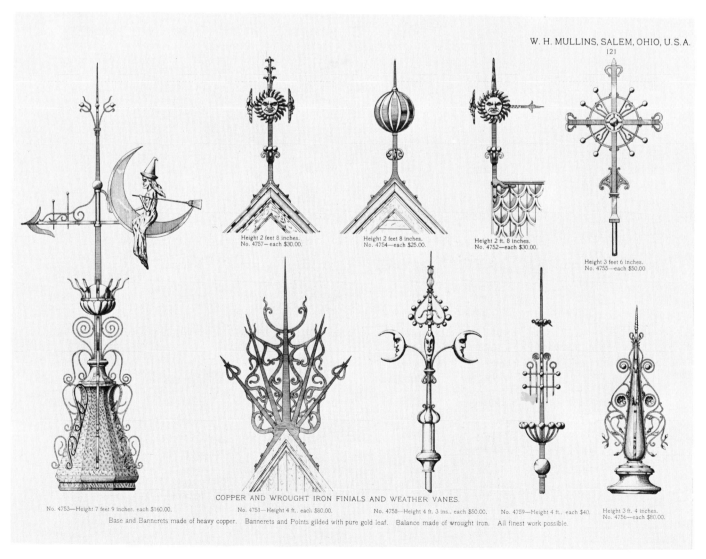

Figure 22. Copper and Wrought-iron Finials and Weather Vanes. *The bases and bannerets of the weather vanes were made of heavy copper, with the bannerets and points of the compass sometimes gilded with gold leaf. The rest of the material in these decorative objects was usually wrought iron. In 1896, these unusual designs, as well as the traditional rooster and eagle, were offered in the catalog of W. H. Mullins of Salem, Ohio. (Library of Congress)*

Figure 23. Pressed Copper Sheet Metal Cornice, Frieze, and Pilasters; Conservatory of the Christian Heurich Mansion, 1307 New Hampshire Avenue, NW, Washington, D.C., 1902; Appleton Clark, architect. *The copper work was assembled from many pieces of sheet copper pressed with low relief designs. (Jack E. Boucher, NAER)*

from 1895 until 1925 when the Garden was demolished. She was constructed of 22-ounce copper, die-struck in sections riveted together then braised to make the form smooth and waterproof. An armature centered on a 7-inch wrought-iron pipe that ran from the head through the toe and 9 feet into the tower supported the statue. With counterweights and a ball-bearing system that allowed her to rotate she weighed somewhat under 1,500 pounds. The statue can now be seen in the Philadelphia Museum of Art. An earlier 22-foot version weighing 2,200 pounds that had proved to be out of scale when placed on the Garden's tower in October 1891 was taken down and sent to the World Columbian Exposition of 1893 in Chicago to grace the dome of Agricultural Hall, which like the Garden was the work of the architectural firm of McKim, Mead, and White. The whereabouts of that statue since the close of the fair is unknown.

The color of antique copper, which is a little more orange than new bronze, was much admired in the late 19th century. Victorian cast-iron hardware was sometimes copper-plated, although brass-plated hardware was more common. Cast-iron stair railings and newel posts (figure 26) were sometimes copper plated. An excellent example is the copper-plated cast-iron staircase, designed by Louis Sullivan in 1894, that was saved from the demolished Chicago Stock Exchange and has been re-erected in the American Wing of New York's Metropolitan Museum.

Today the cost of copper prohibits its extensive decorative use, but it is still used for certain utilitarian systems because of its unique properties. Copper's high capacity for thermal and electrical conductivity accounts for its continued use in buildings in heating and air-conditioning systems, electrical systems, and telephone wiring. Also, its strength and resistance to corrosion by most types of soils and water make it appropriate for use in plumbing.

Figure 24. Copper-Clad Bay Window and Cornice, Thomas C. Whyte House, 1329 R Street, NW, Washington, D.C., 1892; George C. Johnson, architect. *From the first-floor window sills to the cornice above the second floor, the bay window is sheathed entirely with pressed sheets of copper, and there are slender two-story copper pilasters flanking the windows. The spandrel between the first- and second-floor center windows has a shell design and the side spandrels have winged sea creatures. Both the cornice of the house and the cornice of the bay window have copper classical dentils and modillions. (David W. Look)*

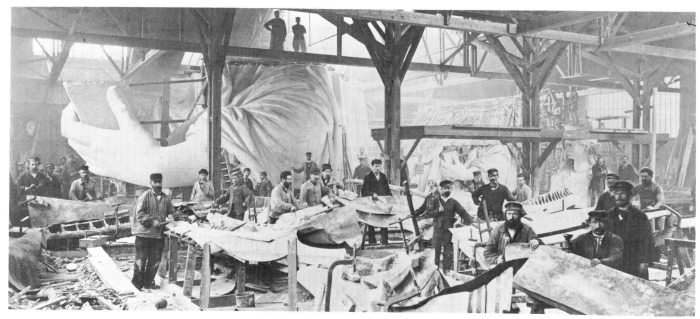

Figure 25. Copper Statue of Liberty, New York City Harbor, 1883–1886; Frederic Auguste Bartholdi, sculptor; Alexandre Gustave Eiffel, engineer. *This photograph was taken in the metal shop in France where the sheet copper was fabricated. In the foreground, sheet metal workers are hammering the copper over wooden forms. The temporarily assembled arm and shoulder in the background, were later disassembled and shipped to the United States. Eiffel, who later designed the 984-foot Eiffel Tower of the Paris Exhibition of 1889, engineered the steel armature to support the statue built to the design of Bartholdi. (Rare Book Division, New York Public Library; Astor, Lenox and Tilden foundations)*

Figure 26. Copper-Plated Cast-iron Stair Railing, Christian Heurich Mansion, 1307 New Hampshire Avenue, NW, Washington, D.C., 1892–1894; John Granville Meyers, architect. *This iron railing was sand cast in many pieces, and the flat areas of the design were ground smooth before the pieces were copper plated. Most of the parts were bolted together, but a few pieces of the newell post were brazed. The railing has a brass hand rail. (Jack E. Boucher, NAER)*

Bronze

Copper alloys have been of prime importance for several millenia, especially bronze, the alloy known and used the longest. Copper plus tin forms bronze, a salmon-colored metal seldom seen without a natural green patina or a brown artificial statuary patina. Bronze lent its name to an entire stage in the development of civilization; the Bronze Age was the point at which various groups of people learned to reduce ores and combine different metals to produce superior tools. Bronze was preferred to iron in early civilizations for its hardness and easier mode of production.

Bronze is remarkably impervious to the vicissitudes of time and weather. Old bronze is recognizable by its greenish-brown patina—a natural protection that sometimes occurs evenly on a surface. However, a bronze surface may be marked with grayish-green and black streaks which may detract from its appearance, if it is exposed to wind and rain from one direction for long. Lack of protection from polluted industrial air may endanger the integrity of exposed outdoor bronze sculpture or exterior building details, a danger not usually present with interior bronzework or doors.

The use of bronze in American buildings before the Civil War was very rare. American foundries did cast some bronze cannons, small sculpture, and bells, but large-size bronzework for churches and capitol buildings was still imported. Although American foundries had the capacity, they lacked the confidence and opportunity to produce fine pieces. Near the mid-19th century, sculptors Robert Ball Hughes and Clark Mills cast their own bronze and soon America was producing fine bronzework for art, architectural sculpture, and for architectural elements and details.

About 1845, Hughes modeled a life-size seated statue for the monument of astronomer Nathaniel Bowditch and cast it in his foundry in Boston. Erected in 1847 in Mount Auburn Cemetery in Cambridge, it was probably the first life-size outdoor bronze sculpture cast in America, although it had to be recast in the 1880s because of its deteriorated condition.

The first bronze equestrian statue was cast in America in 1848 when Clark Mills modeled a statue of Andrew Jackson, the hero of the day. Mills cast the statue and it was erected in 1853 in Lafayette Park, Washington, D.C. Cannons captured from the British at the Battle of New Orleans were melted to supply the needed bronze. Mills' work was important not only for the technical skill needed to cast the many pieces of bronze for the statue, but also for his ability to balance the mass on the horse's hind legs. Congress was so impressed with Mills' work that it commissioned him to model an equestrian statue of Washington (which had actually been proposed in 1783), which now stands in Washington Circle not far from Lafayette Park.

The first bronze doors installed in America were the "Columbus Doors" by Randolph Rogers at the U.S. Capitol, (figure 27), which were cast in Germany. The doors of the new Senate wing of the Capitol were the first bronze doors both commissioned and cast in America. Thomas Crawford received the commission for these in 1855. He had completed the plaster cast of one

Figure 27. Bronze "Columbus Doors," Rotunda of the U.S. Capitol, Designed by Randolph Rogers, 1858, installed 1863; Royal Bavarian Foundry, Munich, Germany. *Shortly after Thomas Crawford received his commission for the Senate doors in 1855, Randolph Rogers was commissioned to design the doors of the Rotunda. He proposed scenes based on the life of Columbus. Although Rogers was an American, he modeled the doors in his studio in Rome, sent photographs to America for approval, and had the doors cast in Munich in 1861. These doors were shipped to America and installed on the House side of the Rotunda in 1863, before Crawford's doors for the Senate were finished. Rogers' doors were later moved in 1871 to the main entrance of the Rotunda. (Courtesy of the Architect of the Capitol)*

panel and clay models of four more panels before he died in 1857. The work was eventually turned over to William Rhinehart, who completed the last panel of the Senate doors and all of the House doors based on Crawford's designs. Although Crawford had planned to have the doors cast in Germany, it was later decided to send them to the Ames foundry in Chicopee, Massachusetts, in 1866. The Senate doors were installed shortly thereafter, but the House doors, also designed by Crawford and Rhinehart, were not hung until 1905.

About the same time, the first large bronze statue was placed on top of a major building. Clark Mills cast Thomas Crawford's colossal statue of *Freedom* for the top of the U.S. Capitol dome and it was hoisted into position on December 2, 1863.

From 1870 to 1940, many public buildings included the integrated expressions of sculptors and architects working together, often using bronze as well as other costly materials. The City Hall of Philadelphia, designed by architect John McArthur in the Second Empire style, is a good example. Alexander Milne Calder and his staff modeled hundreds of pieces of sculpture for the building, ranging from architectural details such as carved pilaster capitals, to the gigantic bronze statue of William Penn (figure 28).

Public structures such as libraries, courthouses, post offices, and city halls often had custom-designed metal doors and other decorative features, which included appropriate historical themes. Bronze was frequently the choice for such features because of its strength, its capacity for casting in high relief, and its relatively high degree of weather resistance.

In the late 19th century, American architects used a great deal of bronze in the detailing and decoration of large neoclassical public buildings and commercial buildings such as Marshall Field and Company Department Store (figure 29). Sculptor Daniel Chester French created the large bronze doors of the Boston Public Library to complement the building's Renaissance Revival design by Charles Follen McKim. Bronze appeared in museums, libraries, university buildings, banks (figure 70), stores, and railroad stations, and other post-Columbian Exposition structures made possible by American affluence.

Many American foundries were needed to cast the intricate bronze work. Typical examples were the bronze grilles, tellers' cages, and elevator doors of several banks, such as those by York and Sawyer. Much of their bronze work was crafted by the William H. Jackson Company, and some of the finest work is still extant at the Bowery Savings Bank in New York City (figure 30). McKim, Mead, and White's bronze light standards and detailing, crafted by Hecla Company, ornament their Columbia University buildings, while the Cunard building on lower Broadway presents a vast floor seal created by the Gorham Company. Architect Cass Gilbert used bronze for the stately ornamental gates in the New York Life Insurance Building in 1928 (figure 31), as did Paul Phillipe Cret for the window grilles on the Old Federal Reserve Bank in Philadelphia in 1932.

The surface treatment of bronze works can be varied from a polished finish with high reflectance to a matte finish. One of the oldest treatments is the gilding of bronze to imitate gold, such as the brilliant gold-leafed "Prometheus" designed by Paul Manship and installed in 1934 above the ice skating rink at Rockefeller Center in New York City.

The lobby of the 35-story Koppers Building in Pittsburgh, designed in 1929 by Graham, Anderson, Probst

Figure 28. Bronze Statue of William Penn, City Hall, Philadelphia, Pennsylvania, 1886–1894; Tacony Iron and Metal Works, Philadelphia. *Bronze was chosen by sculptor Alexander Milne Calder, the grandfather of the 20th-century sculptor, for his monumental statue of William Penn, founder of Philadelphia and the colony of Pennsylvania. When Calder had completed the clay sections, his assistants executed a huge plaster model. However, the model stood idly in City Hall for a year and a half because there was no foundry in the United States capable of casting the statue, which would be the largest cast bronze statue in the world at that time. By 1889, the newly founded Tacony Iron and Metal Works was able to handle the project. On November 6, 1892, the completed statue, measuring 36 feet 4 inches tall and weighing 27 tons, was erected in the courtyard of the City Hall for public viewing while the iron clock tower was completed. Two years later, the statue was hoisted in sections to the top of the tower. (Historic photograph courtesy of George Eisenman)*

& White of Chicago, contains a wealth of Art Deco bronzework complemented by polished marble, as do many Art Deco buildings in New York City, including the Chanin Building (figure 33).

Metallurgists have added other metals to the tin-copper mixture to produce special qualities for specific uses. Additions of zinc and lead make a more ductile alloy that allows for very crisp castings. The fine molding quality of bronze is important for architectural detail work and statuary. Aluminum or iron in the bronze mixture makes a harder substance. To achieve bronzes with different colors, the proportions of each metal can be changed.

Like copper and brass, bronze was used for plating cast iron. Sir Henry Bessemer made a small fortune bronzing cast iron by using a "gold" powder. This was before he invented a process for making steel. There were other methods for coating iron ranging from bronze paint to bronze plating. As mentioned in the November 1904 *Architectural Record*, the lamps on the old U.S. Mint on Spring Garden Street in Philadelphia had "wrought-iron electro-bronze plated brackets" fabricated by John L. Gaumer Company. Several catalogues offered bronzed cast iron as well as cast iron ready for painting.

Figure 29. Bronze Clock, Marshall Field and Company Department Store Addition, corner of State and East Washington Streets, Chicago, Illinois, 1907; Graham, Anderson, Probst & White, architects. *This huge bronze clock, weighing 7 3/4 tons and hanging 17 feet above the sidewalk, was designed by Pierce Anderson for the addition to Marshall Field's store. With a 46-inch face and a minute hand measuring 27 inches, the clock and its twin on another corner of the building can be seen for blocks. These magnificent works of art have become part of the city's landscape as a fourth generation of Chicagoans meet "under the clock." (Margot Gayle)*

Figure 30. Bronze Teller Cage and Mailbox, Bowery Savings Bank, 110 East 42nd Street, New York City; 1923, York and Sawyer, architects; William H. Jackson Co., foundry. *The Bowery Savings Bank has been relatively unscathed by "modernizing" and is literally filled with bronzework: doors, elevators, check writing desks, window trim, tellers' cages, gates, and even mailboxes. (a) Although the function of tellers' cages was to provide security, they were transformed into decorative features. (b) During the late 19th and early 20th centuries, functional items such as letter boxes were custom designed for each building and integrated into the total design. (Bowery Savings Bank)*

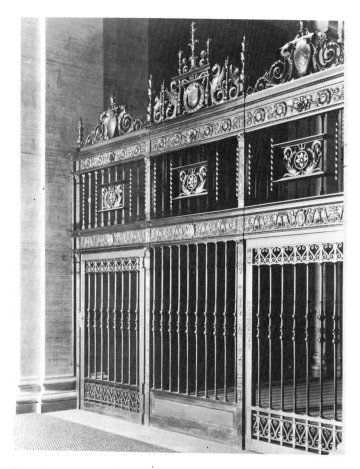

Figure 31. Bronze Screen and Gates, New York Life Insurance Company Building, 51 Madison Avenue, New York City, 1928; Cass Gilbert, architect, William H. Jackson Co., foundry. *The bronze gates in the foyer guard the broad stairway to the first basement and subway entrance. (New York Life Archives)*

Figure 32. Bronze Storefront, Grilles, Spandrel Panel, and Window, Southern Railway Building, 912 Fifteenth Street, NW, Washington, D.C., 1928; Waddy Butler Wood, architect. *This building is typical of many large commercial buildings with extensive use of bronze. Everything from the grilles to the windows and spandrels to the storefronts were fabricated of bronze. Although many storefronts have been remodelled beyond recognition, this one still has its original design and materials. (David W. Look)*

Figure 33. Bronze Ventilation Grille, Chanin Building, 405 Lexington Avenue, New York City, 1929; Sloan and Robertson, architects; lobby design by Jacques Delamarre. *The foyer of this Art Deco style building contains four highly modeled ventilation grilles in an abstract design, in what some designers called the "Futuristic" style. (David W. Look)*

Bronze is still used for doors and windows, frames, railings, elevators, escalators, lamps, and hardware. Today, commercial "bronze" and architectural "bronze" contain zinc rather than tin; these materials are actually brasses but are marketed as bronze because bronze is generally considered a more prestigious metal. One example of this is the "bronze" clad Seagram Building (figure 34) in New York City by Mies Van der Rohe.

Brass

Brass is an alloy resulting from the mixture of copper and zinc. The color of brass varies, depending upon the amount of zinc in the mixture and whether or not other metals are added. Brass with relatively large amounts of zinc are yellow in color; the addition of aluminum makes a light golden color; a small percentage of manganese produces a bronze-like color; and the addi-

Figure 34. "Bronze" Curtain Wall, Seagram Building, 375 Park Avenue, New York City, 1958; Ludwig Mies Van der Rohe, architect. *The curtain wall consists of 4 1/2- by 6-inch extruded architectural "bronze" (really brass: 57% copper, 3% lead, and 40% zinc) I-beam mullions (2 1/2 inches larger than the largest bronze sections extruded to that time), Muntz metal spandrels (brass also: 60% copper and 40% zinc), and pink-gray, heat- and glare-resistant glass in story-high architectural bronze frames. The 26-foot-long architectural bronze I-beams were extruded rather than built up with welded plates to avoid waviness in the sections. The architectural bronze, which only resembles real bronze with a statuary brown patina in color, is regularly rubbed with oil to prevent the bronze from forming a natural green patina. (Ezra Stoller)*

tion of nickel results in a silvery metal called nickel silver (for further information on nickel silver, see chapter 6).

A hard, durable, and utilitarian metal, brass makes excellent castings, can be worked hot, and extruded. A very workable brass can be made by adding a little lead. The process of extrusion is most commonly used, especially to produce large architectural pieces, including doors and elevators, and in such elements as window frame sections, hand rails, and balustrades. Brass was also used for architectural members because of its corrosion resistance.

In colonial America, public buildings and fine homes often had brass hinges, door knobs, door knockers, chandeliers, and fireplace andirons; however, almost all of the brass hardware was imported from England until after the Civil War. In the Victorian era in England and America, brass was used for light fixtures, plumbing fixtures, and every type of builder's hardware. Although much of the hardware (figures 35 and 36) was solid brass, some was cast iron plated with brass. Even such mundane fixtures as siamese connections were crafted from brass (figure 37).

The Commercial Style buildings that appeared with the increase of commerce and manufacturing in the late 19th century brought new uses of brass and other metals. The great architects of office buildings and early skyscrapers, such as Burnham and Root and Adler and Sullivan, used large quantities of brass to enhance the appearances of theaters, company headquarters, banks, and stores. Corporations and municipalities commissioned craftsmen and architects to beautify their structures; polished brass was a favorite for handrails on stair railings and in elevators, lobby furniture, bulletin boards, lobby mailboxes, name plaques, and building directories (figure 38).

As the Beaux Arts and Neoclassical styles became popular in the early 20th century, apartment buildings, hotels, and government offices were often decorated with brass in the private as well as the public spaces. It was the beauty of brass, its gleam and color, that influenced the choice rather than its more practical quality of resistance to corrosion. The Beaux Arts City-County Building in Pittsburgh (1915-1917) displays a traditional use of brass in its elevator doors, and an innovative and visually powerful use of brass-sheathed columns (figure 39). The Utah State Capitol of the same period (1913-1916) has exterior brass doors (figure 40).

In the 1920s and 1930s, some architects preferred using white metals (see nickel silver, Monel metal, stainless steel, and aluminum) to accent their designs, but other architects used brass in nontraditional ways to achieve special design effects such as the brass strips on the interior of the Hotel Edison in New York City (figure 41).

Today brass is still used for hardware, plumbing fixtures (usually chrome plated), doors, windows, elevators, and escalators. It is available in a variety of finishes—highly polished, stained, brushed, and so on. Usually the finish is protected with lacquer to prevent tarnish and eliminate the need for polishing.

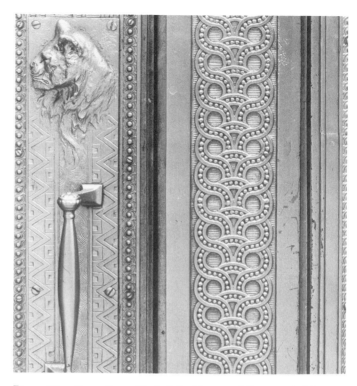

Figure 36. Brass Puma Pushplate, Door and Surround, Marquette Building, 140 Dearborn Street, Chicago, Illinois, 1893–1894; Holabird and Roche, architects; Edward Kemeys, sculptor. *The entrances and lobbies of early skyscrapers were not only finished in high-quality materials, but also were sometimes decorated by well-known artists and sculptors who were commissioned to design individual elements and details. Kemeys, who created animal sculptures for the 1893 Columbian Exposition in Chicago including the lions in front of the Art Institute on Michigan Avenue, sculpted the puma heads for the pushplates on the doors leading into the Dearborn Street lobby. (Barbara Crane, Courtesy of the Commission on Chicago Historical and Architectural Landmarks)*

Figure 35. Brass Doorknob and Escutcheon Plate, Old United States Mint, San Francisco, California, 1869–1874; Alfred B. Mullet, architect of the Treasury. *Throughout most of the 19th and into the early 20th centuries, hardware was often specially designed for significant public and some private buildings. This doorknob displays the seal of the U.S. Treasury and reflects the tastes and styles of the time by combining classical and Victorian motifs on the escutcheon plate and keyhole cover. (General Services Administration)*

Figure 37. Brass Siamese Standpipe Connection, Rookery Building, 209 South LaSalle Street, Chicago, Illinois, 1886; Burnham and Root, architects; W. D. Allen, manufacturers. *Brass fittings can be functional and very attractive when kept well polished. Even though the natural weathered dark patina on brass is protective, it is generally considered to be unsightly and great effort is expended to recapture the metallic gleam. (Margot Gayle)*

Figure 38. Brass Lobby Directory, City Hall and County Building, Chicago, Illinois, 1911; Holabird and Roche, architects. *A dual purpose lobby directory and light standard, this piece of brass lobby "furniture" displays the capacity of brass to take the most opulent and ornamental cast shapes. This design is in keeping with the elaborate style of many neoclassical buildings erected in the early years of this century. (Office of the Mayor, City of Chicago)*

b.

a.

Figure 39. Brass Elevator Doors and Brass-Sheathed Columns, City-County Building, Pittsburgh, Pennsylvania, 1915–1917; Palmer, Hornbostel and Jones, architects; Edward B. Lee, associate architect; Tiffany and Co., designers (for columns only). *(a) Brass was used extensively for interior decorative features in 19th- and 20th-century buildings, and was especially popular for statuary, large-scale furniture, and elevator doors in government and office buildings. This set of highly modelled brass doors tells the story of Pittsburgh's development as reflected in its important buildings. (b) The large structural steel columns that support the barrel vault of the lobby are sheathed in brass—an unusual choice of material for columns. Over the years the fluted shafts and stylized capitals had acquired a dull, dark patina, but when the lobby was restored in 1972, the columns were polished and lacquered to return them to their original appearance. (Pittsburgh History and Landmarks Foundation)*

Figure 41. Brass Wall Trim, Edison Hotel, 228 West 47th Street, New York City; 1929–1930, Herbert J. Krapp, architect. *Here is a very unconventional use of brass. Thin strips of brass on the walls and ceiling along with mirrors, murals, and chrome-plated railings, all contrast and contribute to the precise composition of this Art Deco interior. (Stan Shaffer)*

Figure 40. Brass Doors, Utah State Capitol, Salt Lake City, 1913–1916; Richard Kletting, architect. *Brass was not used for exterior doors as often as bronze, although many doors that are reportedly bronze may actually be brass. These highly polished exterior brass doors, make a strong architectural statement reinforcing the overall design of the building. Classical motifs include Roman grate windows, circular shields in the lower panels, and a scallop design in the transom. (Margot Gayle)*

Chapter 6: Nickel and Nickel Alloys

Nickel is a hard, silvery-white metal familiar to most Americans because of its use in coinage. However, the U.S. 5-cent piece, commonly called a "nickel," is an alloy of 25% nickel and 75% copper. Canada is by far the world's largest producer of nickel; the United States has only minor deposits in Missouri, Oregon, and Alaska.

Although electroplating with nickel was accomplished as early as the 1840s, the nickel plating industry was not established in America until the 1870s. Although somewhat rare, nickel has been used for plating architectural details, such as religious decorations, letters for signs, and hardware. The copper-plated facade of the cast-iron building designed by Richard Morris Hunt in New York City had sections that were nickel plated. Designed by Long and Kees and completed in 1889, the Minneapolis Public Library (demolished in 1950s) had nickel plated stair railings fabricated by Winslow Brothers Company of Chicago. Architects Hollabird and Root used a stair railing of "flat" nickel for the LaSalle-Wacker Building in Chicago in 1930.

Nickel is more frequently used for building components in the form of alloys: nickel silver, Monel metal, and stainless steel. Today over 50% of the nickel produced goes into the fabrication of nickel-steels and nickel-chromium steels, commonly called stainless steels. The properties and uses of stainless steel will be discussed in a later chapter (see chapter 7).

Nickel Silver

The ancient Chinese developed a nickel-copper alloy called "Paktong," which was first imported to England in the 17th century. Decorative items made from this metal, such as fireplace screens and candleholders, became popular in England and its colonies. In Charleston, South Carolina, the Miles Brewton House has a nickel silver fireplace screen purchased in 1730. By the early 19th century, English and German metalworkers were producing the white metal in their own countries. "Merry's Metal Blanc" was produced in Birmingham and "German Silver" in Berlin. The latter name was in common use until World War I, when the generic term nickel silver replaced it. Both of these terms were misnomers because the alloys contained little nickel and neither contained any silver, but each had a silver-white appearance.

Nickel silver sometimes has been called "white brass" but probably should be termed "nickel brass" because it generally contains 75% copper, 20% nickel, and 5% zinc. Different percentages result in a range of colors and improved properties for specific fabrication methods such as casting or extrusion. Shades of nickel silver can range from silvery-white to pale yellow but can also be produced with a slight blue, green, or pink tone to harmonize with other building materials or to contrast with other metals. For instance the Squibb Building at Fifth Avenue and 58th Street in New York City has a pink-toned nickel silver specially formulated by Anaconda Brass. Designed by architects Buchman and Kahn in 1930, the entrance, elevators, stair railing, and elevator doors were fabricated of nickel silver to harmonize with the warm tones of the lobby's stone veneer.

When nickel silver was cast earlier in this century, a small amount of tin and lead were added and the zinc content was kept below 20% to improve the casting

Figure 42. Nickel Silver Doors, Manufacturers Hanover Trust, 481 Seventh Avenue, New York City, 1930; Sugarman and Berger, architects. *Cast in yellow nickel silver, the Art Deco style doors on this bank look like brass and are in striking contrast to the bronze door surround and red granite walls. (David W. Look)*

properties. The metal was popular for sculpture, decorative panels, plaques, chandeliers, doors, grilles, and railings (figures 42, 43, and 44). The terms *white bronze* and *nickel bronze* were used for cast nickel silver hardware, not necessarily because of the low tin content (2½% to 4%), but because of a cultural preference for the more prestigious bronze.

Nickel silver hardware was popular in the United States during the Art Deco and Depression Modern periods. Architects and designers preferred nickel silver because it could take and retain appropriate finishes, and it resisted corrosion. For the same reasons, cast nickel silver was used for fine plumbing fixtures and water fountains in monumental public buildings, hotels, and even custom-designed homes. It was also usually the base material for nickel-plated fixtures.

Strips of nickel silver have been used to separate different colors of terrazzo flooring. Nickel silver door frames, window frames, and parts of storefronts were usually fabricated from extruded sections that contained 8% to 15% nickel and 40% to 50% copper, with a large percentage of zinc making up the balance. Doors and spandrels, above and below windows, generally were rolled, pressed, or cast. Many companies have produced and promoted nickel silver under numerous trade names, such as "Nevada silver," "Queen's metal," "White metal," and "Wolfram brass." F. B. Howard-White gives a partial list of trade names in his book *Nickel: An Historical Review*.

Designed by architects Schultz and Weaver, the Waldorf Astoria Hotel in New York City is a *tour de force* of nickel silver works. The entrance, fabricated from cast, rolled, and extruded shapes, displays a great variety of color and finishes from white to a brassy yellow and from satin to a highly polished finish.

In addition to its having a wide range of natural color, nickel silver was frequently contrasted with other metals. In the U.S. Post Office Department Building on Pennsylvania Avenue at 12th Street, in Washington, D.C., architects Delano and Aldrich in 1934 set up a progression of color and contrast to achieve a varied design experience. This progression included exterior ornamental doors of bronze; ventilation grilles of nickel silver with bronze stars immediately inside the doors; inner vestibule doors of nickel silver, bronze, and glass; "Pony Express Rider" elevator doors of nickel silver; and identical bronze doors adjacent to the stair tower. The nickel silver used in the building is very white and the bronze is yellow, without a brown statuary patina.

In the first National City Bank in New York City, pale yellow nickel silver is contrasted with red bronze (figure 45). Probably the most elaborate set of nickel silver doors were those of the Goelet Building. The tympanum above these doors used the contrasting colors of nickel silver, copper, bronze, and brass (figure 46).

Two fine outdoor sculptures displayed at the Museum of the City of New York were made of nickel silver containing 16% nickel. The two statues, weighing about one ton each, are of Alexander Hamilton and De Witt Clinton. They were designed by Adolph A. Weinman and cast by the Roman Bronze Works. Today, these statues

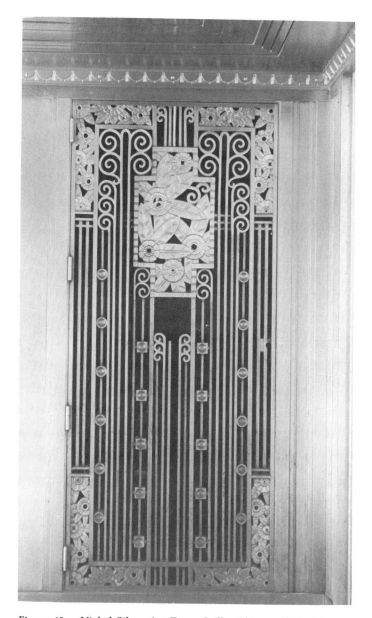

Figure 43.   Nickel Silver Art Deco Grille, Chicago Daily News Building (now Riverside Plaza Building), 2 North Riverside Plaza, Chicago, Illinois, 1929; Holabird and Root, architects. *Nickel silver, one of the polished "white metals" popular in the Art Moderne movement, now called Art Deco, was used in this building for radiator grilles, elevator doors, directory cases, and stair railings. (Margot Gayle)*

have a patina similar to the bluish-green color of weathered bronze.

Nickel silver is still used for a variety of architectural elements, but not as frequently as it was in the 1920s and 1930s. Today only a white alloy of nickel silver is readily available; however, other colors can be custom ordered to match existing original work. For cast nickel silver, manganese is now substituted for tin in the formula.

Figure 45.   Nickel Silver Check Writing Desk and Teller Cages, City Bank Farmers Trust Company (now First National City Bank), 6 Hanover Street, New York City, 1931; Cross and Cross, architects. *To achieve subtle definition and emphasis, architects frequently contrasted materials and colors in Art Deco designs. The nickel silver entrance doors and transom (not shown) of this building are accented with red bronze plaques. The grille of the teller windows (background) also has details in bronze, while the desk (foreground) is mono-chromatic, using only nickel silver. (David W. Look)*

Figure 44.   Nickel Silver Railings, Texas Commerce Bank, Gulf Building, Houston, Texas, 1929; Alfred C. Finn, Kenneth Franzenheim, J. E. R. Carpenter, associated architects; Gorham Co., foundry, Providence, Rhode Island. *The doors to the banking rooms, elevators, and shops and all radiator grilles were cast by the Gorham foundry, well-known for its fine art metal work. The nickel silver railings in the lobby galleries reflect the enthusiasm for Egyptian designs in Europe and America following the discovery of Tutankhamen's tomb. (Ed Stewart Photography and Associates, Inc., courtesy of Texas Commerce Bank)*

a.

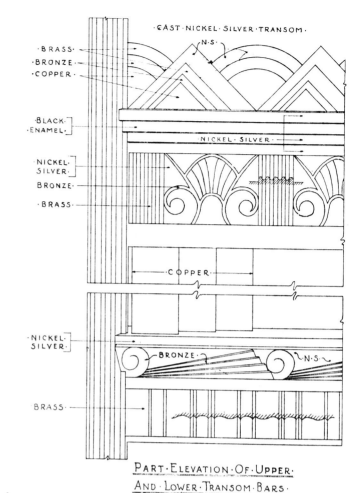

b.

Figure 46.   Nickel Silver Doors and Tympanum, Goelet
Building, New York City, 1932; E. H. Faile, architect; General
Bronze Corp., foundry, Long Island, New York. *(a) This Art
Deco-style entrance features silvery-yellow geometric doors
which are almost overshadowed by the exuberant swan and
fountain design in the tympanum with its array of colorful
shapes. (b) The effect was achieved with a combination of copper, bronze, brass, nickel silver, and black enamel as indicated
on the original drawing. When the first-floor facade was
remodeled in 1966, the doors were removed and stored; the
tympanum was taken to Newport, Rhode Island, to be
reinstalled in a private club. (International Nickel Company)*

Monel Metal

Monel metal is an alloy of approximately two-thirds nickel and one-third copper. It is not a nickel silver because it consists of more nickel than copper and does not contain any zinc. It is similar to platinum in color.

Until the 20th century, nickel from Canadian mines was sold mainly for the production of nickel silver. Before that, copper-nickel alloys were produced by refining the copper and nickel separately and then recombining them. Later an effort was made to refine the copper and nickel at the same time and produce nickel silver or a metal to compete with it.

Early in 1905, Robert C. Stanley succeeded in driving off the sulphur through a roasting process, and then smelted the copper-nickel ore together to produce a sample of a new nickel-copper alloy. The first bar was stamped "Monell Metal" in honor of Ambrose Monell, then president of International Nickel. When the name was registered as a trademark one "l" was dropped because the law prohibited the use of a family name as a trademark.

Monel metal has been called a natural alloy since the proportion of nickel to copper is the same in the ore and metal; each contains roughly 68% to 72% nickel and 28% to 32% copper. The properties of this new alloy, its methods of production, and its possible uses were studied simultaneously.

Monel metal was ductile, yet stronger than mild steel and more resistant to corrosion from sulfuric acid or saltwater than bronze. In fact, Monel pioneered many of the present uses of stainless steel. The first architectural use of Monel was for roofing of the Pennsylvania Railroad Terminal in New York City in 1909 (figure 47).

Over 300,000 square feet of rolled sheets were used to cover the station. Although the iron and steel bridges and skylights on the roof had deteriorated and were replaced with ones made of Monel in 1936, the roof was still in excellent condition when the building was demolished.

The Chicago Northwestern Railroad Station, also built in 1909, has Monel metal skylights, ventilators, and smoke hoods, features which through the years were exposed to a polluted atmosphere produced by steam engines belching smoke and soot. In 1936 the copper roof on the New York City Public Library at Fifth Avenue and 42nd Street was replaced with a Monel metal roof.

Figure 47.   Monel Roof, Pennsylvania Railroad Terminal, New York City, 1907–1910; McKim, Mead and White, architects; International Nickel Company. *The first architectural use of Monel metal was the sheet roofing of the Pennsylvania Station, which was completed in 1909. When the station was demolished in 1965, the Monel roof was in excellent condition, having needed no major repairs since its installation. (International Nickel Company)*

There were several advantages of Monel roofing: it could be brazed, welded, or soldered in place to provide a watertight, continuous cover; it had a low coefficient of expansion and, with proper expansion joints, resisted fatigue failure well; and it could be seamed if desired, using double-lock seams similar to those used for soft metal roofs, such as copper. Monel did not corrode and stain adjacent materials; it was stronger than mild steel, which permitted wider spans and fewer structural supports; and it was durable, permitting the use of lighter-gauge metal sheets. Monel metal flashing has also been used with other roofing materials such as lead as at the National Cathedral in Washington, D.C., and with built-up roofing as at the Pentagon.

Monel metal can be worked by every other method of metalworking except extrusion and joined by every known method of connection. The finishes of Monel can range from highly polished to hammered and sand-blasted, or from etched to brushed. All of the Monel metal doors in the nonpublic areas of the National Archives Building in Washington, D.C., have mirror-like finishes.

Designers in the Art Deco and Depression Modern periods strongly favored the white metals, especially when contrasted with yellow metals such as bronze. Monel metal, like nickel silver, was very popular for decorative exterior and interior metalwork. The Union Trust Building in Detroit is an extravagant example of Monel metalwork (figure 48). A monumental screen of Monel metal separates the bank from the lobby entrance, and all the other metalwork—elevator doors, grilles, gates, teller cages, and check-writing desks—are of Monel.

Artistic effects could be achieved with Monel metal. The sculptural panels on the nickel silver doors of the United Nations Building in New York City were cast of Monel (figure 49). Like bronze, Monel can be etched, as the elevator doors were in the Walker Building in Washington, D.C. (figure 50).

Monel-clad steel was first introduced in 1930, but its use does not appear to have been very extensive, probably because of cost. During World War II, large quantities of nickel and copper had to be diverted to the war effort and the supply of Monel was greatly reduced. After the war, stainless steel and aluminum replaced Monel because of their lower production cost. However, 42,000 pounds of Monel and 42 ounces of gold leaf were used in 1959 to cover the dome of the Georgia State Capitol in Atlanta. The drains, downspouts, and sheathing of the base of the dome were also of Monel. Today Monel metal is still produced, but it is not frequently used in architecture since it is more expensive than stainless steel.

a.

Figure 48. Monel Entrance Screen, Elevator Door, and Tellers' Cages, National Bank of Commerce (now Michigan National Bank), Union Trust Building (now Guardian Building), 500 Griswold, Detroit, Michigan, 1928; Smith, Hinchman and Grylls, architects; Gorham Co., Providence, Rhode Island. *(a) Over 40,000 pounds of Monel metal were used in this Art Deco bank and office building for such features as the Monel clock, two-story grille, gates, railings, and signs of this monumental entrance screen. (b) The design of the elevators was executed in Monel metal and colorful favrile glass from Tiffany. (c) In the banking area, Monel was used for tellers' cages, grilles, gates, check writing desks, screens, and even switch plates. The commercial areas were similarly enriched with Monel. (a and b) Smith, Hinchman and Grylls, architects; (c) Allen Stross, NAER)*

b.

c.

Figure 49. Monel and Nickel Silver Doors, United Nations General Assembly Building, First Avenue between East 42nd and 48th Streets, New York City, 1953; Ernest Cormier, designer, Montreal. *The contrasting pale yellow nickel silver and platinum-colored Monel metal doors were a gift from Canada to the United Nations. The seven nickel silver doors were fabricated from extruded sections by the Anaconda American Brass, Ltd.; and the Monel metal sculptural panels representing Truth, Peace, Justice, and Fraternity were cast by Robert Mitchell Company, Ltd. (David W. Look)*

Figure 50. Etched Monel Metal Elevator Doors, Walker Building, 734 15th Street, NW, Washington, D.C., 1937; Porter and Lockie, architects, Baltimore. *The Egyptian Revival design was etched into the highly polished Monel metal doors, providing a subtle decorative effect. (Walter Smalling, Jr.)*

Chapter 7: Iron and Iron Alloys

The metallic element iron is called *ferrum* in Latin, hence the term ferrous metal for iron and steel. Iron ores constitute approximately one-twentieth of the Earth's surface; it has been known and used by many civilizations through the centuries. The role of iron has expanded from that of a material for tools, firebacks, pots and kettles, wagon rims, nails, cannons, and machines to that of an important architectural building component. It has been used in three common forms—as cast iron, wrought iron, and more recently as steel.

Cast iron was a major 19th-century building material of the Industrial Revolution, while wrought iron was used for minor structural and also decorative elements from the 18th century on. Introduced to the construction industry at the end of the 19th century, steel and its specialized alloys provide some of the basic structural materials for buildings of the modern world.

The tell-tale sign of a ferrous metal is rust. Application of a magnet to a painted or even rusted metal surface will reveal the presence of iron. It is found in a pure state in nature only in meteors. Iron used in construction is usually one of the three principal iron-carbon alloys. The percentage of carbon makes the difference: *wrought iron* contains little carbon (not over .035%); *steel* has a moderate carbon content (between .06% and 2%); and *cast iron* has a high carbon content (2% to 4%).

Wrought Iron

Iron that is worked or wrought at an anvil, or shaped by machines at a larger forge, is called wrought iron. Wrought iron constituted the major use of this metal until around the mid-18th century when in England, and to a lesser degree in France, new technologies increased the production and availability of cast iron. Wrought iron is tough and stringy; it has the elasticity and tensile strength needed for bolts, beams, and girders.

Wrought iron is also remarkably malleable, which means it can be reheated and hot-worked again and again to the desired shape. The more wrought iron is worked the stronger it becomes; it is also easily welded. The final product can be a thing of beauty, as in the case of hand-wrought gates and grilles. It can also be something as simple and utilitarian as a kitchen ladle, a spade, a plow, a fireplace spit, a shoe-scraper for a porch stoop, or a length of fencing.

Until the mid-19th century, the use of wrought iron in buildings was generally limited to relatively small items such as tie rods, straps, nails, and hardware, or to

decorative ironwork in balconies, railings, fences, and gates. Around 1850 its structural use became more widespread as iron mills began to roll rails, bulb-tees, and eventually, true I-beams.

Decorative Wrought Iron

American wrought-iron artistry is the direct descendant of centuries of work in this medium in other countries where, besides making utilitarian equipment, the smiths made iron objects that sometimes displayed the quality of jewelers' work. Examples include "chased," carved iron boxes, ornamented by engraving or embossing; elaborate door hinges, locks, and doorknobs; and ingeniously wrought doorknockers. Sometimes the iron objects were "damascened" or inlaid with silver or gold, as in the best armor work.

Fences, gates, railings, and balconies have been traditional architectural uses of wrought iron. The iron combines the strength and ornamentation desired in each of these items. The wrought iron balcony at Congress Hall in Philadelphia (figure 51) was signed and dated by the craftsman, S. Wheeler, in 1788. Wheeler also made and signed the ornate gates of Christ Church in Philadelphia (figure 52). Although such identification became common for cast iron, it was rare for wrought iron.

Toward the end of the 18th century, small castings of rosettes, bows, spearheads, and anthemions—first in lead and later in cast iron—were made as part of wrought-iron fence designs. The influential British architects Robert and James Adam designed composite wrought- and cast-iron fences which became popular, first in England and later in the American colonies. Adam-style ironwork can still be seen in older American cities such as Boston, Philadelphia, and Charleston.

The visual effect achievable with wrought iron ranged from simple, straight, geometric designs to curvilinear, organic designs (figure 53). Since each part is individually hand made, no two are identical. The subtle variation in shape and tool marks adds to the unique artistic expression of each piece of ironwork. In general, wrought iron is light in appearance and uses only enough material to achieve the desired design. In contrast, cast iron usually appears more massive (larger designs were usually hollow but appear solid) with highly repetitive design elements.

Many nonstructural uses of wrought iron were only minimally decorative. Some utilitarian objects such as wrought iron shutters were made of rolled sheets of iron and were quite plain (figure 54).

Figure 51. **Wrought-iron Balcony, Samuel Wheeler, blacksmith; Congress Hall, 1787–1789, Chestnut Street at 6th Street, Independence National Historical Park, Philadelphia, Pennsylvania.** *Built as the Philadelphia County Court House, this building was used by the Federal Congress from 1790 to 1800. In 1961, the National Park Service removed many layers of paint from the balcony over the front door prior to its restoration. During the process, the name and date "S. Wheeler 1788" was discovered. The inscription was located on the inside of the balcony facing the window. Just a few layers of new paint have already obscured the marking. (Jack E. Boucher, NAER)*

a.

b.

Figure 52. Wrought-iron Gates, Samuel Wheeler, blacksmith; Christ Church, 22-26 North Second Street, Philadelphia, Pennsylvania, 1727-1744; attributed to Dr. John Kearsley, builder-architect. *(a) The wrought iron was heated, hammered, bent, and twisted to achieve the various parts of the design. The verticals were split and then bent to form the scrolls, rather than bent and attached to the verticals. (b) Like the balcony on Congress Hall (see figure 51), these gates are signed and dated; "S. Wheeler 1795" appears on the edge of the gate, seen only when the gates are open. (Jack E. Boucher, NAER)*

Decorative work in wrought iron was popular throughout the United States. Beautiful grilles, galleries and stair railings, both interior and exterior, remain from the late 18th and early 19th centuries in many eastern seaboard cities and in towns throughout the South. An early surviving design, the grille on the Old City Hall and Market in Mobile, Alabama, combines wrought-iron woven wire with cast-iron fasteners (figure 55), a technique widely used for grilles and fences.

Later 19th-century buildings display decorative wrought-iron and cast-iron stair railings, porches, balconies, verandas, roof cresting, lamps, grilles, fences, and canopies (figure 56).

At the end of the 19th and beginning of the 20th centuries, there was a rebirth of the crafts in America, of which ironworking was a part (figure 57). Fine artistic expressions were achieved in wrought iron by blacksmiths such as Samuel Yellin in and around the Philadelphia and Washington, D.C., areas (figure 58). Wrought iron was used on every type of building from residences, to Art Deco office buildings and stores. Although most blacksmiths used traditional methods, commercial ironworking firms began to use welding instead of rivets and collars and to use machines to bend and twist bars.

Structural Wrought Iron

In addition to ornamental uses, wrought iron, was also widely used in small-scale structural forms such as the rods or strapwork for strengthening devices in buildings of stone, brick, or wood. The most pervasive use of wrought iron was for hand-forged iron nails, which were used until the 19th century. Craftsmen also devised wrought-iron cramps to hold stone veneer onto brick bearing walls and to anchor wooden elements into masonry walls.

Figure 53.   Wrought-iron Fence, Frederick Ames Mansion, 306 Dartmouth, Boston, Massachusetts, 1872; John Sturgis, architect.
This fence was fabricated by hand from iron bars; square and round sections were hot-worked into spirals, circles, and scrolls. Even the fence posts are compact spirals of strong rods shaped about a central support to make them rigid. (Esther Mipaas)

Figure 54. Wrought-iron Shutters, Arch Street Meeting House, 302-338 Arch Street, Philadelphia, Pennsylvania, 1803–1804; Owen Biddle, architect and master builder. *The shutter is on the window of the "fireproof" vault used to store records. The iron shutter has a frame of hand-forged rectangular bars to which a series of rolled sheets was riveted. (George Eisenman)*

Figure 55. Wrought-iron Guard, Old City Hall and Market, 111 South Royal Street, Mobile, Alabama, 1853; ironwork by J. B. Wickersham, New York City. *Wickersham produced some of the earliest iron foundry catalogues, with his first published in 1855. It was probably through his catalogue advertising that he generated so much later business in the South. Although his catalogues carried everything from iron beds to verandas, his fences were most popular and can be found almost everywhere. Most of these designs were based on his patent for bending bars and then fixing them in place by casting rosettes onto the intersection of the bars. (NAER, Library of Congress)*

Figure 56. Wrought-iron and Glass Canopy, 1734 N Street, NW, Washington, D.C., ca. 1885. *Iron is found in a variety of forms from strap hinges to fragile glass and iron combinations—such as the canopy protecting the entrance of this elegant townhouse. Glass panels were set in an iron frame with fleurs de lis on the front edge and flourishes as supporting brackets. (David W. Look)*

Figure 57. **Wrought-iron Door, Joslyn Castle, 3902 Davenport Street, Omaha, Nebraska, 1902–1904; Winslow Bros., foundry, Omaha.** *The one-ton iron door to the entrance hall of this Scottish baronial-style mansion is precison balanced and swings easily. A hand-forged wrought-iron grille consisting of scroll and vine motifs is set in Gothic cast-iron framing. (Robert Peters)*

Figure 58. **Wrought-iron Entrance Gates, Packard Building, southeast corner of Chestnut and 15th streets, Philadelphia, Pennsylvania; 1924, Ritter and Shay, architects; Samuel Yellin, artist and blacksmith.** *In the 20th century, the name Yellin stands for excellence in ironwork in America. Although he called himself a blacksmith, he was much more—an artist with iron for his medium. An immigrant from Poland, Yellin executed most of his major commissions between 1920 and 1940. He used every method of metalworking—cutting, splitting, twisting, scrolling, punching, incising, repoussé, and banding— to achieve unique designs. (David W. Look)*

Figure 59. **Wrought-iron Tie Rods with Cast-iron Star Anchors.** *Wrought-iron tie rods were added to buildings to prevent the walls from buckling or separating from interior walls. The rods were bolted to cross beams or to a parallel masonry wall. They were always made of wrought iron to take tension. To prevent horizontal forces from pulling the tie rods through the wall, they were connected to cast-iron stars, rosettes, or "S" anchors on the outside of the wall. The anchors, which spread the force over a greater area, were the only visual evidence of the presence of the tie rods. As a precaution, tie rods and anchors were sometimes included in original construction; but the more usual use was their addition when an outer brick wall began to lean or buckle. The addition of a tie rod could not bring the wall back to its original vertical alignment, but it prevented the wall from moving further. (David W. Look)*

Often the hidden iron bars, straps, pins, U-shaped bridle-irons, and tie rods are revealed only at times of alteration or demolition. Star-shaped anchors on the exterior brick walls of old buildings mark the location of wrought-iron tie rods, sometimes called straps, which may be tied to wooden joists inside or may run through the structure to hold the wall in plumb. Often the anchors, which are of cast iron, take the form of stars, but they may be S-scrolls or fancier devices (figure 59). Occasionally tie rods are visible and are even ornamented, as in the Trolley Station in Seattle's Pioneer Square (figure 60).

Wrought-iron rods were universally used in mid-19th-century wooden and iron trusses for buildings and bridges where the structural member was put in tension. Also, flat link chain and cables of early suspension bridges were made of wrought iron (figure 61).

Cast-iron bow-string trusses with wrought-iron tension members were fabricated by John B. Wickersham in New York, for the Harper Brothers' printing plant with its block-long cast-iron facade, which was erected in 1854. Early that year, Peter Cooper produced in his Trenton, New Jersey, foundry the first large wrought-iron rail beams, which also went into Harpers' innovative building. Both the 7-inch-tall bulbed-T rails, so called because of their shape (the "Cooper Beams"), as well as the 8-inch "I" beams first rolled by Cooper and Hewitt about 1855, were eminently suitable for interior metal framing of large buildings (figure 62).

Soon iron beams were in great demand. John Jacob Astor wanted them for his new library on Astor Place in New York City. The beams were the prototypes of new, mass-produced framing for the trend-setting "elevator buildings" that architects were building taller than the traditional five- and six-story walk-ups. This usage lasted for several decades, certainly well after steel was available. The use of structural wrought iron gradually came to an end as the qualities of structural steel became apparent and as steel was produced in quantity.

From 1855 to 1890, the most frequent structural combination was rolled wrought-iron beams for the horizontal members with cast-iron columns for the vertical members. A great many commercial and public buildings were constructed with this type of framing, for example, the 16-story Manhattan Building, designed by William LeBaron Jenney in 1840, and still standing in Chicago's Loop.

The old Custom House in Wheeling, West Virginia, is an interesting pre-Civil War example of this. The specifications prepared in 1856 by Ammi B. Young, then Supervising Architect of the U.S. Treasury, called for a great deal of iron in its construction, although this is not evident in its three-story limestone exterior. Cast-iron columns and wrought-iron beams support the segmental brick arches which comprise the fire-resistant floor system and a corrugated iron roof that covers the building. Two-hundred thirty-eight iron beams and 44 iron girders for the building were ordered from the Trenton Iron Works of New Jersey.

Wrought iron served as a major structural material in the United States for more than 30 years. Its manufacture was always tedious, as production demanded exhausting labor even after the mid-19th century, when

Figure 60.   Iron and Glass Pergola, Trolley Station, Pioneer Square, Seattle, Washington, 1909. *This station, which has become a symbol of the revival of the city's old commercial area, consists of glass panes held between ribs of wrought iron supported by cast-iron arches and columns, both of which are in compression. The wrought-iron tie rods (top of photo) take the outward thrust of the arches; thus, the rods are in tension. Iron members in tension had to be made of wrought iron because cast iron is suitable only for compressive loads. However, iron members in compression could be of either cast iron or wrought iron, whichever was more economical and convenient for the iron shop to fabricate. By the late 1960s, most of the glass in the pergola was broken and the iron was rusting. Preservationists, planners, and city officials worked together to rehabilitate Pioneer Square with the pergola as its centerpiece. Wooden patterns were carved from which sand molds were made to recast the lost and broken iron parts. With new lamps and fresh paint, the pergola was rededicated in 1973. (John Jochman, Seattle Office of Historic Preservation)*

large rails and beams could be produced mechanically. In 1856, scarcely 3 years after the advance in the rolling of wrought iron, Henry Bessemer in England demonstrated his new means of steel production. About a decade later, William Siemens and his brothers devised their open-hearth steel-making process. Together, these British advances paved the way for the mass production of steel at a moderate cost.

Nonetheless, many American public buildings, particularly those from the period just after the Civil War, have structural wrought-iron framing. Today, very little wrought iron is produced and almost all that is sold as wrought iron is really mild steel.

Figure 61. Suspension Bridge, Public Garden, Boston, Massachusetts, 1867; Elemens Herschel and William Preston, engineers.
Popular among Bostonians, this small suspension bridge originally consisted of plank flooring hung from chains made of flat wrought-iron links. In 1921 the bridge's deteriorated wood was replaced with steel beams; the bridge was reinforced in 1975 with more steel and concrete. Although the deck has been replaced, the masonry piers and the chains hung between them are still largely original. (Carleton Knight, III)

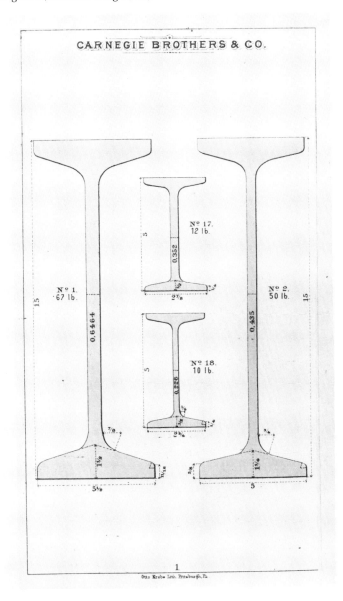

Figure 62. Wrought-iron Beams, Carnegie Brothers and Company's Pocket Companion . . . , 1876. *The earliest known wrought-iron handbook of wrought iron structural shapes was published by Carnegie Kloman and Co. in 1873, some 18 years after the first wrought-iron I-beams were rolled in the United States by the Trenton Iron Works, founded by Peter Cooper. Copies of the 1873 handbook are quite rare; however, the Library of Congress has a copy of the 1876 handbook of Carnegie Brothers and Co. The* Iron and Steel Beams: 1873 to 1952, *published by the American Institute of Steel Construction, Inc., is a valuable resource book because it documents the handbook dates, the sizes, weights, and properties of all rolled beams during this period. The largest beam in the 1873 handbook was 15 inches deep and 67 pounds per lineal foot, the same as the beam shown in this illustration at the far left. (Library of Congress)*

Cast Iron

Perhaps no metal is more versatile than the ferrous metal known as cast iron. Between the mid-1700s and the mid-1800s, improved technology for the production of cast iron increased the supply greatly, while the expanded technology for its use led to its full exploitation in architecture and engineering.

Cast iron is very hard and, because of the flakes of carbon it absorbs during production, it is brittle. At the same time, it is remarkably strong in compression—the reason it would be the standard choice for structural columns for over a century. Cast iron is much weaker in tension than in compression, thus it is not appropriate for structural beams. There are examples of disastrous failures of some overburdened cast-iron beams.

The first bridge of cast iron, completed in 1779 over the River Severn in England, gave its name to the adjacent community, Ironbridge, in Shropshire. All of the cast-iron arches are in compression. The bridge still stands and has been restored recently. Shortly before 1800, structural cast-iron columns were first used in the construction of multistoried factory buildings in England, especially for textile mills. The new iron columns were fire-resistant and strong, allowing for increased distance between columns, thus providing more floor space for looms and other machinery. In domestic buildings, the increasingly available cast iron was made into iron stoves and firebacks for improved heating, into pots and smoothing irons and into iron pipes to conduct water.

At first, English technology predominated, even in America. Many finished iron products were exported to the colonies, but numerous iron casting works were established in New Jersey, Pennsylvania, and Massachusetts before the Revolution.

After the Revolution, many blast furnaces were built which could remelt pig iron (refined iron poured into crude molds to form bars) and form castings in varied shapes. Typical of the work being done was that of New York founder Peter Curtenius who announced in the *Daily Advertiser* of October 17, 1787, that he could make many household items and save the purchaser "the duty of £6 being laid on foreign casting." He and many other founders saw a ready market for the Franklin-type open and closed stoves as well as other heating equipment, machine parts, wagon and other vehicle components, and cooking utensils. In the early decades of the 19th century, these foundries began to turn out cast-iron fencing, fence posts, and simple cast-iron columns for building purposes.

Structural Cast Iron

Columns

Builders started using cast-iron columns instead of the standard timber mill-type construction in early-19th-century industrial buildings. The oldest part of the Middle Mills near Utica, New York, erected in 1825, exemplifies this. The three-story mill with basement was an early example of the American industrial framing system following English models—a combination of iron and wood that would be widely used for more than a half a

century. On each level there was a double row of 12 slender 11-foot-high fluted iron columns. There is no record of where these iron columns were cast. However, they supported wood girders and joists that held floors laden with machinery until recently when the mill was vacated. In the mid-19th century, the framing system became one of cast-iron columns with wrought-iron beams; wood beams were eliminated in favor of the stronger iron.

William Strickland was one of the first American architects to use cast-iron columns. In 1820 he employed them in Philadelphia's Chestnut Street Theatre to support three rows of box seats. A similar treatment was used later by architect Benjamin Latrobe in the gallery enlargement of St. John's Church, opposite the White House in Washington, D.C. In both cases, the new

Figure 63. Cast-iron Gasholder, Petersburg Gaslight Company, Petersburg, Virginia, 1851–1852. *The Greek Revival style gasholder has six pairs of slender Doric columns three tiers high which served as "guides" for the expandable tanks. Cast-iron horizontal members, which provided stability and carried only their own weight, are widest at the centers to resist bending. In this case the top of the beam is in compression and the bottom is in tension. To reduce weight, the beams were perforated with circles graduated in size toward the ends. (Jack E. Boucher, NAER)*

material was strong enough to be used sparingly, permitting a larger seating capacity and better sight lines for the audience.

In 1833, the U.S. Naval Home in Philadelphia, another Strickland design, was opened. The two-tiered verandas were supported by hollow cast-iron columns, 8 inches in diameter, and the iron railings were a lattice of thin-woven wrought-iron strips strengthened with small rosette shaped cast-iron clamps.

Cast-iron columns (figure 63) were often secured from small local foundries. Later, if they could not be procured locally, they were ordered from catalogues published by a number of large firms, such as James L. Jackson Ironworks and Architectural Iron Works, New York (figure 64), Buffalo Eagle Works, and Tasker and Co., Philadelphia.

Building Fronts

In the last century, cast iron was used for building fronts (figures 65 and 66). Its function was both decorative and structural. The ironwork could comprise the entire facade or only the first-floor level (figure 67). It could support its own weight and part of the floor system when used in a building on a corner lot.

As early as 1825 there were cast-iron storefronts in Manhattan. An advertisement appeared in the *New York Evening Post* on March 29 of that year which told of two buildings under construction and soon to be available for rent that had ground floors, or storefronts, constructed of cast iron and upper stories of brick. The buildings stood on the south side of Burling Slip which was the waterside end of John Street at the East River. They were mid-block between Water Street and Pearl Street near the Seventh Ward Bank.

"Store to Let: The subscriber is now building two handsome four story brick stores with iron fronts three doors from Pearl Street in Burling Slip. They are intended for the dry goods or hardware business and will be let from the first of May next. For terms apply to: Richard Patten, Corner of Burling Slip and Water Street."

Buildings with iron fronts, like buildings with expensive stone fronts, displayed these facades to the street only. Behind the facades, the structures usually had walls of brick and floor systems of wood (figure 68).

The full iron front and the one-story iron storefront were American-type commercial structures not found, to any great extent, in other countries. Significant iron front buildings can be found in Louisville, Kentucky; Montgomery, Alabama; Galveston, Texas; Binghamton, Rochester and Cooperstown, New York; Baltimore, Maryland; Portland and Salem, Oregon (figures 69 and 70). Once there were many more of these serviceable and decorative commercial buildings, but thousands were demolished in the 1950s, 1960s, and early 1970s in urban renewal clearances of old business districts.

Virtually all cast-iron front buildings were erected during the mid- to late 1800s. In the late 1840s, James Bogardus introduced the cast-iron facade as a new building type and as a system of prefabricated "fireproof" construction. Although cast iron was known to be non-combustible, it was soon learned that it was not "fireproof." Columns, panels, and decorative elements were

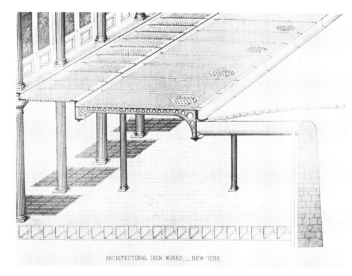

ARCHITECTURAL IRON WORKS — NEW-YORK

Figure 64. "Elevation and Section of Sidewalk Showing Vault Under Street," Plate LXXXIII, no. 45, from Daniel D. Badger's 1865 Catalogue, The Architectural Iron Works of New York City. *The basement areas of 19th-century commercial buildings often expanded into the space beneath their sidewalks and occasionally out under the street. To make this possible, heavy cast-iron columns carried the facade of the building, while additional cast-iron columns supported the sidewalk and vault roof. Getting daylight into the cellars or vaults required imaginative engineering, since lighting with gas or kerosene presented hazards in these enclosed spaces where ventilation was limited and the possibility of fire was ever present. The ingenious invention of the "vault light" Theodore Hyatt patented in 1845—a sturdy type of iron grating plugged with chunky glass blocks—allowed natural light to filter through the sidewalk into the basements yet provided a surface rigid enough to support pedestrian traffic. Such glazed grilles eliminated the need for basement window areaways and allowed passersby to step close to shop windows to examine merchandise. Vertical panels of vault lights were often set into foundations. Library floors and whole staircases were fabricated with this system. (Avery Library, Columbia University)*

cast, polished, checked for fit and given a protective coat of paint in the iron foundry. Then they were shipped as separate pieces to the construction site and bolted together to form an entire facade of iron. Assembly of the prefabricated pieces was much faster than traditional construction methods allowed. Often the foundry cast its name on a facade element, usually on the base of a column, pilaster, or pier (figure 71).

Such prefabricated iron facades could be made in numerous shapes and sizes, reflecting a wide range of architectural styles. Although some were very ornate, they were far less expensive than carved stone facades. To imitate stone, sand was stirred into paint of neutral stone colors to produce a stone-like texture on the cast iron. As cast-iron building designs became less imitative of stone buildings, more imaginative and varied color schemes were used. However, after the Columbian Exposition of 1893 in Chicago, popular taste returned to the more conservative stone colors.

Figure 65. **Cast-iron Haughwout Building, 490 Broadway, New York City, 1856; John P. Gaynor, architect; Daniel D. Badger's Architectural Iron Works of New York City.** *Some of the best iron front buildings stand in the SoHo area of the city. There are excellent examples of the quality and character of mass-produced 19th-century ironwork. Once foundry patterns were prepared, any number of like building fronts could be cast. The facade of the Haughwout Building consists of a single module, Palladian in character, repeated again and again. The result was an impressive design at a moderate cost. (Clover Vail)*

Figure 66. Catalog Illustration, Cary Building, New York City, 1856; John Kellum, architect; Daniel D. Badger's Architectural Iron Works of New York City. *This iron front design depicted in the 1865 catalog of Badger's foundry is still standing in downtown Manhattan. Although the iron is scored to look like ashlar, the slender freestanding colonettes between the windows reveal that the facade is metal, not stone. Many of the rolling metal shutters at the windows have been pulled shut. Badger sold rolled iron shutters before he started promoting cast-iron storefronts. (Avery Library, Columbia University)*

Figure 67. One-story Cast-iron Storefront, 75 Main Street, Cold Spring, New York. *This modest facade is typical of cast-iron storefronts popular for decades after their introduction about 1825. Fabricated by both small local foundries and large nationally known companies, storefronts were available in a variety of styles and sizes, and could be ordered from catalogs. The slender piers and columns could support the weight of several stories, usually masonry, while providing the framework for broad expanses of glass. The open front was perfect for the display of merchandise. (Otto Verne)*

Figure 68. Cast-iron Facade, Capital Hotel (originally the Denkla Office Building), 117 West Markham Street, Little Rock, Arkansas, 1873. *The Italianate office building was converted in 1877 into a hotel. Being located near the state capitol, it became popular with politicians and was often used as campaign headquarters. Note the difference in window size in the facade and the masonry sidewall. The larger windows of the cast-iron front provided a great deal of natural light, which the building's original use (offices) required. Although not apparent from a distance, the top story of the front facade and the cornice are pressed sheet metal, probably galvanized iron. (Earl Saunders)*

Figure 69.   Iron Front Hildebrand Building, 730 Main West Street, Louisville, Kentucky, 1884; Charles D. Meyer, architect. *The elaborate iron front of this five-story commercial building in the old downtown section exemplifies the advantages of cast-iron construction. The tall iron columns and colonettes between windows, slender as they are, take the weight of the materials, allowing large openings and light rooms. Iron manufacturers linked the technical requirements of their material with aesthetically appealing design, a fact which is evident even in this unrestored building. (John Albers and Preservation Alliance)*

Figure 70.   Ladd & Bush Bank (Branch of the U.S. National Bank of Oregon), 302 State Street, Salem, Oregon, 1869, Willamette Iron Works; addition by Skidmore, Owings and Merrill, 1967. *The elaborate iron elements of this bank in Salem were a near twin to the Ladd and Tilton Bank in Portland, also cast by the Willamette Iron Works in 1868. When the latter was demolished, its iron facade was saved and later used for expansion of the Salem bank. Additional parts were cast as needed by the original foundry. Note the bronze doors which were added in 1912. (Donald Sipe)*

The U.S. Army owns one of the most remarkable iron buildings in existence, it is nearly *all* iron. The structure was erected just before the Civil War to serve as a gun carriage storehouse. Measuring some 100 by 200 feet in size, it is located at Watervliet Arsenal, an Army installation on the Hudson River opposite Troy, New York (figure 72).

Domes and Cupolas

Even the most cursory look at the significant mid-19th-century public structures is enough to see how widely iron was used. The Old St. Louis Courthouse has an iron dome which predates that of the U.S. Capitol (1859-1862). It has iron elements from top to bottom. Although the building suffered two fires and underwent several alterations, the iron has survived intact. Architect William Rumbold's plan for the Italianate style iron dome, submitted in December 1859, called for strengthening the existing structure to receive it. He replaced stone columns with cast-iron replicas to support the first gallery in the rotunda. The second and third galleries have 20 slender cast-iron columns alternating with wooden columns painted to look alike (figure 73). This columnar system ran up through the building to the drum of the iron dome, which it supported. The drum itself consisted of a ring of iron columns with Italianate windows between them.

The great dome of the U.S. Capitol, completed in 1865, is the most monumental example of cast-iron architecture in America. Thomas U. Walter, Architect of the Capitol, designed the Renaissance style dome and engineer Montgomery C. Meigs made erection of the dome technologically feasible and supervised its construction. Several iron foundries handled the casting work; innumerable iron pieces were bolted together—smaller assemblies at the foundry, larger ones at the site—to create the pie-shaped sections, curving from base to tip, that form the exterior "skin" of the big dome.

The highly decorated skin was laid over a daringly conceived armature of 36 main radial ribs, each an open-web truss made up of 10 iron sections. These massive trusses can withstand the driving force of winds and the expansion and contraction resulting from temperature changes. The dome of the Capitol stands on an iron drum which is ringed by a peristyle of iron columns cast in Baltimore. Except for the bronze statue of Freedom at its apex, all of the dome structure above the roof of the center pavilion, in both framing system and covering, is iron (figure 74). The influence of the U.S. Capitol's design can be seen in the many state capitols which display Renaissance style domes. Some are totally of iron, while others are sheathed with copper.

Many city halls and county courthouses throughout America have cast-iron domes and cupolas. Built shortly after the U.S. Capitol dome and probably influenced by it, the Baltimore City Hall's cast-iron dome was recently restored (figure 75). The cupola of Brooklyn's Borough Hall burned in 1895; when it was rebuilt, the original wooden cupola was reconstructed in cast iron and sheet metal (figure 76).

Figure 71. Foundry Label: "BARTLETT, ROBBINS & CO., ARCHITECTURAL IRON WORKS, COR. SCOTT & PRATT ST., BALTIMORE, MD." *Foundries often attached labels to their work, a tradition started by bronze founders. A combination of pride and promotion, foundry labels can be found on architectural ironwork all over the country. This label appears on a building in downtown Baltimore. For some years the firm's name was Hayward, Bartlett and Co., under which it cast iron fronts for an attractive row of stores in Richmond, Virginia, recently restored as an office building. (David W. Look)*

Light Courts and Skylights

Before the introduction of electric lighting, it was difficult to illuminate adequately the interior spaces of large public buildings. Many 19th-century capitols, city halls, and other large structures, such as the Library of the Peabody Institute in Baltimore (figure 77), were designed to include ornamental light courts to bring natural light into the core of buildings. These three- or four-story-high spaces were covered by iron and glass skylights. Cast-iron columns typically supported these gallery-like openings in the floors.

Richmond, Virginia's, Old City Hall was designed in 1882 by Elijah E. Meyers, architect of many public structures. The interior is almost entirely of cast iron, including cast-iron columns, galleries, and a monumental staircase (figure 78). The center hall rises to the skylight roof in 4 levels of Gothic pointed arches set on squat cast-iron columns resembling heavy stone.

In Burnham and Root's Rookery Building in Chicago, offices were wrapped around a large light court with an iron and glass skylight just above the foyer (figure 79). The upper floors surrounding the light court look onto an unroofed light well. Los Angeles' Bradbury Building is another instance of filigree cast-iron balustraded galleries (which serve as open corridors) and iron and marble stairs rising five stories. The entire light court is covered with an iron and glass roof (figure 80).

Decorative Cast Iron

Stairs and Elevators

Cast iron had immediate applicability as a fire-resistant material for use on interior stairs. There had been numerous catastrophic fires involving wooden stairs and the only alternative, stone, was too expensive and heavy to be practical. So, with the introduction of cast iron for building purposes, it was soon adopted for interior use on stairs and other elements with repetitive designs.

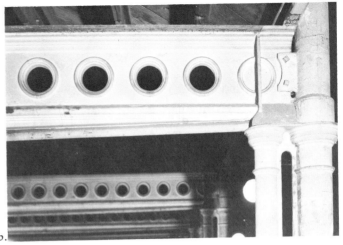

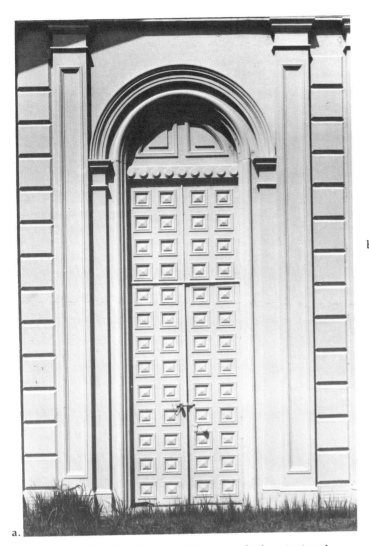

b.

a.

Figure 72. Cast-iron Personnel Door (south elevation) and Girder-Column Detail (interior), Watervliet Arsenal, New York, 1859; Daniel D. Badger's Architectural Iron Works of New York City. *(a) This military storehouse is the most nearly all-iron building in the United States: the walls, window frames, doors, and columns are all cast iron, and the roof trusses are wrought iron. Built as a "fireproof" warehouse for ammunition storage, this classical Greek and Roman building was cast in sections at Badger's foundry and shipped by barge up the Hudson River to be assembled on the foundation in less than three months. (b) The detail shows a cast- and wrought-iron girder connected to a cast-iron column. The cast-iron part of the girder, the top three-quarters, is perforated to reduce the weight of the load and slightly arched to take compressive stresses. The wrought-iron part is at the bottom of the girder to take tensile stresses. (Jack E. Boucher, NAER)*

Figure 73. Rotunda Galleries, Old St. Louis Courthouse, Fourth and Market Streets, St. Louis, Missouri, 1859 expansion; William Rumbold, architect. *The courthouse has many iron elements, including the intricate elliptical cast-iron staircases in the wings and half of the Ionic and Corinthian columns which support the rotunda galleries. Every other column is wood. The cast-iron columns were added to take the increased load of the dome, a major feat of engineering and architectural design. William Rumbold accomplished the detailed engineering of the dome between 1859 and 1862, one and one-half years before the dome of the U.S. Capitol was completed. (Piaget, NAER)*

Figure 74. Stairs between the Inner and Outer Domes, U.S.Capitol, 1856–1865; Thomas U. Walter, Architect of the Capitol; Montgomery C. Meigs, engineer. *The double shell dome construction is supported by 36 radiating, arched trusses. In this view of the stairs to the lantern, every element is cast iron except the wrought-iron tie rods and bolts. To the right is the back side of one of the cast-iron coffers of the inner dome. The center of the coffer can be unbolted for inspection and maintenance of the inner dome. (David W. Look)*

a.

Figure 75. City Hall and the Restoration of the Dome, 100 North Holliday Street, Baltimore, Maryland; 1867–1875; George A. Frederick, architect; Wendel Bollman, engineer; restoration, 1975. *(a) This Second Empire building was designed by Frederick, but the dome and lantern were designed by Bollman, inventor of the Bollman truss and sole proprietor of the Patapsco Bridge and Ironworks of Baltimore, Maryland. By 1970 the dome was in a seriously weakened condition. The sentiment of the townspeople and the mayor to keep the dome and rehabilitate the building was so strong that an $8 million bond issue was approved for the project. (b) All parts of the dome pictured are cast iron. The outer plates were removed for strengthening the ribs. (Filip Sibley, Office of the Mayor, Baltimore; Robert M. Vogel)*

b.

Figure 77.   Cast-iron Interior, Peabody Institute Library, Mount Vernon Place, Baltimore, Maryland, 1857–1878; Edmund George Lind, architect; Bartlett, Robbins and Co., Architectural Iron Works, Baltimore. *A gift from the philanthropist, George Peabody, who started his career in Baltimore, the Peabody Institute included a library which is virtually all cast iron and glass. Although the building's exterior is a traditional Renaissance design in stone, the most innovative materials of the time were used on the interior to safeguard the collection of books and manuscripts from fire. The central area of the library is surrounded by five floors of cast-iron galleries and is covered by one great skylight of glass set in an iron frame. The floors of the five decks are of iron inset with blocks of translucent glass. The decks are supported by cast-iron piers with applied two-story fluted pilasters rising in three tiers from floor to roof. (Peabody Library)*

Figure 76.   Cast-iron and Sheet-iron Cupola, Designed by C. W. and A. A. Houghton, architects, 1898; Hecla Ironworks; Borough Hall, 209 Joralemon Street, Brooklyn, New York, 1846–1851; Gamaliel King, architect. *After the Old Brooklyn City Hall burned in 1895, it was rebuilt within the masonry shell, and a cast-iron and sheet-iron cupola replaced the wooden one that had been destroyed in the fire. It is typical of many such cupolas throughout America. (Esther Mipaas)*

Figure 79. The Rookery, 209 South LaSalle Street, Chicago, Illinois, 1886; Burnham and Root, architects; Hecla Iron Works, Brooklyn, New York. *The central foyer of this early 11-story skyscraper is a fine example of the integration of structural and decorative cast iron. The vaulting beams are perforated to reduce the dead load of the structural members without reducing the strength—the same principle as the truss. The chandeliers were designed by Frank Lloyd Wright in 1905. Unfortunately, the glass roof has been painted over. (Becket Logan)*

Figure 78. Cast-iron Light Court, Old City Hall, bounded by 10th, Broad, 11th, and Capitol Streets, Richmond, Virginia, 1886–1894; Elijah E. Myers, architect. *The great central light court with its tiers of enriched cast-iron columns, spandrels, railings, and brass fixtures ranks as one of the most impressive municipal interiors in America. In imitation of stone, the cast iron has a massive, solid quality consistent with the character of the exterior masonry. (William Edwin Booth)*

b.

Figure 80. Light Court and Detail of Cast Iron Stairs, Bradbury Building, 304 Broadway, Los Angeles, California, 1893; George Wyman, architect; Winslow Brothers, foundry, Chicago, Illinois. *(a) Built for the successful miner Louis Bradbury, this conventional masonry building gives no hint from the outside of its remarkable interior light court with its iron and glass skylight. The five-story open space has bird-cage-like elevators moving in open shafts with the machinery and counterweights exposed. (b) The elaborate openwork design of the galleries was cast in bold relief on both sides of the panels. The railings were cast in many parts and then assembled. Slender beaded balusters take the form of clawed feet where they attach to the staircase. All parts of the railing and galleries are outstanding examples of the art of sandcasting. (Becket Logan)*

a.

For the Federal Custom House in Wheeling, West Virginia, and many Federal structures, architects turned to cast iron because it was not combustible and because the repetitive nature of steps and railings allowed for the efficient use of molds. Ornate designs could be cast rather than carved, and parts of the stairs could be perforated to reduce the weight of the cast iron (figure 81). Iron staircases, sometimes monumental in size and design, often dominate the lobbies and rotundas of large public buildings (figure 82).

Exterior cast-iron stoops, usually modest in scale, were commonplace in 19th-century domestic architecture. Their treads and risers were usually perforated both to save metal and to lighten their weight. This seemed to have been a popular feature in the South, and can be seen in Mobile, New Orleans, Columbus (Georgia) and Savannah and throughout the mid-Atlantic states.

The first passenger elevator was installed by Elisha Graves Otis in 1857 in the still standing iron front Haughwout Store in New York. Open-cage elevators soon developed an architectural style of their own. Because of changing tastes and modern fire and safety laws, however, only a few survive. Vestiges of the metal shaftway grillage can still be found in some older office buildings and public structures. Once out of style, cast-iron elevators are now admired and occasionally a way is found to preserve them in the rehabilitation or adaptive reuse of a building. One such example is the 1905 elevator in the Pioneer Courthouse in Portland, Oregon, where the architects of the 1973 renovation put fire-resistant panels behind the iron grillework of both shaft and elevator cab (figure 83). On the other hand, an original system still survives in the 1893 Bradbury Building in Los Angeles where cage elevators move up and down in open shafts (figure 80).

Lintels and Grilles

Iron was also used in 19th-century buildings for window lintels and sills. It was ideal for this use when the spans were short, no more than 3 or 4 feet across. Since decorative lintels were usually backed by brick arches they did not have to be very thick to hold their own weight. As the iron could be used sparingly, it was a relatively light and inexpensive building material, especially when compared to granite or marble. In the casting process, elaborate shapes could be incorporated in the mold and used repeatedly. Thus iron sills and lintels could be trimmed with Italianate brackets or incised with Eastlake trimming; decorative caps for over doors and windows might be almost florid with elaborate lacework (figure 84). Such iron elements could be bought in great variety from the foundry catalogs of

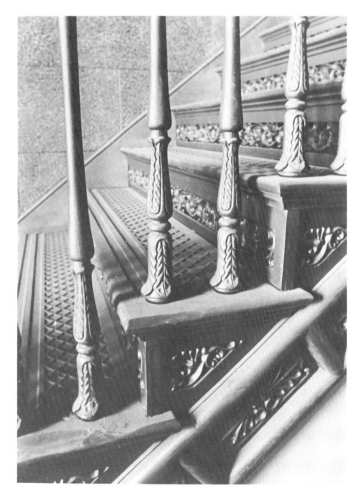

Figure 81. Restored Cast-iron Stairs, Old Customs House (now known as West Virginia Independence Hall), Wheeling, West Virginia, 1859; Ammi B. Young, Architect of the Treasury. *In this building the people of western Virginia declared their independence during the Civil War and joined the Union. These cast-iron stairs and balusters have recently been restored with the recasting of missing or damaged pieces. Perforated stairs were originally designed to combine decorative, functional, and economical detailing; to provide elaborate but strong construction; and to reduce the weight and quantity of iron required. (West Virginia Independence Hall Foundation)*

Figure 82. Grand Stairs and Detail of Cast-iron Railing, Georgia State Capitol, Capitol Square, Atlanta, Georgia, 1884–1889; Willoughby J. Edbrooke and Franklin P. Burnham, architects. *Monumental stairs in public buildings were not only a means of vertical circulation but also a source of public pride and often the site of public ceremonies. (James R. Lockhart, Georgia Department of Natural Resources, Historic Preservation Section)*

the day. Cast-iron window grilles were widely used on houses or public buildings for street-level or below-grade windows that had to be secured, yet where ventilation was desired. Philadelphia abounds in varied cellar window grilles of both cast and wrought iron (figure 85). The glass lights in exterior doors were often covered with custom-fitted ornamental cast-iron security grilles that were both effective and attractive. Many buildings built after 1840 used lacy ventilating grilles set under the eaves. These grilles could be ordered from catalogs, as could cast-iron hot-air registers (figure 86), grating, and panels for use under shop windows.

Figure 84.   Cast-iron Lintel, Ben Whitmire House, 109 Jackson Street, Trenton, New Jersey, 1872. *The scrollwork of the foliated lintel is clearly of cast metal; execution of such a design in stone would be almost impossible. This house also has window lintels and sills of iron, all of which were probably cast at Bottom and Tiffany's Foundry in Trenton. They were often painted stone colors with sand added for the correct texture. Residences, commercial buildings, institutions, and even industrial buildings incorporated ornate lintels and sills in their design. (Ben Whitmire)*

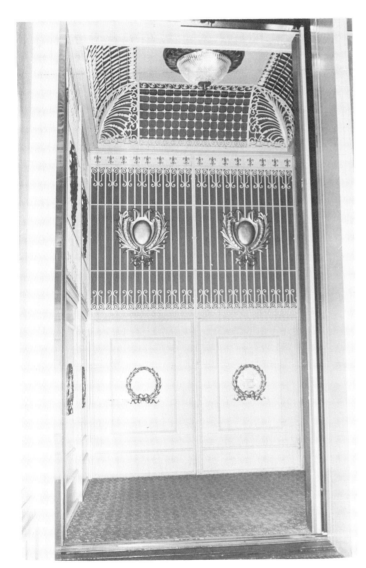

Figure 83.   Cast-iron Elevator Cab, Otis Elevator Company, 1905; Pioneer Courthouse (U.S. Courthouse and Customhouse), 520 Southwest Morrison Street, Portland, Oregon, 1869–1873. *To meet fire code requirements, restoration architects McMath and Hawkins installed a new fire wall inside the elevator shaft in 1973. To give the illusion of openness, the elevator grille and cab were painted a cream color, with gilt shields and wreaths; the fire wall was painted a dark gray, creating the effect of a silhouette. (Mike Henley)*

Figure 85.   Cast-iron Cellar Window Grille, Matthew Quay House, northeast corner of Spruce and 11th streets, Philadelphia, Pennsylvania. *Although little noticed, there is a seemingly endless variety of decorative cellar window grilles in Philadelphia. With the first-floor level several feet above grade and the sidewalks often extending right up to the facade, these articulated iron grilles were installed to protect exposed cellar windows while still allowing ventilation. The grille photographed here displays a motif of cast-iron vines set in a pair of arcaded panels. (Harley J. McKee, FAIA)*

Figure 86.   Exhibit of Cast Iron Furnace Registers, Centennial Exhibition, Philadelphia, Pennsylvania, 1876. *This historic photograph shows the wide variety of sizes and designs of furnace registers available from just one company, the Tuttle and Bailey Manufacturing Co. of New York City. (Smithsonian Institution)*

Verandas and Balconies

Cast-iron verandas and balconies are almost universally identified with the streets and courtyards of New Orleans and with other Southern cities such as Savannah and Mobile (figure 87); but they are also found in many other localities (figure 88). If kept painted, these balconies and verandas can be preserved indefinitely. Sections may deteriorate or get broken, but they can be recast and inserted.

Railings, Fences, and Cresting

In addition to verandas and balconies with railings, many American buildings had two-story spaces with railings on mezzanine levels, primarily department stores and hotel lobbies. Iron railings were not only less expensive and lighter than stone, but they were stronger and more fire-resistant than wood. Iron railings were both functional and decorative.

Closely related to railings in style and composition were the cast-iron fences and cresting. Molten iron could be cast in so many different shapes from simple to elaborate that designers and patternmakers had free rein. They made grapevine fences and fences resembling rows of swords thrust into the ground; there were also fences with Greek key designs for Greek Revival style houses. Railings, fences, and gates done in Gothic tracery were favored for churches, and a favorite cemetery gate motif shows lambs lying beneath a weeping willow tree. Other fences were made to look like a row of corn stalks (figure 89). Many custom designed fences carried symbols related to the structures with which they were associated.

Cast-iron cresting decorated the ridges of roofs and the edges of bay and porch roofs (figure 90). These decorative additions were mass produced and could be purchased in a variety of designs.

Street Furniture and Lighting

"Street furniture" is very much a part of the urban landscape. It applies to various objects on our streets that facilitate public activities, including metal mailboxes and fire alarm boxes, fire hydrants, street lamps, trash containers, and also such amenities as benches (figure 91), drinking fountains, flower planters, and occasionally tall sidewalk clocks. Until recent years, most of these amenities were fabricated of cast iron. A few manufacturers still cast street furniture in Victorian designs or popular later designs.

Gaslighting was introduced in the United States early in the 19th century, and by the Civil War had become the dominant form of street and home illumination. Most American cities chartered a local gas company and brought gas into their commercial districts via simple but utilitarian lampposts. Most of these lampposts were fabricated of cast iron. Churches, businesses, and private owners installed their own exterior iron fixtures, including elaborate and sculptural lamps which were tributes to the founders' art. By the 1890s, electricity was beginning to replace gaslighting. The two forms coexisted for some years, while many municipal gaslamps were converted to electricity.

In the mid-1890s, New York City installed tall iron double-pendant electric lamps along Fifth Avenue from Washington Square to 59th Street. In 1903 several companies contracting to light certain sections of the city adopted the cast-iron Bishop's Crook single-pendant electric lamp that became the basic street light for the city's five boroughs until recently.

Salt Lake City, one of the first American cities to have systematic electric street lighting, developed an elegant type of lamp standard with three lights on a tall fluted shaft. The cast-iron bases of these lamps bear four medallions displaying profiles of Indians in feathered war bonnets (figure 92). The city keeps old lamps and globes in good condition, replicates where necessary, and lines at least one central thoroughfare with them.

Figure 87.   **Cast-iron Veranda and Fence, Ketchum Mansion, 400 Government Street, Mobile, Alabama, 1861; Wood and Perot, foundry, Philadelphia.** *This veranda, skillfully produced in decorative cast iron, as well as the cast-iron railing, fencing, gates, and gate posts, are painted white to contrast with the warm-colored brick of the Italianate mansion. (Jack E. Boucher, NAER)*

a.

b.

No. 108.

Verandah made to order for Z. Jones, Esq., of Washington, D.C.

Figure 88. Cast-iron Veranda, Zephaniah Jones House, 1024 10th Street, NW, Washington, D.C.; Janes, Kirtland and Co., foundry. *(a) It is a rewarding experience to see an advertisement for an architectural feature in a foundry catalog, then to discover the original model is still extant. (b) This veranda appears in Janes, Kirtland and Company's 1870 catalog of ornamental ironwork. The caption reads, "Verandah made to order for Z. Jones, Esq. of Washington, D.C." The veranda, in need of repair, remains on the Jones House over 100 years after its installation. (David W. Look)*

Cast-iron lamps on Canal Street in New Orleans are especially memorable. Erected about 1910, they have triple lights on very tall shafts that rise from high, carefully detailed bases. The base of each lamp displays four sculptured plaques denoting the four national periods of Louisiana history under Spain, France, the Confederacy, and the United States. Lamps damaged in traffic accidents have been restored or replaced.

Sometimes lamps were added to a building many years after construction, but occasionally exterior lighting fixtures were designed as part of the building's facade. This is the case of the lamps on the Boston Public Library, which are an integral part of the building's composition (figure 93).

Tall cast-iron street clocks were popular at the turn of the century, especially as picturesque advertisements for banks and jewelry shops. But they also rendered a public service (figure 94). Many still exist, and several cities, including Milwaukee, San Francisco, and Portland, Oregon, have designated them official landmarks.

Fountains and Statues

Large cast-iron fountains, a feature of public squares and avenues in 19th-century towns and cities, were often opulent, tiered structures decorated with waterbirds, porpoises, tritons, cherubs, and even life-size human figures. Although they were often expensive items and represented a considerable civic investment (figure 95), they were less expensive and more common than bronze. Smaller iron fountains were produced for the lawns of institutions and for private gardens.

The Bartholdi Fountain in Washington, D.C., across Independence Avenue from the U.S. Botanic Garden near the Capitol is a cast-iron fountain of great sophistication. It was exhibited as a work of art at the 1876 Exhibition, after which it was purchased by the Federal government. Three iron classical style maidens hold aloft a large bowl, originally rimmed with gaslights (now with electric lights), from which water cascades. The sculptor, Frederic Auguste Bartholdi, is best known for the Statue of Liberty. His fountain is a rare example in the United States of the work of a major artist in cast iron.

Some Victorian cast-iron fountains were both utilitarian and ornamental. Such is the case with Lotta's Fountain in San Francisco (figure 96). This sentimental 1876 gift to the city from the famous actress Lotta Crabtree incorporates four spigots for drinking water along with a tall decorated column with a light on top. Its base is heavily ornamented with cast-iron medallions depicting gold miners and sailing ships.

The constant presence of water and leaky plumbing has caused trouble for many iron fountains, while others have been dismantled as old-fashioned relics and sold for scrap by shortsighted municipalities. Now these cast-iron extravagances are again being appreciated.

Figure 89.   Cast-iron Fence, Cornstalk Hotel, 915 Rue Royale, New Orleans, Louisiana, ca. 1855; Wood and Perot, foundry, Philadelphia. *In the 1850s, Dr. Joseph Biamenti brought his bride to this New Orleans house, later converted to a hotel. In an effort to keep her from feeling homesick for her native Iowa, the doctor commissioned this cornstalk fence from the well-known Philadelphia foundry. Representing a field ready for harvest, the green and yellow fence sports ripe cast-iron ears of corn on their stalks. Pumpkin vines entwine the stalks and climb up the ironposts to the bundle of corn ears which make up the finials. Once a foundry made patterns, it would usually advertise the new design in its catalog and reuse the molds as orders were received; a rendering of this fence appeared in the 1858 Wood and Perot catalog. In 1859 another cornstalk fence was erected by Wood and Miltenberger, the New Orleans branch of Wood and Perot, at the Short-Favrot House in New Orleans Garden District. (Becket Logan)*

Figure 90.   Cast-iron Cresting, Moran-Bogus Building, 501-509 G Street, NW, Washington, D.C., 1889–1890. *This slate Mansard roof was added in 1890 by George Bogus, the second owner, to a brick commercial building built the year before by J. E. Moran. Cast-iron cresting was a popular ornamental feature on Gothic Revival and Second Empire style buildings, but can be found on other styles of structures during the Victorian era. Note also the galvanized sheet-iron rope molding and dormers with cast zinc ornament. (David W. Look)*

Figure 91.   Cast-iron Benches, Illustrated Catalogue of Or-namental Iron Works, Janes, Kirtland & Co., 1870. *Cast-iron furniture for both indoor and outdoor use enjoyed great popularity with the Victorians, especially for furnishing conservatories, porches, lawns, gardens, parks, public squares, and cemeteries. Benches such as these were cast in 10 or 12 sections, which were assembled and bolted together. After the rough edges were filed away to protect the user's clothing, the benches were painted several times to prevent rust from forming. This page of the catalog illustrates designs in the Gothic, grapevine, Rococo, and rustic styles. (Library of Congress)*

Figure 92.   Cast-iron "Indian Head" Lamps, Salt Palace Complex, Salt Lake City, Utah. *(a) Electric street fixtures began to replace gas fixtures in the 1880s; many of the ornate electric street lamps were erected about the time of World War I. (b) Salt Lake City put up cast-iron street lamps with Indian head medallions on the bases. With the recent revival of interest in the downtown area, the Utah Power and Light Company refurbished the surviving lamps and had others made. (Hal Rumel Studio; Utah Power and Light Co.)*

Figure 93. Iron Lamps, Boston Public Library, Copley Square, Boston, Massachusetts, 1895; Charles Follen McKim, architect. *The Boston Public Library contains many forms of metal ornamentation: bronze doors by Daniel Chester French, wrought-iron gates and grilles, and Strozzi-type wrought- and cast-iron lamps which flank the three entryways. Repeated casting from the same molds made ornamentation worthy of a Renaissance palace affordable in the 19th century. (Esther Mipaas)*

Figure 94. Cast-iron Post Clock, Boylston Street, near the corner of Berkley, Boston, Massachusetts, ca. 1900; E. Howard Clock Co. *The iron post clock was a familiar item of street furniture for over a century, and was used nationwide as a form of advertising for merchants, especially jewelers, and for banks. This clock in the Boylston Street shopping area was manufactured by the noted New England clockmaker Edward Howard, whose company also made street clocks, steeple clocks, and watches long after his death in 1904. Other examples of such clocks can be found in Milwaukee, St. Louis, Salt Lake City, and Portland, Oregon. However, the post clock is a vanishing amenity, its useful life shortened by street widenings, abandonment of inner cities, and the ravages of the automobile. (Esther Mipaas)*

Figure 95. Cast-iron Fountain, Plate Number 5, Illustrated Catalogue of Ornamental Iron Works; Janes, Kirtland and Co., 1870. *Large cast-iron fountains became part of America's urban landscape after the 1851 London Crystal Palace Exhibition, where several iron fountains attracted attention. A French example was said to have inspired this design, which was first made for the city of Savannah, Georgia. In 1856, the fountain was installed in Forsyth Park where, with the benefit of a recent restoration, it exists today. Janes, Beebe and Co., maker of the fountain and forerunner of Janes, Kirtland and Co., offered it in the 1858 catalog for $2,500 plus the cost of the basin. Poughkeepsie, New York, and Madison, Indiana, have similar fountains. The tri-level fountain was made of hundreds of pieces of cast iron, which were shipped to the site, bolted together, then caulked and painted. The lowest level displays large trumpeting Tritons, the second waterfowl, and the top a figure holding a water-spouting torch. (Library of Congress)*

There are relatively few cast-iron statues that are not a part of a larger monument such as a fountain. A large statue of Henry Clay by Wood and Perot was erected in 1855 in Pottsville, Pennsylvania; and the residents of Eatonton, Georgia, honored native son Joel Chandler Harris by placing a cast-iron statue of Br'er Rabbit on the courthouse lawn. Also unique is the 56-foot-tall cast-iron figure of *Vulcan,* Roman god of the forge, standing on a mountain overlooking Birmingham, the iron and steel center of the South. Said to be the largest cast-iron figure in the world, *Vulcan* was cast in many sections by several Alabama foundries and shipped to St. Louis where the statue represented the state at the 1904 World's Fair. Small animal sculptures, such as dogs, deer, and lions, were quite popular in the Victorian era and were often ordered from catalogs.

Tombs

One of the finest examples of the founder's sculptural art is the 1859 iron tomb marking the grave of President James Monroe. In Richmond, Virginia's, Hollywood Cemetery on a prominence overlooking the James River, this Gothic style cast-iron masterpiece was designed by German-born Richmond architect Albert Lybrock and cast in the foundry of Wood and Perot in Philadelphia (figure 97). "Cast iron Mausoleums of beautiful design and finish" were advertised by Wood, Miltenberger and-Co., the New Orleans branch of Wood and Perot. Several splendid iron tombs exist in New Orleans' historic cemeteries, while others, apparently stock designs, can be seen in Mobile, Alabama. Examples of modest-scale cast-iron architecture, these elegant little buildings were made of parts separately cast and bolted together by the same methods employed for iron front warehouses, hotels, and stores. Like their commercial counterparts, some tombs were individually designed and others could be ordered from catalogues.

The heyday of cast iron lasted well into the 20th century. As discussed, the metal had a wide variety of uses. Some architectural historians labeled the early popularity of cast iron as "ferromania" and dated its decline in the 1870s due to the discovery that it has limited fire resistance. Although non-combustible, cast iron can be weakened in a fire. Cervin Robinson has pointed out, however, that the vast number of cast-iron facades built in the 1890s testified to their renewed popularity. As late as 1904 multistory cast-iron facades were erected in the SoHo area of New York City. Their brief decline in the 1880s could be attributed to stylistic changes; buildings were being designed with fewer repetitive elements, which were so economical when mass produced in cast iron.

Other uses of cast iron continued uninterrupted until new styles eliminated their use or they could be more economically made of new materials. Two late examples are the Charles Scribner's Sons Bookstore on Fifth Avenue in New York City, which has an iron and glass storefront built in 1913, and the doors of the Cheney Brothers Silk Store, which were cast in iron in 1925 (figure 98). Cast iron was even used in the Art Deco period, when many new metals were becoming available.

Figure 96. Cast-iron Drinking Fountain, intersection of Market, Kearny, and Geary streets, San Francisco, California, 1875. *Cast iron took many shapes in the 19th-century urban landscape. One of the more interesting is this public drinking fountain given to the city by Lotta Crabtree, a grateful citizen who had acquired fame and fortune there as an actress. The fountain was restored and rededicated on its 100th birthday in 1975. (Becket Logan)*

Today, cast iron is used for plumbing fixtures and piping in new construction, and its structural and decorative use is being revived through the preservation of historic buildings.

Rolled Sheet Iron and Steel

Surfaces of iron and steel exposed to the atmosphere will develop a crust of iron oxide, commonly known as rust. Unlike bronze, which oxidizes to form a patina that generally protects the surface from further oxidation, iron and steel form a highly corrosive coating. Rust is a porous substance that allows deeper and deeper layers to oxidize until the entire object is consumed by it. In thin sheet metal, corrosion can be quite rapid, with resulting reduction of the object's strength and usefulness.

Figure 97. Cast-iron Tomb Enclosure, Grave of President James Monroe, Hollywood Cemetery, Richmond, Virginia, 1859; Albert Lybrock, architect; Wood and Perot, foundry, Philadelphia. *The ceremonial enclosure of the tomb of James Monroe is a particularly fine example of cast-iron design and craftsmanship. In the 1850s the state of Virginia took steps to move Monroe's resting place from New York to his native state. The Gothic Revival design chosen for the tomb was that of German-born Richmond architect Albert Lybrock. Perhaps more important was the selection of Wood and Perot, manufacturers of ornamental iron, to prepare the patterns, make the molds, and cast the separate parts that would compose this work of art. The words "Robert Wood, Maker" can be found at the edge of the enclosure. In later years, Wood and Perot presented sketches of the tomb cover in its sales catalog. It measures 7 feet wide by 10 feet long, with a perforated canopy rising 20 feet to a finial of crockets. Four miniature corner towers enclose side panels filled with Gothic arches and trefoil patterns. (F. Heite, Library of Congress)*

Figure 98.
Cheney Brothers Silk Store (now Merrill Sharpe, Inc.), 181 Madison Avenue, New York City, 1925; Howard Greenley, designer; Ferrobrant, foundry. *Originally fabricated under the direction of Jules Bouy for Cheney Brothers Silk Store. These doors were later moved in 1928 to their present location, the Madison Belmont Building. Edgar Brant of Ferrobrant fabricated the additional metalwork for the new building. Note that the parts of the frame and transom painted gold (the lighter color in the photo) are actually cast bronze, recently restored and polished. (David W. Look)*

In the United States, the first sheet iron was rolled in a Trenton, New Jersey, mill owned by Robert Morris. He roofed his never-finished home in Philadelphia with sheet iron around 1794. In 1814, architect Benjamin Latrobe wrote a Captain Wooley recommending sheet iron roofing rather than lead or tin. Latrobe assertedthat a sheet iron roof he had installed on Nassau Hall at Princeton College in New Jersey after a fire was "as good as the day when it was put on. . . ." Although he did not mention any protective coating, the roof was probably painted. The slate roof on the White House was replaced with sheet iron in 1804. How widespread sheet iron roofs became is not clear, but they were available until the end of the 19th century. Some of them had pressed designs (figure 99). Shingles and pantiles were also available in painted sheet iron and steel (figures 11 and 12).

As mentioned previously, a method for corrugating iron was first patented in England in 1829. As early as 1834, William Strickland planned to use corrugated sheet iron for his design of the market sheds in Philadelphia. Early corrugated iron was painted or blackened with pitch, but galvanizing, when discovered, was a better protection (see chapter 4). Corrugated iron was adopted quickly, as its extra rigidity and stiffness allowed for lighter roof framing, and horizontal roof supports could be spaced further apart and made smaller. Corrugated sheets as large as 2 by 5 feet were soon available, allowing for 10 square feet of roofing to be installed at a time. The sheets were placed on purlins with the furrows sloped downward to provide drainage.

Corrugated iron and later steel had other uses besides roofing; the most important was in floor construction. Arched sheets of corrugated metal were placed on the bottom flanges of beams spaced 4–5 feet apart (figure 100). Concrete was then poured over the beams and sheets to provide a flat floor. Previously, brick arches had been used between the beams, but the corrugated sheet iron or steel was faster to install. Both types were usually plastered to provide a finished ceiling for the room below.

As early as 1868, sheet iron was used for ceilings, probably to provide some fire protection. The early ceilings were corrugated, and sheet iron and steel was also sometimes stamped with designs (figure 101). Although commonly called "tin ceiling," these pressed sheets were not usually tin plated for indoor use, but were always painted to protect them from deterioration. Some galvanized sheet iron or steel ceilings were produced. Pressed metal ceilings were popular through the first two decades of the 20th century. They are still available today. At least one company now makes pressed metal ceilings that are tin-plated.

Steel

Structural Steel

In the mid-19th century, advancing technology had brought tall buildings into the realm of architectural possibility. Builders and manufacturers turned to steel, which was stronger than cast iron in compression and wrought iron in tension. Steel had been known and used to some extent for centuries. What was lacking was a way to produce it cheaply and in quantity. This challenge was met when the Bessemer process was developed in England in 1856. Shortly thereafter, the open-hearth process was invented.

The industrial application of the new methods and materials moved with remarkable speed, especially in England. In the United States, the Civil War held up the introduction of large-scale steel production; cast and wrought iron were the major construction materials until the 1870s. About 1865, Alexander Holley engineered a steel making system in America based on the Bessemer patents. Andrew Carnegie and others soon developed the industry further and laid the groundwork for the United States to become the largest producer and user of steel.

The first major American construction project in which steel was used was the Eads Bridge which crossed the Mississippi River at St. Louis, Missouri. In 1867 James Buchanan Eads designed and began construction of the 1,524-foot multiarched steel truss bridge. Although steel was a major component, some iron was used in this and other early steel bridges.

In 1868, John A. Roebling, having built several bridges with iron wire cables, designed steel cables for the proposed Brooklyn Bridge across the East River in New York. Roebling had patented the first traversely wrapped wire cable in 1841 and developed a method for galvanizing wire in 1876. He did not live to see completion of the Brooklyn Bridge, which at 1,596 feet was the longest suspension bridge in the world when it opened in 1883.

Railroad companies were among the first to recognize the superior qualities of steel. By the end of the 1880s, most rails and railroad bridges were made of steel; the last wrought-iron rails were rolled in 1884. For several years the railroads used so much steel that it was in short supply for building construction.

In 1885 William Le Baron Jenney used the first steel beams in the upper floors of his partially completed Home Insurance Building in Chicago. Regarded by architectural historians as the first skyscraper, the 11-story building was demolished in the 1930s. Its iron and steel framework carried the entire weight of the structure, including the exterior masonry walls which were supported at each floor level. This construction allowed for much thinner exterior walls, especially on the lower floors, and increased the available rental space. Steel framing made larger windows possible for better lighted shops and offices.

The transition from iron to steel was gradual, and for years many buildings used both iron and steel. The first completely steel-framed structure, the Rand McNally Building in Chicago, was completed in the early 1890s. Burnham and Root's Monadnock Block, completed in Chicago in 1891, illustrated the need for steel frame construction in urban settings. The traditional load-bearing masonry walls at the ground-floor level of the Monadnock Block were 6 feet thick. The materials and labor involved added to the expense of construction and the thick walls took up a large part of the rental space. Steel frame construction soon became the standard construction for structures of more than a few stories (figure

ILLINOIS ROOFING AND SUPPLY CO., CHICAGO, ILL. 33

Cluster Tiling or Shingles,

—FOR—

ROOFING, MANSARDS, GABLES AND SIDING.

Attractive. Cheap. Durable.

MADE OF SHEET STEEL PAINTED OR GALVANIZED.

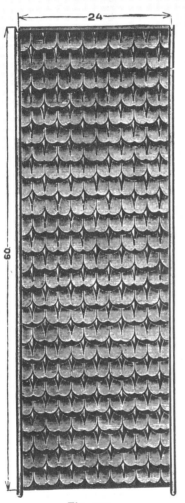

Fig. 139.

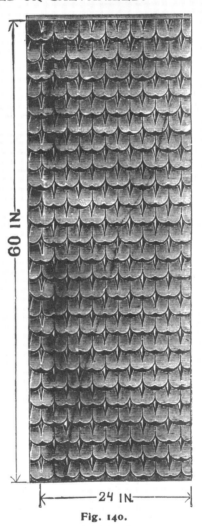

Fig. 140.

Fig. 139 shows Cluster Shingle, with pressed standing seam edges, applied with cleats.

Fig. 140 shows Cluster Shingle in sheets. This is particularly adapted for gables, mansards and siding. The side lap is made by lapping one-half of a shingle and is perfectly water-tight when properly nailed.

A Square consists of ten (10) sheets 60 inches long each by 24 inches wide, covering width.

Figure 99. Pressed Sheet Steel Roofing and Siding, Illinois Roofing and Supply Co., Chicago, Illinois, 1896, page 33. *Sheet metal was often pressed with decorative patterns to imitate shingles. These sheets, 24 by 60 inches, were available in either painted or galvanized sheet, and were recommended for gables, Mansards, and siding. (Library of Congress)*

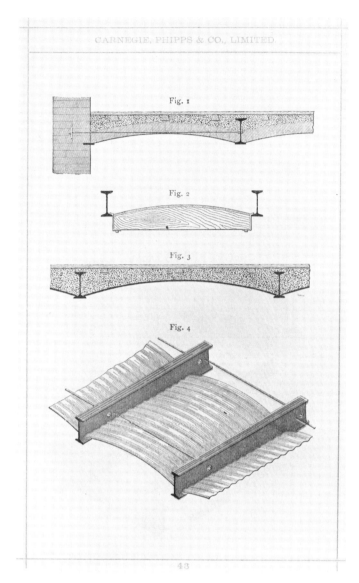

CARNEGIE, PHIPPS & CO., LIMITED.

Fig. 1

Fig. 2

Fig. 3

Fig. 4

43

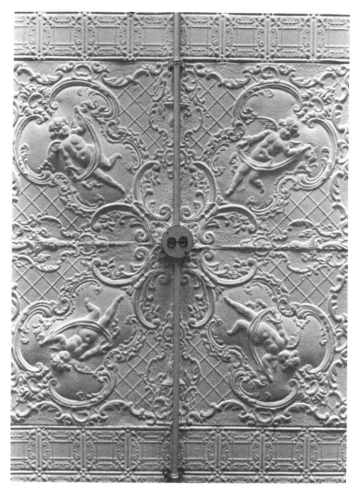

Figure 100. Corrugated Iron Arched Floor Construction Pocket Companion . . . , Carnegie, Phipps and Co., Ltd., Pittsburgh, 1890, p. 43. *In an effort to reduce the time needed for arch construction (figures 1 and 2), the corrugated iron arch was introduced (figures 3 and 4) with a concrete fill. The sheets of corrugated iron, bent to a radius, were sprung between the bottom flanges of the I-beams. Note the tie rods between the beams to keep correct spacing and beam alignment. Even though iron is noncombustible, these floors were not "fireproof" because the iron arches and beams lost their strength and collapsed when exposed to the high temperatures of a fire. (Library of Congress)*

Figure 101. Pressed Metal Ceiling, 212 West Main Street, Johnstown, New York. *Mistakenly called "tin ceilings," pressed metal ceilings were stamped sheet iron and later sheet steel; only one or two isolated companies coated them with tin. Pressed metal was sometimes galvanized with zinc, especially when used outdoors or as porch ceilings. It was sold by the sheet with the patterns fitting neatly together for covering ceilings and sometimes walls or wainscotting. Accessory pieces, such as ceiling medallions, were available. Cornices provided the transition from ceiling to walls. (Becket Logan)*

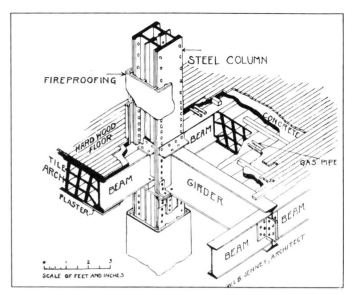

Figure 103. Detail of a Column-and-Girder Connection and Floor Construction, The Fair Store, South State, West Adams, and South Dearborn Streets, Chicago, Illinois, 1892; Jenney and Mundie, architects. *This is a connection of the type used in many iron and steel connections. Note the "fireproofing" of the columns, which consisted of terra-cotta tile and plaster. The floors were constructed of lightweight, flat tile arches covered with a concrete topping slab with wooden sleepers to receive the hardwood floor. The bottom of the flat tile arches was plastered to provide the finished ceiling of the room below.* (Industrial Chicago, *volume 2, 1891, facing page 842; Library of Congress)*

Figure 102. Iron and Steel Skeleton Frame, Unity Building, Chicago, Illinois, 1891–1892; Clinton J. Warren, architect. *One of the best-known contributions of Americans to the development of architecture is the skeleton frame, pioneered by architects of the "Chicago School" in the late 19th century. Before the steel skeleton, construction of buildings of even moderate height required thicker and thicker walls to bear the increased load. With the new method, the weight of the building is carried on the frame, not the walls. The skeleton frame allowed buildings to rise to tremendous heights without using increasing amounts of floor space for wall thickness, thus decreasing rental income. Construction documents of this period reveal other records. Construction of the Montauk Building was continued through the winter of 1881 by covering the frame with canvas and heating the space with steam. Electric lights allowed crews to work around the clock. Construction records were set when steel for the top ten stories of the Reliance Building were erected in 15 days, from July 16 to August 1, 1894. Once the frames are fireproofed, they are not seen again until a building is rehabilitated or demolished.* (Industrial Chicago, *volume 2, 1891, facing page 234, Library of Congress)*

102). The exterior walls were "hung like curtains" on a lighter but stronger frame. A whole new vocabulary of building connections was developed for anchorage of the curtainwalls to the skeleton and for the complex connections between columns, beams, and girders (figure 103).

Although iron and steel are not combustible, they lose strength in a fire if they are not protected from the heat. Almost all structural steel has to be "fireproofed" in some manner, utilizing a cladding of terra-cotta, tile, plaster, poured concrete, sprayed concrete or sprayed insulation. Therefore, once covered most structural steel is not seen again until hit by the wreckers ball.

Ferro concrete, commonly called reinforced concrete, was developed in Europe in the late 19th century when steel wire was added to concrete. Concrete is good in compression but poor in tension, whereas steel is good in both tension and compression. Therefore, steel bars were imbedded in wet concrete where it had to take tension, as in floor slabs, beams, and girders (figure 104), and where there were large compression loads, as in columns. Ernest Leslie Ransome during the late 1880s, used reinforced concrete floors and iron columns in construction of the Academy of Science in San Francisco. The first large-scale uses of reinforced concrete for both floors and columns came at the Leland Stanford Jr., Museum in 1890 and later at the Pacific Borax Company, both by Ransome. In the 20th century, reinforced concrete buildings became as common as steel frame buildings.

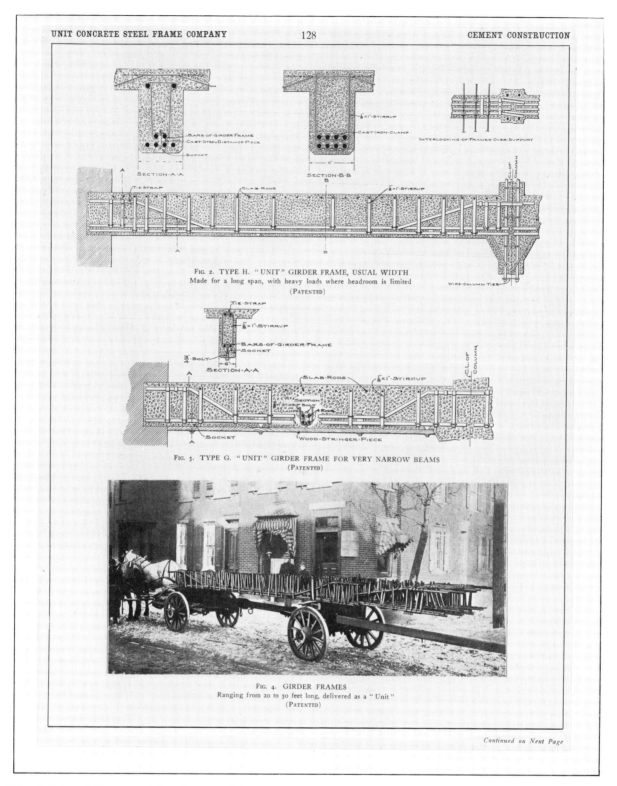

FIG. 2. TYPE H. "UNIT" GIRDER FRAME, USUAL WIDTH
Made for a long span, with heavy loads where headroom is limited
(PATENTED)

FIG. 3. TYPE G. "UNIT" GIRDER FRAME FOR VERY NARROW BEAMS
(PATENTED)

FIG. 4. GIRDER FRAMES
Ranging from 20 to 30 feet long, delivered as a "Unit"
(PATENTED)

Continued on Next Page

Figure 104.   Reinforced Concrete, Advertisement of the Unit Concrete Steel Frame Company, Philadelphia, Pennsylvania, from "Sweet's" Indexed Catalogue of Building Construction, 1906, p. 128. *This company specialized in the prefabrication of reinforcing for concrete girders ranging from 20 to 30 feet long, delivering them as a "Unit" to the construction site by horse-drawn wagon. Reinforced concrete girders and beams, consist of concrete (which is good only in compression) reinforced with bars of steel (which is good in both compression and tension). Most of the steel bars are placed at the bottom of the girder at the center of the span where the top part of the girder is in compression (to be taken by the concrete) and the bottom part of the beam is in tension (to be taken by the steel rods). Slab rods are only for controlling shrinkage of the slab. The opposite situation appears at the ends of the girder where it passes over a support. There the bottom part of the girder is in compression and the top part is in tension, explaining why some of the bars are bent up at an angle toward the ends of the girder. Note the cast-iron clamp and cast-steel distance piece which hold the reinforcing bars in correct vertical and horizontal alignment when the wet concrete is poured around the bars in the temporary wooden formwork (not shown). The 1/8- by 1-inch stirrups take shear loads.*

In recent years, high strength, high carbon steels have been developed, as well as very sophisticated steel framing systems such as the massive diagonal bracing on the John Hancock Building by I. M. Pei in Chicago. Likewise, pretensioned and posttensioned conrete using steel cables in tension has been developed to keep the concrete in compression. In these materials the concrete is constantly in compression. Precast concrete also uses steel for reinforcement and for anchorage to the framework of buildings in a manner similar to the anchors designed to hold stone or glazed architectural terra-cotta curtain walls in place.

There are countless decorative uses of steel in construction including staircases, window frames, doors and door frames, elevator doors, railings, and grilles. Most of these elements come painted or primed from the fabricator, and many have baked-on finishes.

Stainless Steel

Since the late 19th century, metallurgists have performed countless experiments to test the characteristics of hundreds of steel alloys to find new metals with superior properties. Industry needed these metals for machinery that would be strong even at high temperatures, hard enough to take the wear of moving parts, and corrosion-resistant to reduce maintenance costs. Much research was done to find better metals for the automotive, airplane, and electric industries. Later many of these alloys were adapted to the construction field.

At the turn of the century, interest centered on nickel steel, chromium steel, and later chromium-nickel steel, now called stainless steel. Between 1903 and 1912, scientists Harry Brearly of England, F. M. Becket of the U.S. and Benno Strauss and Eduard Maurer of Germany shared in the initial development of chromium-nickel steel. Its most important property is its resistance to corrosion. Stainless steels containing about 18% chromium and from 8% to 12% nickel are the most widely made. Their tensile strength, ductility, hardness, and resistance to creep and oxidation at high temperatures vary slightly with the composition. They can be cold worked, heat treated, cast, forged, welded, brazed, and soldered. However, stainless steel is expensive; hence, it is used primarily as a nonstructural metal or where there is a high potential for corrosion.

In 1928 architects Howe and Lascaze specified stainless steel, because of its high strength, for the grille and gate to the safety deposit room of the Philadelphia Savings Fund Society (PSFS) Building, which is now a National Historic Landmark. The stainless steel makes a very subtle contrast with the copper-clad walls.

Stainless steel sheets have been used for roofing, flashing, gutters, leader heads, downspouts, and cladding. One of the most extensive early uses of stainless steel was in the Chrysler Building in New York City. Architect William Van Alen originally intended to use aluminum to clad the building's Art Deco pinnacle (figure 105a), but finally decided in favor of stainless steel. The gargoyles were cast of stainless steel; the main entrance and storefronts are fabricated of rolled sheets and extruded sections of the same material. The elevator doors are stainless steel inlaid with wood (see figure 105b). Also in the Chrysler Building is a branch of Manufacturers Hanover Trust which is a *tour de force* of cast stainless steel (figure 106).

In the late 1920s and 1930s, the use of white metals increased with the rise of Art Deco, Depression Modern, Streamline Modern, and the International styles. Mirror finish chromium-plated metalwork was frequently used, but the plating often wore through to the base metal in high traffic areas such as entrances and lobbies. Since stainless steel is very hard, can be highly polished, and requires little maintenance other than periodic washings, it was a good choice for doors and storefronts. Some designs for stainless steel doors that became standard stock models can be found on several buildings, including the Versailles Apartment Building in Brooklyn (figure 107). Others were custom designed such as the stainless steel gates on the Federal Trade Commission Building in Washington, D.C., modeled by sculptor William McVey (figure 108).

Although there has been a long search for a noncorrosive material for bridge construction, stainless steel has not been used extensively, probably because of cost. As early as 1909, some nickel steel was used in construction of the Queensboro and Manhattan bridges crossing the East River in New York City. In 1937, 3,680 tons of 3.5% nickel steel were used for structural members of the San Francisco-Oakland Bay Bridge and 370 tons of stainless steel were used for pins in the cantilevered portion of the bridge. However, a total stainless steel bridge has never been built. After World War II, stainless steel replaced Monel metal for dairy, hospital, kitchen, restaurant, and laboratory equipment for economy. During the 1940s and 1950s, the stainless steel diner became a familiar part of American cities (figure 109).

There are many other uses for stainless steel including louvers, screens, railings, fascias, and cables. Fastening devices of stainless steel are also useful as anchors for masonry and metal curtain walls, and for restoring terra cotta and cast iron architecture. In 1964 Eero Saarinen used stainless steel to clad the Gateway Arch at the Jefferson National Expansion Memorial in St. Louis, Missouri.

Frequently stainless steel is used in modern sculpture, such as "News" in 1940 by Isamu Noguchi at 50 Rockefeller Plaza, New York City. A new gold-colored stainless steel developed recently has been used for storefronts in London and may soon be available in America.

Copper-Bearing Steels

Copper-bearing steels contain from 0.15% to 0.25% copper. Compared to ordinary steel, these metals develop increased resistance to atmospheric corrosion by forming a protective oxide coating. This "skin" has a uniform deep brown color and texture.

Copper-bearing steels were perfected in the 1950s and used in culverts and railroad grain cars before an architectural application was found. Architect Eero Saarinen noticed some railroad grain cars with the rich brown color and pleasing texture, and upon closer examination found the surface was unpainted. He learned that the material was specially developed for loading and transporting grain. Because sharp edged grain such as shelled corn eroded the paint on railroad cars, causing expensive maintenance programs, the railroad industry used this special steel, which rusted to a limited depth. The rust then formed a protective patina which prevented any further oxidation. Saarinen used this copper-bearing steel in the exterior of the Deere and Company Administrative Center at Moline, Illinois, and carbon steel on the interior where it was covered with fireproof material (figure 110). This was the first extensive architectural use of "Corten" manufactured by U.S. Steel. Weathered copper-bearing steel is also produced by Bethlehem Steel under the trade name of "Mayari R."

a.

Figure 105. Stainless Steel Dome, Gargoyles, and Elevator Doors, Chrysler Building, 405 Lexington Avenue, New York City, 1928–1929; William Van Alen, architect. *(a) The Chrysler Building was the first extensive use in America of chromium-nickel steel, now commonly called stainless steel, as an exterior finish on a large commercial structure. There are many types of stainless steel with different properties; the type used here was Nirosta, K.A.2 (Krupp's formula), installed by the sheet metal contractor, Benjamin Riesner, Inc. According to the architect, "The sheet metal covering for the needle or upper third of the spire (not shown) was attached directly to the structural steel frame. A base of "nailing" concrete was provided for the sheet metal work, completely covering that portion of the dome and spire below the needle, and extended down on both sides of the circular-head dormers to the 59th floor level. The sheet metal ribs were fastened to fireproofed wood nailing strips placed on top of the concrete and fastened to the structural steel frame. Standing or lock seams, made without solder, were used throughout, except where they were impossible or undesirable, where soldered seams were used. The radial ribs on the fronts of the metal-covered dormers of the dome and similar ribbed construction are formed by sheet metal-covered wooden battens. Contact between dissimilar metals was avoided by using Nirosta steel nails, screws, bolts, nuts, and rivets for fastening the sheet steel in position." (b) Influenced by the discovery of the King Tut's tomb, these stainless steel elevator doors are inlaid with rare woods in a stylized Egyptian design featuring a lotus blossom at the top. (Cervin Robinson)*

b.

Figure 106. Cast Stainless Steel Entrance, Manufacturers Hanover Trust, Chrysler Building, New York City, 1931; Cooper Alloy Foundry, Elizabeth, New Jersey. *The gate, door, frame, lamps, night deposit, and lettering were cast in Nirosta stainless steel. (David W. Look)*

Figure 107. Typical Stainless Steel Doors, Versailles Apartment Building, 1717 Avenue N, Brooklyn, New York, 1936; Kavy and Kavovitt, Inc., architects. *The doors were fabricated from sheets of stainless steel with etched and frosted glass in the window. The stainless steel frame was produced from rolled sections and inset with glass blocks. Identical doors with clear glass can be found on the Majestic and Gynwood apartment buildings in Washington, D.C. (David W. Look)*

a.

Figure 109.   Stainless Steel Empire Diner, 210 Tenth Avenue, Chelsea, New York City, 1943, altered, 1976; Carl Laanes. *(a) Early diners were horse-drawn wooden wagons, but after the advent of the automobile they soon became stationary. Although companies built diners in a range of sizes and styles, and of various materials, the stainless steel diner became the ultimate expression in diners. The exterior of the Empire Diner has panels and strips of white and black enameled steel which contrast with the polished stainless steel. (b) Although some early diners had wooden interiors and Monel metal equipment, most diners were paneled with pressed stainless steel and had stainless steel equipment by the 1940s. (David W. Look)*

Figure 108.   Stainless Steel Gates, Lamps, and Lettering, Federal Trade Commission, Sixth and Constitution Avenue, NW, Washington, D.C., 1937; Bennett, Parsons, Frost, architects; William McVey, sculptor. *During the 1930s stainless steel was frequently used for monumental doors and ornamental gates on government buildings. Noted sculptors were employed to design custom ornamental metalwork. The lamps, lettering, and window grilles (not shown) are all stainless steel. (David W. Look)*

b.

Figure 110. "Corten" Steel, Deere and Company Administrative Center, Moline, Illinois, 1964; Eero Saarinen, architect. *The Deere and Company building, which received many architectural awards, was among the first to make extensive architectural use of this unpainted, corrosion-resistant material for exterior steel members. (Deere and Company)*

Chapter 8: Aluminum

Aluminum was not available at a reasonable price or in sufficient quantities for architectural uses until after the beginning of the 20th century. It is the third most abundant element on Earth, exceeded only by oxygen and silicon. Like most metals, it never occurs in nature as a pure element but always as a compound. The name of the aluminum-rich ore, bauxite, came from the French village Les Baux, where a deposit was found in 1821. Four years later, Danish physicist Hans Christian Oersted produced the first few ounces of aluminum. It was considered so precious that Frederick VII, King of Denmark, had a royal helmet made of polished aluminum and gold.

Figure 111.   The Setting of the Aluminum Tip on the Washington Monument, Washington, D.C. *The first architectural use of aluminum was the small pyramidal cap of the Washington Monument, which was set in place on December 6, 1884. At that time, aluminum was still considered a precious metal. (Engraving in* Harper's Weekly, *December 20, 1884; Martin Luther King Library)*

In 1855 at the Paris Exposition aluminum was introduced to the public. Napoleon III had pocket watches and a table service designed of it, and during the American Civil War, General Ulysses S. Grant received an aluminum medal from the U.S. Congress. One hundred ounces of the rare metal were cast to form the small pyramidal cap of the Washington Monument in Washington, D.C. Before ceremonial positioning of the cap atop the monument on December 6, 1884 (figure 111), it was displayed in Tiffany's window in New York City. The monument cap was the first American architectural use of aluminum.

Until a method was found to separate the pure aluminum from the bauxite ore in large quantities and at a moderate cost, it could not be used for anything other than small items. Metallurgists were intrigued by the attractive, lightweight, corrosion-resistant metal and foresaw many commercial and industrial applications. The modern electrolytic method of producing aluminum was discovered in 1886 almost simultaneously by Charles Martin Hall in the United States and Paul L. T. Heroult in France. The essentials of the Hall and Heroult processes were identical and have become the basis of the modern aluminum industry. Initially Hall found little support for the commercial development of his process, but fortunately he met another metallurgist, Captain Alfred E. Hunt, who convinced a small group of steel producers to establish the Pittsburgh Reduction Company in 1880. Early production soon reached 50 pounds of aluminum per day at the small plant; tea kettles and cooking utensils were some of the first products.

In 1893 Winslow Brothers, Company, of Chicago, Illinois, published a photographic essay of their previous work, probably for the Columbian Exposition. The book not only gives the names of buildings that contained their work and the architects who designed the buildings, but also identified in detail the metals, alloys, plating (if any), and other finishes. Of special interest are the Monadnock (figure 112) and Venetian (now demolished) Buildings in Chicago which contained cast aluminum stairs, elevators, and grilles dating from 1891 and 1892, respectively. Also listed, but not illustrated, is the Isabella Building of 1893 which also has original aluminum work.

As production increased and other companies were founded, the cost of aluminum decreased, but by 1895, aluminum was still five times as expensive as copper. In spite of the cost, aluminum was used in 1895 to sheath the dome and roof of the Church of San Gioacchino in Rome, Italy. Seventy years later, the roof was still in excellent condition.

The engine of the Wright Brothers' plane at Kitty Hawk was made of aluminum. By the time World War I began, aluminum was in use for military aircraft because of its relative lightness and strength. Production increased enormously and the costs continued to decline. Architectural use of aluminum slowly increased in the 1920s, mainly for decorative detailing. Aluminum was one of the white metals popular in the modern movements of architecture and art.

When it was proven that aluminum could be shaped by most known methods of metal working, its inclusion in architectural and industrial settings surged. Since it could be rolled into sheets, it was used for roofing, flashing, gutters, downspouts, wall panels, and spandrels; it could also be extruded into lengths of specialized profiles or cross sections for use in window mullions and frames, storefront surrounds, and doors. Because it was a favored color and could be cast, aluminum was chosen for interior trim in public buildings and commercial structures in the 1920s and 1930s.

Figure 112. Cast Aluminum Staircase, Monadnock Building, 53 West Jackson Boulevard, Chicago, Illinois; Burham and Root, architects; Winslow, Brothers, Co., foundry. *Although the Monadnock Building is widely known as the last skyscraper with load bearing walls, few people know that it contains the second known architectural use of cast aluminum in America. The first story staircase, including the newell posts, electroliers, balustrade railing, facias, and stringers, are all cast of aluminum. The lamps have been removed. Aluminum ventilation grilles near the exterior doors are also illustrated, but have also been removed. (plate 4, Collection of Photographs of Ornamental Iron Executed by Winslow Bros., 1893, Library of Congress)*

Art Deco designs were often fabricated in cast aluminum, as can be seen in the Post Office in Cincinnati. Frequently neoclassical designs were executed in aluminum, as in the Mellon Institute of Pittsburgh. In both buildings, the ornamental door trim, window details, revolving doors, lobby fixtures, and elevator doors were fabricated of patterned silvery aluminum.

The perforated Gothic spire of the Smithfield Street Congregational Church was cast in Pittsburgh and affixed to the church in 1926 (figure 112). Another exterior use of aluminum was in the 1929 Springfield, Illinois, Post Office where decorative aluminum panels are set into the walls, and bold stylized anthemions stand along the roofline.

The first extensive use of aluminum in construction was the Empire State Building, completed in 1931. The entire tower portion is aluminum, and architects Shreve, Lamb, and Harmond also included it in their design of the entrances, elevator doors, ornamental trim, and some 6,000 window spandrels. Flanked by ribbons of stainless steel, these panels of "deplated" aluminum are a dark gray color.

In 1933 almost 65,000 pounds of aluminum sheets were used to roof the Union Terminal in Cincinnati. That same year the architectural firm of Ritter & Shay. designed the U.S. Custom House on Chestnut at Second Street in Philadelphia, which had aluminum light standards and sculptural bas-relief figures in tympanum panels over the doors (figure 113). In Washington, D.C., sculptor Carl Paul Jennewein modeled the aluminum work for the Department of Justice Building (figure 114).

During World War II, aluminum moved into fourth place among metals in production and use. Roofing of the Mormon Tabernacle in Salt Lake City, Utah, in 1947, was an important post-War example of the use of aluminum. Today aluminum ranks second to steel in production.

Although the process for anodizing aluminum was invented in 1923, it was not used for architectural elements until the 1950s. Anodizing is a special electro-chemical bath that provides a tough oxide coating for greater resistance to atmospheric corrosion, and can also be used to add a colored finish. Aluminum siding with a baked-on paint finish came on the market about the same time as anodized aluminum. The 30-story Alcoa Building, erected in 1951-1952 in Pittsburgh's Golden Triangle, was the first multistoried building to employ curtain walls of aluminum. Rising 410 feet, the walls consisted of 6- by 12-foot sections mechanically stamped from 1/8-inch aluminum sheets. Each section has a reversible pivot aluminum window above a pyramidal stamped panel, backed by aluminum lath and sprayed perlite plaster. The lighter weight of the curtain wall reduced the size of the structural steel members and the foundation, resulting in a 30% savings on these two items. The exterior panels were given an irridescent gray anodized coating. There was a deliberate attempt to make use of aluminum in as many ways as possible, even including aluminum strips in the terrazzo floors. Innovative major uses included all-aluminum wiring; aluminum pipes for plumbing, heating, and air conditioning; and an aluminum cooling tower (figure 112).

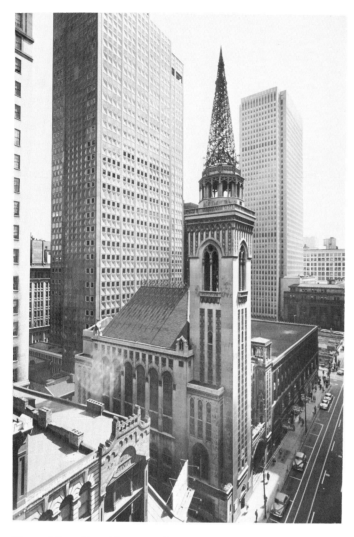

Some 2,500 tons of aluminum were used in construction of the U.S. Air Force Academy in Colorado Springs, Colorado, in the 1950s. The chapel of the Academy has aluminum exterior panels, windows, handrails, and grilles, but the most spectacular aluminum members are the 17 roof spires made up of 100 giant, preformed tetrahedrons. In 1953, Henry Ford financed F. Buckminster Fuller's first aluminum and plastic geodesic dome. Within a few years, thousands had been constructed around the world.

Because of its durability, aluminum was used in construction of the Vehicle Assembly Building completed in 1965 at the NASA Launch Complex, Kennedy Space Center, Florida, which is listed in the National Register of Historic Places. Enclosing 10 acres of land and over 45 stories tall, the building is clad with ribbed aluminum sheathing specially designed to withstand 125 mph winds.

Today aluminum is used extensively in construction for everything except major structural members, and is available in a wide variety of colors and finishes.

Figure 113.   Cast Aluminum Spire, German Evangelical Protestant Church, Pittsburgh, Pennsylvania, 1926; Henry Hornbostel, architect. Also Alcoa Building (background, left), Golden Triangle, 1952; Harrison and Abramovitz, architects. *The perforated spire of the German Evangelical Protestant Church, now the Smithfield Street Congregational Church, consists of 22 filigree aluminum castings. The Alcoa Building is the first multistory structure with an aluminum curtain wall. The other tall building (right) is the United States Steel-Mellon Building. (Carnegie Library of Pittsburgh)*

Figure 114.   Aluminum Bas-Relief Sculpture in Tympanum and Lamps, U.S. Customhouse, bounded by Chestnut, Second, and Third streets, Philadelphia, Pennsylvania, 1933; Ritter and Shay, architects; Edward Ardolino, sculptor. *In the 1920s and 1930s, architects frequently chose one of the white or silvery metals for their buildings; those designing in the Art Moderne, now called Art Deco style, especially considered gold or bronze colored metals "old-fashioned." The highly stylized bas-relief mural in the typanum is flanked by cast aluminum and glass lamps. (Esther Mipaas)*

Figure 115.   Aluminum Doors and Lamps, U.S. Department of Justice, Ninth and Constitution Avenue, NW, Washington, D.C., 1934; Zantzinger, Boris, Medary, architects; Carl Paul Jennewein, sculptor. *The monumental doors, fabricated of cast lions and rolled sections of aluminum riveted together, are opened back into pockets of the walls of the entrance showing the inner set of aluminum and glass doors and transom. Flanking the entrance are cast aluminum lamps with stylized eagles, buffaloes, and dolphins. The work was executed by Anthony D. Lorenzo. (David W. Look)*

Conclusion

Much can be gained from studying trade catalogs and contemporary accounts on the subject of metals in America's historic buildings. The foundry catalog traditionally played an important role in the marketing of metals in the United States as prefabricated building materials, and was part of the revolution in building techniques that took place during the 19th century. Catalogs brought good-quality standardized products within the grasp of builders across the country and resulted in lower prices for products shipped directly from the iron factories and foundries.

The first foundry catalogs seem to have appeared in America in the 1850s. Most metal products were manufactured in cities where they contributed to both commercial and residential growth patterns. The products offered unquestionably added to the variety of buildings that could be constructed in every community served by railroad, canal, or coastal waters.

The items usually advertised were columns, storefronts, entire building fronts, stairs, brackets, window sills and lintels, overdoors, railings, shutters, verandas, balconies, posts, fences, and cresting. Some catalogs were also sources for heating, plumbing, and lighting equipment.

The best known catalog is that of the Architectural Iron Works of New York City, issued in 1865 (reprinted in 1970, see bibliography). Another reprinted foundry catalog is that of Janes, Kirtland and Company, which in 1870 was marketing decorative cast-iron fountains,

urns, verandas, trellises, garden furniture, and lawn animals. Recently the 1857 J. B. Wickersham New York Wire Railing Company was republished by the Philadelphia Athenaeum under the title *Victorian Ironwork.*

For various reasons, few catalogs have survived to the 20th century. Some early catalogs were printed on poor quality paper little better than newspaper. Those that have survived are usually on quality paper. A few were beautifully done with hand-colored drawings, and some of the later catalogs included photographs.

A few catalogs list previous clients and their buildings to advertise their designs and satisfied customers. Examination of a collection of catalogs from a foundry such as J. L. Mott, J. W. Fiske, W. H. Mullins, or Wood and Perot shows the repetition of certain designs from catalog to catalog and can indicate which designs sold more and how long their popularity lasted.

Contemporary accounts give details on how these metal components were made, installed, and used. The bibliography lists these accounts to help architectural historians, historical architects, preservationists, craftsmen, and industrial archeologists find information on topics germane to preservation projects.

The second part of this report will discuss the physical and mechanical characteristics of these architectural metals, examine the reasons for their deterioration, and suggest methods of keeping them from environmental and human damage.

Opposite: Replication of the original c. 1815 Philadelphia gutter at The Octagon in Washington, D.C. utilized hand-cast lead sheets and traditional application techniques. (John G. Waite)

Part II. Deterioration and Methods of Preserving Metals

by John G. Waite, AIA

Chapter 9: Preservation of Architectural Metals

The metals used most commonly in historic American building construction have been lead, tin, zinc, copper, bronze, brass, iron, steel, and to a lesser extent nickel alloys, stainless steel, and aluminum. While they have been employed in a variety of ways, these metals have been used primarily for structural systems, sheathing, roofing, siding, and decorative elements. The first part of this report provided a pictorial survey and historical description of these metals and their architectural uses. This part will discuss the deterioration, preservation, repair, and maintenance of metal building components.[1]

Like other building materials, metals can deteriorate over time or be damaged and require conservation or replacement to continue to serve their intended functions. The problems of size and weight or the integration of these metals into the structure of a building can complicate conservation attempts.

Before steps can be taken to analyze or treat deterioration, it is necessary to know which metal is involved. Determining the metallic composition of an architectural component may not be easy, especially if it is inaccessible or encrusted with paint. If possible, the original architect's specifications and any correspondence relating to the structure should be checked for any references to foundries, catalogs, or stores where building materials might have been purchased. If these resources prove fruitless, a preservation consultant or historical architect may be able to help.

When deterioration has set in, prompt action to halt or correct the damage is essential. But first, the exact cause of the problem must be found. If water, oxidation, *galvanic action* (destructive corrosion between two dissimilar metals), or a host of other conditions continue to exist in a building system, it may be that no amount of corrective action will be sufficient to save it. These problems must be accurately diagnosed before any restoration or rehabilitation is undertaken. For example, many buildings in the past were constructed with unfortunate combinations of dissimilar metals, which resulted in destructive reactions. Builders then did not always know enough about the properties of various metals and the potential for reactions with each other and with other materials such as certain types of wood, masonry, and coatings. Once the causes of deterioration have been identified and the damage repaired, a regular maintenance program is needed to prevent recurrence. Records of the structural investigations and all changes, including additions and subtractions from the building, should

be kept. When records are kept, later problems with materials or remedial measures will be easier to detect and inappropriate treatments easier to avoid.

After a general discussion of metal deterioration, this part of the report will discuss methods of stabilizing metal components that are currently available and will recommend steps toward their preservation and maintenance. The metals most widely used in historic buildings will be discussed for specific properties, deterioration characteristics, and preservation and repair techniques.

Metals are, in general, those inorganic substances that have luster and hardness, can conduct heat and electricity, are opaque, and possess certain mechanical properties, the most valuable of which is the ability to resist deformation. All metals[2] have crystalline structures and are somewhat malleable and ductile; that is, they can be shaped by hammering or rolled into thin sheets and drawn into wire. Metals have tenacity, resist separation of individual particles, and are fusible; that is, they become liquid when heated at a high temperature. Metals also have high specific gravity or relative weight.

In chemistry, a *metal* is defined as an element that yields positively charged ions in aqueous solutions of its salts. Another definition is that a metal is a lender of electrons; that is, a metal loses electrons during a chemical reaction. Different types of metals have different chemical properties and consequently react in various ways with elements of the environment.

The preservation architect must be knowledgeable about these physical and chemical properties and their relationship to the agents of deterioration in the building's environment in order to choose proper stabilization or restoration techniques. If the properties of the metal are not fully understood, an inappropriate treatment that, in the long run, may cause more deterioration than it corrects, might be selected. (table 1).

In order to be used successfully for architectural purposes, the metals selected must maintain their functional integrity over a long period of time and must also be aesthetically acceptable. The long-term performance of metal architectural elements depends upon the metals' intrinsic physical and chemical properties, the climates to which they are exposed, and the specific design details that determine their relationship and proximity to other metallic and nonmetallic building components. Properly selected, installed, and maintained, metal architectural elements are among the most durable and permanent building materials. However, metal elements that are not properly suited for the chosen function or are not properly cared for can be very fragile and short lived.

Table I.

Metal	Symbol	Atomic Number	Atomic Weight	Relative Density	Melting Point Degrees C	Specific Heat	Heat Expansion Per °C	Heat Cond'y % of Cu	Elect. Cond'y % of Cu	Coef. of Elect. Res. Per °C	Modulus of Elast'y psi
Lead	Pb	82	207.1	11.38	327	0.031	.000029	9.	7.8	.0041	800,000
		50	118.7	7.28	231.8	0.054	.000020	16.	15.		6,000,000
Zinc	Zn	30	65.37	7.14	420	0.094	.000029	29.	28.2	.0040	13,700,000
Copper	Cu	29	63.5	8.89	1083	0.093	.000.17	100.	100.	.0040	16,000,000
Phosphor Bronze				8.66		0.104	.000018		36.	.0039	16,000,000
Brass				8.46	900	0.088	.000020	28.	28.	.0015	13,800,000
Nickel	Ni	28	58.6	8.85	1440	0.130	.000013	15.5	16.	.0041	30,000,000
Nickel Silver				8.75	1110	0.095	.000018	7.6	5.2	.0003	17,000,000
Monel Metal				8.80	1315	0.127	.000014	6.6	4.	.0019	26,000,000
Iron	Fe	26	55.8	7.7	1535	0.110	.000013	15.	15.	.0062	25,000,000
Cast Iron				7.2	1000-1200		.000010	10-12	2-12		12-27,000,000
Steel				7.9	1400		.000013	6-12	3-15		30,000,000
18/8 Cr/Ni Iron (stainless steel)				7.9	1400	0.118	.000017	3.6	2.8		28,600,000
Aluminum	Al	13	27	2.7	660	0.218	.000024	52.	56-59	.0042	10,000,000

Table I. Properties of Metals Used in Building Construction.

The information in this table is of special interest to preservationists because it includes alloys commonly used in construction. The metals and alloys in this table are listed in the same order as they appear in this report. This order was devised to avoid repetition, that is, the discussion of elements would precede the discussion of bronze and brass. The relative density has no units because it is a ratio and expresses the relative weight of equal volumes of metals to the weight of the same volume of a standard. The melting point is of interest because it has a bearing on the ease or difficulty of casting, soldering, brazing, and welding. Historically, copper has been used as a standard for comparing the properties of heat conductance and coefficients of electrical resistance because of its excellent ability to conduct heat and its extensive use in electrical wiring. Other tables use silver or hydrogen as a standard, but these are not used in construction and are more difficult to relate to for people in the construction industry. The modules of elasticity is a measure of the rigidity of a metal, that is, its ability to resist deformation until the elastic limit (point at which the metal will not spring back to its original position after the load or weight has been removed; therefore, permanent deformation) of the metal has been reached. (Adapted from *Practical Design in Monel Metal*, (p. 10, published in 1935 by International Nickel Company.)

In scientific terms, *deterioration* is generally defined as a decrease in ability of the material to fulfill the function for which it was intended.[3] It usually refers to the breakdown of a material because of natural causes, although deterioration can also be either directly or indirectly caused by man. Although deterioration usually implies a chemical change, under some conditions, the change can be physical.

Corrosion

Corrosion, in one form or another, is the major cause of the deterioration of architectural metals. Often called oxidation, it is the chemical reaction of a metal with oxygen or other substances. Metals are constantly undergoing change. With exposure to the atmosphere, heat, moisture, pressure, and other agents, they tend to revert from a pure state, such as iron and copper (elements), to their natural ores, such as iron oxide and copper sulfide (compounds). The deterioration of metal architectural elements is a complex process because the types and degree of corrosion are affected by minor variations in environment, contact with other metals and materials, and the composition of the metal itself.[4]

Upon exposure to the atmosphere, almost all new or newly cleaned metals become coated with a thin complex film, which is a result of the reaction of the metal with oxygen in the air. This film may modify the properties of the metal and make it less susceptible to further corrosion. As the film thickens, it may tend to insulate the metal from moist air or other corrosive agents. The inherent nature of the metal to resist corrosion and the nature of the film determines to what degree the corrosion of the metal is controlled. With some metals such as aluminum and copper, the oxide coating can form a protective membrane which restricts the passage of metal ions out of it or oxygen into it and through it. With other metals, such as iron, the oxide does not form a protective film, but rather promotes the continued corrosion of the metal.

Architectural metals are attacked by corrosion in several ways, including the following:[5]

Uniform Attack is where the metal corrodes evenly when exposed to corrosive agents.

Pitting is the localized corrosive attack on the metal (see figure 180 and 181).

Selective Attack can occur where a metal or alloy is not homogeneous and certain areas are attacked more than others.

Stress Corrosion Cracking can occur where stresses were induced into the metal in the pulling or bending process of metalworking and the metal was later subjected to a corrosive environment. For example, wrought brass can crack if small quantities of ammonia are introduced into the environment; stainless steels can crack in chloride-containing environments; and carbon steels in nitrate, cyanide, or strong caustic solutions.[6]

Erosion occurs when the corrosion-resistant film or oxide or layers of protective corrosion product is removed by abrasion, exposing fresh metal to the corrosive agents.

Galvanic Corrosion is an electrochemical action that occurs between two different metals in electrical contact in the presence of a common electrolyte forming an electrical couple (where there is a flow of electrons). Positive ions can travel through an electrolyte such as ionized water (which must be present). A galvanic action will occur only (1) when there are two dissimilar metals having a difference in a potential, (greater and lesser degree of nobility), (2) when the two dissimilar metals are in electrical contact so there can be a flow of electrons, and (3) when there is an electrolyte so that ions can move from one metal to the other (figure 116). In some cases, the electrolyte may be moisture or condensation on the surfaces of the metals. If any of the three conditions are not present, then galvanic action will not take place.[7]

Table II is a galvanic series from the ASTM Standard Guide G82-83 (Development and Use of Galvanic Series Predicting Galvanic Corrosion Performance).[8] It is based on actual potential readings in sea water, a standard corrosive environment used to test many metals. Although few architectural metals are found in contact with sea water, this table is still useful because the positions on the list would change little if the metals were subjected to other corrosive environments such as urban pollution.

The severity of galvanic corrosion is also a function of area size: if the more noble metal is much larger than the baser metal, the deterioration of the baser metal will be more rapid and severe; if the more noble metal is much smaller than the baser metal, the deterioration of the baser metal will be much less significant. For example, if two copper sheets fastened together with iron rivets are placed in a corrosive environment, the iron rivets will deteriorate rapidly. On the other hand, if two iron sheets fastened together with copper rivets are placed in the same corrosive atmosphere for an equal period of time, the iron plates will only show a slight amount of deterioration and the copper rivets will be unaffected.[9]

Oxygen Concentration (Galvanic) Cell is an electrolytic cell set up where oxygen is trapped between two metals such as between tin and steel on a sheet of tinplate, or between a metal and a nonmetal, such as between a metal and a gasket or between a metal gutter and tree leaves.

Atmospheric Corrosion is an electrochemical reaction resulting from a film of moisture on the surface of the metal which serves as an electrolyte. The film contains gases absorbed by the water. Here the potential difference is between two points on the same metallic surface. This type of corrosion is the most common form of corrosion to which architectural metals are exposed. The rate of atmospheric corrosion generally increases with the humidity levels. Once a critical humidity level is reached, corrosion proceeds rapidly. Generally, an increase in temperature also increases the rate of corrosion.

Industrial atmospheres contain (along with oxygen, water, and carbon dioxide) other corrosive agents including soot, fly ash, and sulfur compounds produced by the combustion of sulfur-containing fuels, especially coal. Common sulfur compounds include hydrogen sulfide (H_2S), sulfur dioxide (SO_2), sulfur trioxide (SO_3), and particles of ammonium sulfate $[(NH_4)_2SO_4]$[10] or salt ($NaCl$) near the sea coast.

Sea water is especially corrosive. Marine atmospheres and sea water contain several corrosive agents including chlorides and other salt particles which can be deposited on the surface of the metal (figure 182). These corrosive agents can affect metals as far as 60 to 70 miles from the sea (depending on weather patterns). Chloride ions are also found in some de-icing salts and in some forms of industrial pollutants. Metals immersed in water are also subject to corrosion by dissolved solids and gases, especially oxygen.

Soils also contain a number of metal-corroding agents including acids, alkalis, dissolved salts, water, oxygen, and sometimes anaerobic sulfate-reducing bacteria.

Corrosive agents other than oxygen and sulfur compounds which attack architectural metals include salts, especially halides such as fluorides, chlorides, bromides, and iodides, and organic compounds such as bird droppings. These agents are found in many substances, such as scum, mud, and marine plants as well as sea water and fresh water.

Mechanical Breakdown

Metal architectural elements can also fail from purely physical causes such as abrasion, or a combination of physical and chemical attack, such as weathering and stress corrosion cracking.

Abrasion is the erosion of the metal (figure 149) caused by the impact of dirt, dust, sand grit, sleet, rain, and hail, or by rubbing with another architectural or human element. Abrasives can also encourage corrosion by removing the protective corrosion deposits from the metal surface. Abrasion is an especially critical problem with metal flashings and valleys used on slate roofs. As the slate deteriorates, particles break off and are washed down the valleys, causing erosion. Other examples of abrasion are when the patina, push plates and rail on bronze and brass doors (figure 117), chrome plating on railings, and brass thresholds are worn by pedestrians.

Fatigue is failure of a metal by the repeated application of cyclic stresses below the elastic limit—the greatest stress a material can withstand without permanent deformation after removal of the load. It results from a gradual or progressive fracture of the crystals. It has been estimated that approximately 90% of the structural failures of metal railroad bridges are fatigue failures which develop late in the life of the structure.[11] One of the major causes of the failure of copper roofs is fatigue

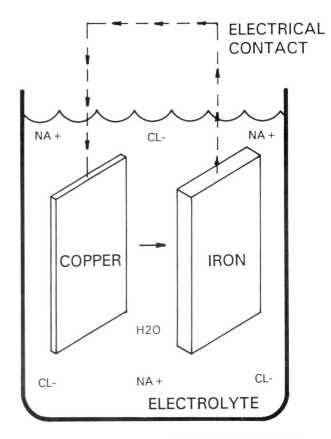

MECHANISM OF COPPER / IRON GALVANIC CORROSION

ARROWS INDICATE ELECTRON FLOW PATH

Figure 116. Galvanic Corrosion. *A galvanic action occurs between the copper and iron with the water serving as the electrolyte. (Texas Instruments)*

Figure 117. Human Abrasion. *At the Old Post Office in Baltimore, Maryland, the bronze and glass doors show the abrasive effect of human hands on the natural patina combined with a residue of dirt and oil (from skin, which contains a minute amount of acid). This wear with accompanying superficial discoloration is only a minor problem. Over the years, these doors have received inadequate maintenance and inappropriate changes (to the hardware) and repairs. Such doors should be thoroughly cleaned to the bare metal; the holes plugged, ground down, and polished; and new chemical artificial bronze patina applied and protected by a lacquer with a corrosion inhibitor and/or with periodic applications of wax or oil (see section on bronze Chapter 15). (David W. Look)*

Figure 118. Fatigue Failure. *This is an example of fatigue cracking of the copper roof of the Senate House, Kingston, New York. Repeated expansion and contraction due to daily and seasonal temperature changes has caused this sheet-copper roof to crack. Note cracking both at the joint and on the planar surface. (John G. Waite)*

cracking caused by lack of provisions to accommodate thermal expansion and contraction (figure 118).

Creep is the continuous flow or plastic deformation of soft metals under sustained stressing, sometimes under relatively high temperatures. It tends to distort the metal, causing thin areas that may fail by rupture. Creep is characterized by inter-crystalline fracture and a lack of strain hardening. The stressing may be related to thermal expansion and contraction and the weight of the

Figure 119. Creep. *Deterioration of milled sheet lead roof on a 19th century canal warehouse and office at Nantwich Basin of the Shropshire Union Canal at Nantwich, Cheshire, England. The failure has been caused by creep and the expansion and contraction of the lead. (John G. Waite)*

metal. The problem of creep is often associated with sheet lead roofing (figure 119), lead statuary, and pure zinc.

Fire can cause unprotected metal (iron and steel) framing members to become plastic and fail rapidly (figure 120). Lead roofs have melted during fires, and sheet metal decoration can buckle from heat and fall off buildings when its anchorage is lost. Structural iron or steel that has survived a fire without deformation is usually safe to reuse, but any questionable member should be load tested.

Overloading is the stressing of a metal member beyond its yield point so that permanent deformation, fracturing, or failure occurs. The member can fail through the application of static loads, dynamic loads, thermal stresses (figure 121), and settlement stresses either singly or in combination. "Buckling" is a form of permanent deformation from overloading which is usually caused by excessive weight but can also be caused by thermal stresses. Members can also be overloaded if their support is removed and loads are redistributed to other members which can become overstressed and deformed (figure 122).

Weathering

A metal architectural element subjected to the weather is exposed to various chemical and physical agents at one

Figure 120. Column Buckling from Fire. *In 1906 San Francisco was shaken by a severe earthquake, followed by fires that raged out of control for hours. In the Fairmont Hotel, the metal lath and plaster that covered the columns was probably damaged by the earthquake and was not sufficient to protect the steel from the intense heat. Portions of this building settled down approximately 7 feet from their original position because 37 columns buckled from the heat in this manner. (From* Trial by the Fire at San Francisco: The Evidence of the Camera, *1906, Library of Congress.)*

time. The result is a kind of synergism where the total effect is greater than the sum of the individual effects.[12] For example, the rate of corrosion accelerates with increases of temperature, humidity, and surface deposits of salts, dirt, and pollution.

Connection Failure

The failure of the connections of metal architectural elements, especially structural members, can also be caused by a combination of physical and/or chemical agents. The most common type of connections used for metal structural elements of historic buildings include bolting, riveting, pinning, and welding. These connections can fail through the overloading, fatiguing, or corrosion of the connectors (figure 123). Common examples of this type of failure include the corrosion, usually by the galvanic effects, of nails, bolt heads, rivets, and areas covered by fastening plates. The effective cross-sectional area of the connectors is often reduced by corrosion, making the connectors more susceptible to stress failure.

Figure 121. Overloading. *The copper gutter on the Senate House, Kingston, New York, installed in the 1920s, has been distorted by ice and snow; the seams between gutter sections have opened. The problems were compounded by the lack of stiffness of the gutter and the absence of adequate provisions for expansion and contraction. The steel restaining straps are deteriorating because of an electrolytic reaction (galvanic corrosion) with the copper (the more noble metal). (John G. Waite)*

Figure 123. Anchorage Failure. *The nails holding down this section of embossed galvanized sheet-iron roofing have deteriorated and the wind has lifted up the corner of the sheet, allowing water to leak through the roof sheathing. Other sections (not shown in the photo) had flapped in the wind until the sheet metal cracked with fatigue failure and tore loose. In 1977 this roof at St. Edward's University in Austin, Texas, was cleaned and supplemented with reproduction "shingles" where needed. (St. Edward's University)*

Figure 122. Structural Failure. *This 19th-century wrought-iron truss bridge at Brunswick, New York, partially collapsed because the cut-stone abutment supporting it washed away. Once the support was removed, the bridge twisted. (John G. Waite)*

Chapter 11: General Preservation Methods

Introduction

Unfortunately, much of the technology that has been developed by the museum conservator for treating small metal artifacts in a carefully controlled laboratory environment is not always transferable to the preservation of architectural metals. When dealing with historic buildings, the architect is often confronted with deteriorated metal elements used either as structural members or as weather protection, such as roof coverings, flashings, and wall cladding. When these elements deteriorate or actually fail, it is not practical to treat them as museum objects under laboratory conditions because of their size or position. These elements are integral parts of buildings and, therefore, cannot be easily removed and replaced. Also, laboratory treatments may not replace lost material; thus, the components would be too weak to use.

The big difference between the treatment of museum objects and architectural components is that once a museum object is cleaned and treated, it is returned to a controlled environment and is never used. The opposite is true of metal architectural components. Once they are treated *in situ*, they remain in their original environment and must function as originally intended. For example, if a roof fails it is not just the roofing material itself that is affected (figure 124). The structure and fabric of the rest of the building as well as the contents of the building can also be damaged. Therefore, it is not surprising to find that architectural metals that have failed are usually removed and replaced with new material.

a

b

Figure 124. Successive Failure. *If a metal architectural element such as a tinplate roof fails, more than just the tinplate may be destroyed. (a) Deterioration is evident in the original framing and roof sheathing of the Schuyler Mansion entrance wing in Albany, New York. The entrance wing was added to the building about 1817 and reroofed with tinplate sheets during the 19th century. The tinplate gutter liners eventually deteriorated and were replaced with copper during the 1930s. However, the tinplate roof remained and electrolysis occurred along the roof perimeter where the copper and tinplate were in contact. (b) Consequently, the tinplate was completely corroded away (as seen here) when the deteriorated roofing was removed. This resulted in major damage to the sheathing, framing, and masonry walls of the entrance. (John G. Waite)*

A practical reason for this approach is cost. The preservation architect normally deals with construction trades which, although skilled in conventional building techniques, have neither the training, experience, nor facility with scientific techniques for conserving historic building materials *in situ*. It is often less expensive to replace the deteriorated metal than to experiment with its preservation, which even if successful, may add only a few years to its life expectancy. If the replacement method is adopted and the original material is significant, it should either be left in place and covered or carefully removed and its location documented; the component (or at least a portion of it) should then be retained as a historic object.

A number of methods have been developed to inhibit the start of corrosion in metals as well as to control corrosion once it has begun. These methods, which will be discussed individually, include the following:[13] proper installation of the metal elements; control of the environment by the use of inhibitors; dehumidification; cathodic and galvanic protection; the use of metallic, ceramic, and organic coatings; and various options for replacement.

Maintenance is the key to the long-term preservation of metal architectural elements. It is far more desirable to retain genuine old building material through continuous maintenance than to replace it with even the highest quality of modern reproduction material. Professional conservation advice should be sought concerning the most effective preservation techniques, especially those relating to the application of paint as a preservative. In the case of metal structural systems, periodic structural inspections should be made using modern, nondestructive methods of examination to detect the first signs of failure.[14]

Proper Design

Much more is known about metals today than when they were first used in construction. In preserving and restoring historic buildings with metal components, proper design may be used to eliminate the cause of deterioration or reduce its effect. A number of factors must be considered, including the following: avoidance of physical or electrolytic contact between dissimilar metals; the selection of new metals that are compatible with the existing metals; the selection of suitable corrosion-resistant materials, when possible; provisions for the removal and prevention of trapped water; and the control of metallurgical factors such as heat-treatment, especially for stress-relief where needed. Proper design should also take into account provisions for expansion and contraction to reduce internal thermal stresses in the metals caused by sun and shade. When working with historic buildings, it is often necessary to balance historical accuracy with sound modern construction practices. Compromises may have to be made to insure that the techniques used do the least damage to the historical, aesthetic, and structural integrity of the building.

Proper design may also include the over-sizing of architectural components that could be attacked by corrosion. A structure with oversized components will still have the structural capacity necessary to fulfill its function even though corrosion may occur, reducing the cross-sectional area. For sheet metals, extra thickness or the use of sacrificial components may be desirable in certain areas, such as flashing in valleys or other area where abrasive erosion may be anticipated.

Control of the Environment

Control of the environment generally is not possible for the preservation of architectural metals because it usually requires placing an air-tight envelope around the components being treated. However, some techniques to limit the destructive effects of the environment are currently in use. The following are brief descriptions of some of these:[15]

Dehumidification is the process of controlling the amount of moisture in the air surrounding a metal element so that water will not condense and dissolve the salts or acids on the surface to form an electrolyte. This is achievable with interior air-conditioned spaces, because air conditioning dehumidifies and filters as it cools. Metal components in air-conditioned spaces corrode less rapidly than metals in noncontrolled environments. (Caution should be exercised when dehumidifying a building because of the effect it may have on the building envelope.)

Cathodic Protection provides an electromotive force which counters the normal flow of current where corrosion is occurring. Such a system is used on ships or steel bridges in sea water where low voltage impressed current is supplied to the objects, effectively reducing corrosion. Both the impressed current anode and the structure to be protected must be in the electrolyte. A similar mechanism is used when a sacrificial metal is coated on a metal architectural component, such as iron galvanized with zinc. Since the zinc is more active than the iron, the zinc will corrode sacrificially and the iron will be cathodically protected.

Corrosion-Inhibitor is any substance which when added in small amounts to a corrosive environment, effectively decreases the corrosion rate of the metal or alloy; examples are zinc chromate and red-lead paints.

Protection with Applied Coatings

Architectural metals can be protected by the factory application of coatings of other metals and ceramic materials, and the factory or field application of organic substances (paints). Metal coatings can be factory applied in the following ways to protect and isolate them from corrosive mediums: electrodeposition (plating); metal spraying; deposition from a vapor phase; dipping into molten metal; adhesive-metal powder techniques; metallic paints; and metallurgical bonding through rolling.[16] Metallic coatings commonly used in construction include galvanizing (zinc), sherardizing (zinc), aluminizing, terne (tin-lead), hot-dip tin, and lead coatings (dipped and rolled).[17] A more noble metal coating will accelerate corrosion of exposed areas of base metals.

Metal structural elements can be protected from fire damage by the installation of insulative masonry cladding, such as brick, clay tile, or concrete. There are also compounds (paints) which intumesce (expand) during a fire to add thermal insulation to steel that has been coated with them thus providing some fire resistance.

The deterioration of metal architectural elements caused by abrasion can be slowed by painting the metallic surface. For example, as a slate roof deteriorates, minute particles of slate break off and slide down the copper valley, eroding the valley until it is worn through. Painting the copper will prolong the useful life of the valley by providing a renewable surface that protects the copper beneath. Ultimately, however, replacement of the damaged member may be necessary.

In the case of human wear and tear, lacquer, wax, and oil have been applied to brass and bronze to resist corrosion and provide a renewable surface. Replaceable plastic guards may be installed over the metal to prevent wear in high pedestrian traffic areas.

The practice of protecting architectural metals with organic coatings (paints) is very common. Generally the success of the coating depends upon surface preparation, type of primer and finish coating, and the method of application. Paints reduce corrosion by permitting only a sluggish movement of ions through the paint film lying between the metal and corrosive environment. Expanded discussions on paint are contained in the sections on individual metals.

Cleaning methods in preparation for painting can be divided into three categories—chemical, thermal, and mechanical. Chemical methods include acid pickling and phosphate dipping. Since the use of acid may predispose the metal toward subsequent corrosion, it is especially important to remove all traces of the acid thoroughly from the metal elements after treatment. When working with acids, care must also be taken to protect workers and materials, such as glass, masonry and landscape elements, which surround the metal component.

The thermal method involves heating a corroded surface with oxyacetylene burners which crack off the corrosion products, or change their chemical nature and cause them to powder away.

Mechanical methods include various uses of abrasive materials or abrasive tools and equipment, such as scraping, sanding, wire brushing, glass bead peening, or wet or dry grit blasting. For large-scale, very hard metal building components (such as cast iron), dry grit blasting may be preferable because it is more thorough, relatively easy, and therefore, more economical. Unlike wire brushing, dry grit blasting, commonly called sandblasting, does not introduce the risk of subsequent corrosion caused by putting another type of metal in contact with one being cleaned. A common technique, that should be avoided, is the use of a wire brush or steel wool on nonferrous metals, which may cause galvanic corrosion or abrasion of the softer metal by the steel. (For further information on sandblasting iron and steel, see section entitled, Iron and Iron Alloys, in Chapter 12.)

Another more delicate method of cleaning some of the harder metals is glass-bead blasting or peening. (See discussion of abrasive cleaning of bronze and brass in the chapters on copper.)

Most metals used structurally and/or decoratively on historic buildings, with the exception of iron and bronze (and some brasses), generally should not be cleaned mechanically because they are quite soft and or thin and pliable, and would be deformed, or their finish would be abraded by such a process. It is usually preferable to clean these softer metals (such as lead and zinc), sheet metals (such as sheet copper), and plated metals (such as tinplate, terneplate, chromeplate, and galvanized iron and steel) with a chemical or thermal method. Stainless steel and aluminum that were originally given a sandblasted finish may usually be cleaned by sandblasting, but if they originally had a high polish, they should not be sandblasted.

Once the surface of the metal has been cleaned of all corrosion products (standards exist to determine the degree of cleaning), a primer coat consisting of a liquid vehicle and a corrosion-resisting pigment is applied. The primer should be applied as soon as possible after cleaning. When the primer is thoroughly dry, the finish coats, which generally consist of lacquers, varnishes (resins in solvent), enamels (pigmented varnishes), or special coatings, are applied. (For more detailed information, see discussions on each metal.)

Other organic coatings include catalyzed or conversion coatings which consist of an "epon" that may be modified with other resins such as vinyls, alkyds, polyesters, et cetera; polyfluorinated ethylenes (Teflon); synthetic rubber; neoprene; rubber based on organic polysulfide (Thiokol); bituminous materials; and high-temperature organic paints formulated from silicone resins, ceramic-type pigments, and inert fillers.

Mechanical Repairs

Metal architectural elements that have deteriorated or failed because of corrosion or physical breakdown, especially fatigue or overloading, can sometimes be repaired by patching, splicing, or reinforcing.

Patching requires mending, covering, or filling a deteriorated area with another piece of material. Depending on the type of metal and its location, the patch can be applied by soldering or by using mechanical connections, such as rivets. For example, a copper cornice with localized deterioration or damage may be patched with sheet copper which has been folded or pressed to match the design of the section of the cornice being patched. Often patching refers to the repair of nonstructural architectural elements. To prevent galvanic corrosion, the patch material should be a very close match to the original material or it should be insulated from the original metal with nonporous insulation.

Splicing refers to the repair of an architectural element, usually structural, by the replacement of the deteriorated section with new material. For example, a deteriorated or damaged section of the web or flange of a steel beam or column may be cut out and a plate of an appropriate thickness welded in its place. Needless to say, all loads must be temporarily supported and the frame braced when structural members are repaired by splicing. The new material is connected to the existing construction in a manner that permits the connection to transfer the loads so that the repaired composite element acts as an integral unit.

Reinforcing is the repair of a damaged or deteriorated element by supplementing it with new metal material. For example, a damaged vertical truss member of a bridge may be straightened and reinforced with plates bolted to the member where it was formerly bent. The new metal does not replace the deteriorated element but is added to it so the old material can still serve its intended purpose while carrying only a proportion of the total load.

Duplication and Replacement

When metal architectural components are beyond repair or when the repairs are only marginally useful in extending the functional life of the member, replacement of the deteriorated element with reproduction material is often the only practical solution. If the metal has deteriorated to a point where it has actually failed, duplication and replacement is the only course of action. Architectural components that have been removed for a long time, such as parts of cast-iron storefronts, can be replaced by new cast-iron members which are reproductions of the original (figures 169-174).

Where deteriorated metal components, such as sheet roofing, are visually important to the building, they should be replaced with materials that duplicate the appearance of the old by matching the original material in composition, size, and configuration of details. However, if a metal building component is seldom seen from normal viewing angles, it may be acceptable to use a substitute material that does not match the original.

Where historic metal structural elements have deteriorated slightly, the elements may not have to be replaced, but can be preserved by changing the use of the building and/or reducing the live loading. This is often done by posting signs to limit the number of people and/or weight of the contents. However, if deterioration continues, some type of remedial treatment will be necessary. Where the deterioration is severe, structural architectural elements can be replaced with new members in most instances if the existing loading can be temporarily supported.

Chapter 12: Lead Preservation and Repair

Identification

Blue-gray in color, lead is a malleable, ductile, and heavy metal—the heaviest of the common metals. It is not magnetic, has no load-bearing capacity because it has little tensile or compressive strength, and is so soft it can be scratched with a fingernail. Lead is easily recovered from scrap materials for recycling, is relatively impenetrable to radiation, and is toxic to humans and animals.[19] Lead combined with tin to form a protective coating on sheet iron or steel is known as terneplate (see Tin, Chapter 13). The weight and high cost of sheet lead and the development of more versatile metals have meant its near abandonment as a common building material. However, lead is currently used widely for radiation shielding and as a protective coating on sheet copper for roofing, rain gutters, and downspouts.

Causes of Deterioration

Lead is stable and does not react with most common chemicals: therefore, it is highly resistant to corrosion. When exposed to air, it forms a protective patina that may be a thin, whitish film of basic lead carbonate, or a thick, darker coat of lead sulfate, both of which usually resist further corrosion. Hence, lead does not need to be painted. The resistance of the lead towards a particular corrosive agent depends on the solubility of the coating formed during the initial attack: if the coating is soluble to corrosive elements in solution, corrosion will continue, while an insoluble coating will resist further attack.

When lead is exposed to alkalis, such as lime and cement mortar, a reddish lead oxide results. Reaction with carbon dioxide and organic acids, such as those present in damp wood, form a whitish basic carbonate or lead formate coating, both of which permit further corrosion of the lead.[20] But, this corrosion is very slow and could take decades to severely damage most lead building materials.

Lead is highly resistant to corrosion by atmospheric pollution. Sulfur fumes common in urban areas react with lead to form a sulfate layer, which protects the lead from further attack.[21] Lead resists corrosion by many acids including chromic, sulfuric, sulfurous, and phosphoric; however, it is corroded by hydrochloric, hydrofluoric, acetic, formic, and nitric acids.[22] Acetic acids are present in fumes given off by breweries, pickle factories, and saw mills.[23] Ants and other insects contain formic acid, and certain beetles and squirrels have been known to eat through lead.

Figure 125. Lead Came Damage. *One of the most common uses of lead is the cames in stained glass windows, transoms, and skylights (see figure 8). Although lead cames are sometimes damaged by corrosion, especially where rain or condensation might collect at the bottom border came (a very slow process), they usually are damaged by creep and fatigue. The weight of the lead and glass in the entrance transom pictured above has caused the cames to creep, resulting in a noticeable sag and outward bulge. This transom did not have iron support bars found on many stained glass windows. The bars (sometimes called saddle bars) were usually set into the frame and attached to the lead cames with copper wires. Transoms are adversely affected by the vibrations of slammed doors and the outward force of compressed air in a vestibule. To complicate things further, the difference in the expansion and contraction coefficients of the lead cames and lead-tin solder has resulted in fatigue cracking, usually at joints. (H. Weber Wilson)*

Figure 126. Lead Came Replacement. *(a) On the table is a tracing of the original pattern of the lead cames of a late 19th-century stained glass window from the Pilgrim Congregation Church, Cambridge, Massachusetts. Because of the severe deterioration of the original lead cames, it was necessary to replace them with new cames that matched the original configuration. (b) This is a detail of the fitting of the new cames around the original glass. (Cummings Studios)*

Care should be taken to protect lead elements from contact with oak building members, as tannic and other acids in the wood attack the metal. Acids produced by other woods such as elm and cedar also attack lead.

Lead flashings and gutters are attacked by acid-charged washings from lichen growing on roofing slate. These washings can score the lead and eventually form grooves and holes. Lead is also attacked by carbon dioxide dissolved in ground water (a situation possible with lead used for damp-proof coursing); however, lead is stable in water containing calcium sulfate, calcium carbonate, or silicic acid.[24] Lead resists corrosion by sea water, salt solutions, neutral solutions, and many types of soils.[25]

Although lead is resistant to most types of corrosion, it can fail because of mechanical breakdown. Lead, like copper and other soft metals, is subject to damage by erosion and abrasion. Lead roof flashings and valleys are especially vulnerable to abrasion from dirt particles, sleet, hail, and rain.

Because lead has a relatively high coefficient of thermal expansion (three times that of steel), it is subject to buckling and fatigue cracking caused by daily and seasonal temperature changes. Creep (figure 119) is damaging to lead roofs, especially where the sheets are of an excessive size, improperly attached, and/or the pitch of the roof is steep.

Fatigue is accelerated by irregularities in the roof sheathing. It is also accelerated by the use of bituminous or asphaltic building paper that can adhere to the metal preventing free movement that can result in buckling. A smooth and even sheathing surface minimizes fatigue, but promotes creep by helping to provide freer thermal movement. As the lead becomes more fatigued, it becomes more brittle until it can eventually fail. Although creep and fatigue are independent deterioration processes, they are commonly found together and one may accelerate the other.

Electrolysis is not often a problem with lead because the protective patina acts as an electrolyte insulator. Normally copper, zinc, and iron (if painted) can be used in contact with lead. For example, copper nails are traditionally used with lead sheets without galvanic corrosion and lead is frequently used to waterproof ironwork where it is fitted into stone[26] (figure 127).

Historically, lead used for roofing was cast on sand beds or casting tables approximately 6 feet by 10 feet[27] and was considerably thicker than the milled sheets of lead that are frequently used today. Although less expensive than traditional cast lead, milled lead has certain disadvantages. The rolling of lead rearranges its crystalline structure and may cause discontinuities in the form of laminations or folds which can increase its susceptibility to deterioration. Also, it will not match the appearance and texture of cast lead, which was almost invariably used on American buildings of the late eighteenth and early nineteenth centuries.

Methods of Preservation and Repair

The decision to repair or to replace a lead roof may not be easy. Generally, a lead roof should be repaired unless the lead is excessively brittle and/or has failed through creep or corrosion over a wide area. If the deterioration is localized (from either cracking or corrosion for instance), the damaged section can be removed and a new section inserted by "burning" (localized melting in a hydrogen flame) or welding. Solder should never be used to repair lead because it has a different coefficient of expansion from lead and will eventually break away. Extreme caution is advised when burning or using any method that is a fire hazard. Lead burning should not be carried out *in situ* on a historic building. When lead burning is needed, the section of lead should be removed from the building and the burning carried out in a remote location, which can be made secure. The extensive damage to Uppark, a National Trust property in England in 1989, caused by lead burning on the roof, has resulted in new guidelines for the protection of historic buildings undergoing lead roof restoration. These guidelines were followed during the recent lead roof restoration work at The Octagon in Washington, D.C. and Monticello in Charlottesville, Virginia, where lead burning was only permitted on a remote scaffolding tower, separated from the building and construction scaffolding by a fire-proof barrier.

If creep has occurred but the sheet has not cracked, it is sometimes possible to drive the lead back into place. A steeply pitched lead roof is usually more difficult to repair than a flat roof because the creep is more serious and will tend to recur. With steep roofs, it may be necessary to replace the roof with hardened lead—a lead-antimony-tin alloy, which is more resistant to creep and fatigue.

Where the lead is partially deteriorated from erosion, abrasion, or corrosion, a protective coating of paint, or sacrificial layer of copper could be attached in localized areas.[28] These would prolong the life of the lead, but at best, are only temporary repairs. However, mastics or asphaltic or bituminous roofing compounds should not be used because they adversely react with the lead.

Existing lead roofing can be taken up and relaid if repairs to the understructure are necessary. However, if much of the lead is deteriorated, it is desirable to melt and recast the old lead into new sheets. Before the lead is melted down, any solder or other nonlead patches must be removed.

Where historic lead elements are missing, new cast lead should be installed based on surviving evidence of the original. Often fragments of the old roofing are found beneath the roof sheathing boards and within the cornice construction. This evidence can be studied to determine the character and extent of the original work, which can be replicated using new cast-lead sheets.

When the new lead sheets are laid, rosin building paper should be used between the lead and the sheathing to permit thermal movement. When new lead roofs are installed, provisions should be made for adequate expansion joints. Under no circumstances should lead sheets more than 9 feet in length or 24 square feet in area be used. Generally, the thinner the sheet of lead, the smaller the sheet should be. Traditionally, cast roofing lead was code-numbered 6, 7, or 8, weighing approximately 6, 7, and 8 pounds per square foot respectively.

Figure 127. Lead Packing. *At the U.S. Treasury Building in Washington, D.C., the iron fence is supported by stone posts. The iron rails are fitted into pockets in the stone. Water seeped into the pockets and the iron rusted, causing it to expand. Rust, plus freezing and thawing action, caused the stone to spall. To remedy the situation, the iron fences were removed; the ends of the rails were cleaned of rust and repainted; and the fence was re-erected with lead packing. This lead is soft enough to accommodate thermal expansion and contraction of the iron. It also waterproofs the ends of the bars. (John Myers)*

Sometimes it is necessary to clean lead. If repairs are to be made to lead and if it is desirable to remove the crust from a small lead object because the crust contains agents that accelerate corrosion, then the object can be soaked in Versene powder (tetrasodium salt of ethylenediaminetetra-acetic acid), Versene acid, and water.[29] The process cleans and stabilizes the object, providing all the crust is removed and the atmosphere to which the newly cleaned metal is exposed is free from acetic and formic acids.

Chapter 13: Tin; Preservation and Repair

Identification

Pure tin is soft, ductile, malleable, bluish-white in color, nonmagnetic, and fairly resistant to corrosion.[30]

By far the most common use of tin in buildings is as a protective coating on iron or steel plates. The plates are called "tinplate" or "bright tin" if the coating is pure tin and "terneplate" or "leaded tin" if it is a mixture of lead (75-90%) and tin (10-25%). Both types of material are commonly called just "tin" or "tinplate." Tinplate and terneplate were most commonly used in sheets 10 inches by 14 inches or in multiples thereof (14 inches by 20 inches, 20 inches by 28 inches, and so forth) for roofing and wall cladding.

Cases of Deterioration

When pure tin is heated at low temperatures for long periods of time, it deteriorates by disintegrating and crumbling to a nonmetallic gray powder.[31] Called "tin pest" or "tin plague," this type of deterioration is usually not a problem with tinplate sheets used for architectural purposes.

Tin by itself is mechanically weak and is, therefore, used for coating stronger base materials. The tin and terneplatings on iron sheets are stable coatings that resist corrosion caused by oxygen, moisture, sulfur dioxide, and hydrogen sulfide, when properly protected.[32]

When exposed to the atmosphere, tin readily develops a thin film of stannic oxide, which helps resist corrosion. Although pure tin is mildly corroded by exposure to acids, marine atmospheres, and certain alkalis, tinplate roofing is generally very durable as long as the tin or terne coating maintains its integrity. Once the plating has been broken and the iron or steel is exposed to oxygen, the deterioration begins and is accelerated by the galvanic action between the tin and iron. The more active tin acts as a cathode to the iron. This protects the iron from corrosion but accelerates the deterioration of the tin, exposing more of the iron to be corroded. Tin and terneplate roofing and flashing will deteriorate when in contact with copper, for instance, in gutters. Also they can be corroded by asphaltic and bituminous roofing compounds and building paper (figures 128 and 129a), as well as by paints containing acids, bitumen, asphalt, or aluminum. Tinplate roofing can corrode on the underside from water vapor condensation if the tin is not protected by a coating of paint and/or a nonacidic vapor barrier (figure 129b).

Figure 128. Deterioration of Tinplate by Asphalt Coating. *The tinplate flashing of the roof hatch has been corroded away (between the corner and the vent) by the action of the asphalt coating and water. (John G. Waite)*

Methods of Preservation and Repair

Techniques for repair range from small localized patches to wholesale material replacement. If a joint in tinplate roofing opens up, or a nail head pops up and punctures the tinplate, it should be repaired by cleaning and resoldering using a solder of 50% pig lead and 50% block tin applied with a rosin flux (figures 131a and b).

Tinplate sheets should be fastened using only tinplate cleats and galvanized iron or steel nails. Copper alloy cleats and nails should not be used because of the potential for galvanic corrosion.

It is not normally practical to replate a deteriorated sheet of tinplate under field conditions. However, at Lindenwald (Martin Van Buren National Historic Site), the terneplate roof installed during the 1848 renovation under the direction of architect Richard Upjohn was cleaned and the coating was repaired *in situ* (figures 133a and 133b). Rust, paint, and asphalt coatings were removed by low-pressure abrasive cleaning using walnut shells. Where the original terne coating had failed, small areas of the iron sheets were recoated with a tin-lead mixture applied with a specially designed soldering "copper." (Historically, a small soldering tool is called a soldering "iron" and a large soldering tool is a soldering "copper.") After this partial recoating, the entire roof was painted.

Priming and Painting are mandatory, and for optimum protection, both sides (not just the exposed face) of the new tin or terneplate roofing should be shopcoated with one coat and preferably two coats of an appropriate primer, such as a linseed oil iron oxide primer. Although seldom done, it is a good idea to apply a coat of compatible, high-gloss oil-base finish paint prior to installation as an added measure of protection, especially for the bottom side.

A finish coat should be applied immediately after installation, followed by another in two weeks. Finish coat paint used on tin roofs should employ only "metallic brown" (another name for iron oxide), "Venetian red" (ferric oxide, calcium carbonate, and ferrous sulfate),[33] or red iron oxide (ferric oxide) pigments. Although red lead pigments were used in the past and are very effective protection in the prime coat, they are in now seldom used because it has been found that they can constitute a serious health hazard. They have largely been replaced by alkyd-based iron oxide primers. Graphite and asphaltic base paints should not be used on tinplate or terneplate because they can encourage corrosion.

Replacement of tinplate or terneplate sheets which have rusted through may be the only practical preservation solution. Damaged sections should be removed and replaced with new materials of similar composition, configuration, and construction (figures 132a, 132b and 132c). Materials other than tinplate or terneplate should not be used to patch tinplate because galvanic corrosion will occur. However, if all of the tinplate roofing or siding must be replaced, it may be desirable to replace the old tinplate or terneplate with units of terne-coated stainless steel or lead-coated copper (figure 134) because these materials are more durable and easier to maintain than tinplate. Although both are more expensive than terne-coated steel in initial cost, they last longer and cost less to maintain if not painted. Either of these materials, if used in visible areas, should match the size, configuration, and construction details of the original roof, and should be painted to match the original color. Although lead-coated copper has been used successfully as a replacement material for tin and terneplate (figure 135), recently terne-coated stainless steel has proven to be a better replacement for tinplate.

If the lead-coated copper is not applied using appropriate methods, its appearance will not duplicate that of a tinplate roof. Many sheet metal workers have a tendency to apply solder freely to the joints over the surface of the lead-coated copper which results in a rough seam that may be an inch or more in width. This contrasts greatly with historic tinplate seams where often no solder was visible on the surface of the metal. Also, 16-ounce lead-coated copper, the thinnest, readily available gauge, is considerably thicker than historic tinplate, resulting in bends that are not as crisp or sharp. Improperly manufactured lead-coated copper may also promote galvanic corrosion, leading to deterioration of exposing the copper base.[34]

Historically, seams of tinplate roofs were often not soldered. Instead they either were installed dry, as was the case with the tin roofs designed by Thomas Jefferson (figure 136), or the seams were filled with white lead

paste. Today, white lead paste is difficult to obtain and constitutes a health hazard. Consequently, modern caulking compounds are used to fill the joints.

Figure 129. Corrosion Failure of Terneplate Roofing. *Hyde Hall, built between 1817 and 1833, near Cooperstown, New York, was roofed with flat-seam terneplate. (a) The plates have deteriorated because of a lack of proper maintenance. Unfortunately, the exposed (top) surface of the terneplate was painted with asphalt coating, which accelerated the corrosion of the roofing. (b) The terneplate also corroded from the underside. When installed, the terneplate was not painted on the underside as it should have been. Condensation formed on the unprotected bottom side of the metal roof and could not evaporate, an ideal situation for corrosion. (John G. Waite)*

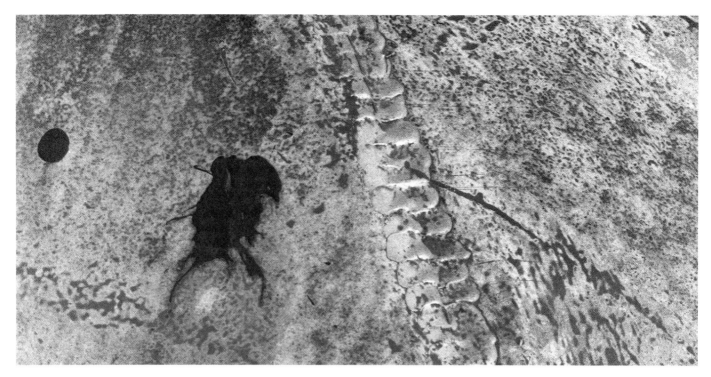

Figure 130. Modern Solder Joint on a Terneplate Roof. *Solder was used to make watertight joints at the edges of terneplates on flat-seam roofs. Nineteenth-century soldered joints were almost invisible, that is, the solder was confined to the seam. These wide-soldered joints are on the Old Pension Building in Washington, D.C. The problems with wide-soldered joints are: (1) they facilitate galvanic corrosion because they provide a wider surface area with which the plates can react, and (2) they tend to fail because of the different coefficients of expansion and contraction of the solder and the terneplate. The black spots to the right of the solder are asphalt or a bituminous roof patching compound, which may cause deterioration of the terneplate and should be removed. (David W. Look)*

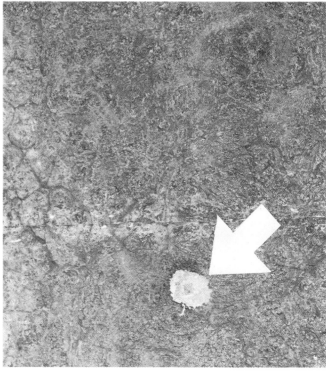

Figure 131. Salvaging a Flat Seam Terneplate Roof. *(a) The roof of the Henry E. Bradford House Carriage Barn (c. 1860s) in Bennington, Vermont, had been covered with an asphalt coating (background) which obscured the true cause of the leaking roof. Once the asphalt coating was scraped from the surface (foreground left), it was noticed that the nails in the sheathing had "popped up" (light spots) and had cut through the terneplate. (b) After the asphalt coating had ben scraped away and the nail holes repaired with solder (left foreground), the roof was then painted with red-lead primer (right foreground). The primed roofing was given two finish coats of iron oxide paint. (John G. Waite)*

Figure 132. Repair and Replacement of Terneplate Roofing. *(a) The ends of the original terneplate batten covers at Lindenwald were badly corroded and could not be replated. (b) The unsalvageable sections were cut out and replaced with terne-coated stainless steel soldered in place. (c) The deteriorated terneplate valley was replaced with sheets of terne-coated stainless steel; the terne coating allowed the valley to be soldered to the original roofing plates. Although terne-coated stainless steel was a good choice, in theory, it proved to be a difficult material to work with in the field. (Correctly, the availability of thinner gauges and a more malleable stainless steel have improved the workability of this material.) (d) The original terneplate had rusted through completely in some areas, requiring reroofing. New sheets of terne-coated stainless steel, duplicating the pattern of the original terneplate, are being laid over rosin paper. (John G. Waite)*

a

b

Figure 133. Abrasive Cleaning of Terneplate Roof and Replating. *(a) Sections of the original terneplate roof at Lindenwald (Martin Van Buren National Historic Site) in Columbia County, New York, designed by architect Richard Upjohn in 1848, were cleaned with a low-pressure blasting of crushed walnut shells to remove accumulated paint and rust before replating with a lead/tin alloy. (b) The new terneplating was applied in localized areas (only where the original terne had been damaged by falling slates or removed because the sheet iron underneath had corroded. The new terneplating was applied where the bare iron was exposed using a soldering "copper" (a large soldering tool) fabricated for the project. After cleaning and replating, the restored roof was painted. (John G. Waite)*

Figure 134. Replacing Flashing and Gutters. *Workmen replaced the deteriorated terneplate flashing and gutters at Olana, built between 1870 and 1874 near Hudson, New York, for the noted artist Frederic E. Church. The polychromed slate roof was restored to the original pattern, and lead-coated copper was substituted for the original terneplate flashing and gutters because of ease of maintenance - it does not require painting, unless there is a need to match the terneplate in color. The original terneplate was painted. (John G. Waite)*

Figure 135. *Complete Substitution of Lead-Coated Copper Roofing for Terneplate Roofing. The 1864 wing addition of Lyndhurst, Tarrytown, New York, originally had a terneplate roof. In an attempt to find a more permanent roofing material, a lead-coated copper roof was substituted for the terneplate, duplicating the pattern and sheet sizes of the original roof. In such substitutions, details may have to be redesigned because of differences in expansion and contraction rates and differences in workability of the material. The color of lead-coated copper is not the same as terneplate because terneplate roofing was never left unpainted. Therefore, lead-coated copper roofing substituted for terneplate should also be painted if it seen from normal viewing angles (usually from street level). (John G. Waite)*

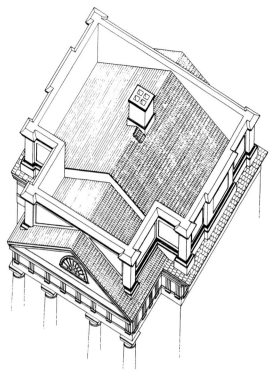

a. Pavilion X roof (Mesick•Cohen•Waite Architects)

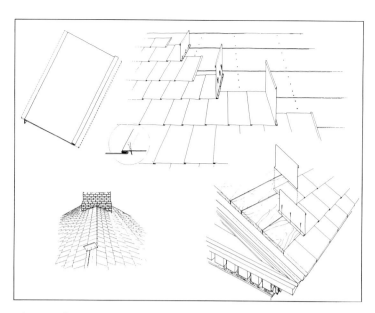

b. Installation techniques (Mesick•Cohen•Waite Architects)

c. Original tinplate roof beneath slate (John G. Waite)

d. New roofing (Clay S. Palazzo)

Figure 136. Replacement of a Thomas Jefferson Tinplate Roof on Pavilion X. *Most of the pavilions constructed between 1817 and 1826 at the University of Virginia originally had tinplate roofs applied with a unique system which did not use soldered seams (a). Consisting of thinly rolled wrought-iron sheets dipped in tin, the edge of each plate was fitted into the fold of the adjacent plate, folded over, and nailed to the wood roof sheathing. It was a very simple system that only required basic carpentry skills to install (b).*

In 1985, during investigations of leaks in the roof of Pavilion X, the entire original Jefferson tinplate roof was found intact beneath a later slate roof (c). The original tinplate roof was preserved in situ and encapsulated by new plywood sheets. A new roof, identical in detailing, was applied over the plywood and a neoprene sheet membrane (d). Using 6-3/4 by 10 inch sheets of stainless steel with a terne coating, the roof exactly duplicates the appearance of the original. Terne coated stainless steel was used because tinplated wrought-iron sheets are no longer available.

Thomas Jefferson installed similar roofs on Monticello and Poplar Forest.

Chapter 14: Zinc, Preservation and Repair

Identification

Zinc is a medium-hard, bluish-white metal character-ized by its brittleness and low strength. It is also subject to creep.[35] Historically, zinc has been widely used for architectural purposes, both in its pure form and as an alloy with other metals, and as a protective coating for iron and steel architectural components using the proc-esses of galvanizing and sherardizing (see definitions). Pure zinc architectural elements are often mistaken for tin-plated or galvanized sheet iron; however, zinc is eas-ily identified because it is softer than iron and is non-magnetic. Zinc can be hot rolled, formed, extruded, spun, punched, cast, machined, riveted, soldered, and welded.[36] It is not ductile at normal temperatures.

As in the past, zinc is still widely used as a protective coating for iron and steel. A major advantage of zinc coating on iron is that if the zinc is worn away or broken and the iron is exposed to the atmosphere, galvanic cor-rosion of the baser zinc occurs, protecting the more noble iron.[37] The following are the most common meth-ods for applying protective coatings of zinc to iron and steel.[38]

Hot-Dip Galvanizing is the immersion of iron or steel in molten zinc, after the surface of the iron has been prop-erly cleaned. This process gives a relatively thick coating of zinc that freezes into a crystalline surface pattern known as spangles. During the hot-dip process, a multi-ple-layered structure of iron-zinc alloys is formed be-tween the inner surface of the zinc coating and the iron. These middle layers tend to be hard and brittle and may peel or flake if the iron element is bent.

Electrogalvanizing is the immersion of iron or steel in an electrolyte, a solution of zinc sulfate or cyanide. Elec-trolytic action deposits a coating of pure zinc on the sur-face of the iron. The thickness of the coating can be accurately controlled using this process. However, the thick coatings provided by the hot-dip galvanizing proc-ess are not usually possible with this method.

Sherardizing is the placing of a thoroughly cleaned iron or steel element in an air-free enclosure where it is sur-rounded by metallic zinc dust. The architectural element is then heated and a thin, zinc alloy coating is produced which conforms to the surface configuration of the ele-ment. This process is usually limited to relatively small objects.

Metallic Spraying is the application of a fine spray of molten zinc to a clean iron or steel element. The coating can then be heated and fused with the surface of the iron to produce an alloy. The coating is less brittle than those produced by some of the other processes and will not peel or flake on bending. However, the coating is more porous than those produced by the other processes and becomes impermeable with time as products of corro-sion fill in the pores.

Another, less effective form of zinc coating is the use of paints containing zinc dust pigments. These can be applied *in situ*.

Causes of Deterioration

Zinc is not resistant to acids or strong alkalis and is par-ticularly vulnerable to corrosion by sulfur acids pro-duced by the hydrogen sulfide and sulfur dioxide pollution in urban atmospheres. Zinc is also attacked by acids found in redwood, cedar, oak, and sweet chestnut, and can be corroded by plasters and cements, especially Portland cements containing chlorides and sulfates.[39] Condensation on the underside of zinc plates and pon-ded water on the exterior surface of zinc architectural ornament can also corrode (figure 137). Zinc also deterio-rates on contact with acidic rainwater run-off from roofs with wood shingles, moss, or lichen.

Although zinc develops a carbonate on its surface by exposure to the atmosphere and by the action of rain-water, the film is not dense or adherent enough to pro-tect the zinc from continued attack.[40] The carbonate becomes brittle and crusty and eventually splits, expos-ing fresh zinc for corrosion. Thermal movement of the zinc is also damaging to the carbonate film. In industrial atmospheres, the zinc carbonate film is broken down by the same acids that attack zinc. These acids convert the carbonate to zinc sulfate, which is water soluble and washes away with rainwater,[41] often staining adjacent building elements (figures 130 and 143).

Zinc has a relatively high coefficient of thermal expan-sion and is therefore vulnerable to fatigue failure. Be-cause zinc is relatively soft, it is also vulnerable to abrasion damage (figure 139), especially in roof valley areas where it can be worn paper-thin.

Although zinc is not damaged by electrical contact with lead, galvanized iron and steel, tin, or aluminum, it is damaged by galvanic corrosion when it comes in elec-trical contact with copper and pure iron in a common electrolyte (figure 138).

Figure 137. Deterioration of Zinc. *At the 1874 Cohoes Music Hall, Cohoes, New York, the original zinc window lintels and belt course were cleaned by sandblasting, resulting in pitting and corrosion of the metallic surface. Note the whitish corrosion products caused by the abrasive cleaning and subsequent exposure to the weather. The lintels had been painted originally but were left bare after the cleaning. Zinc and galvanized sheet iron should always be primed and painted with paints especially formulated for zinc. (John G. Waite)*

Figure 138. Zinc Deterioration and Staining. *On the First Presbyterian Church in Alexandria, Virginia, the engaged columns, arch molding, corner blocks, and the sill molding are fabricated of cast zinc and galvanized sheet iron (the windows and frames are wood). The paint has deteriorated, leaving the surface of the metal bare in some places. The zinc or zinc coating on iron has oxidized. Notice the whitish corrosion stain on the brick from the zinc carbonate coating which continues to wash over the surface of the bare metal and then down over the bricks. The metalwork should be scraped down to remove all loose zinc carbonate. Joints should be caulked and/or resoldered, and repainted with a zinc chromate primer. (Baird M. Smith)*

Figure 139. Zinc Corrosion, Erosion, and Inappropriate Repairs. *In construction of the Nott Memorial at Union College in Schenectady, New York, during the 1870s, architect Edward Tuckerman Potter used "illuminators" in the ornamental slate roof. These were slate-sized zinc plates with a small colored-glass disc 1 3/4 inches in diameter inserted in the center. Barely discernible from the outside, they transformed the vaulted dome within a "heaven" of red, yellow, purple, orange, and green stars. Shown here is a cluster of three illuminators, each consisting of a zinc plate with a small colored-glass insert and the connecting tube through the metal deck and plaster to the interior. The zinc was inaccessible and not kept painted. Small fragments of slate broke off and tumbled down with gravity. The wind and rain eroded away the layer of corrosion from the zinc surface. The left plate is missing (see dotted line), showing the connecting tube. The corner of the lower right plate is missing because it became brittle and fractured off. Unfortunately, modern roofing cement applied over the zinc plates is accelerating the deterioration. (John I. Mesick,* The Nott Memorial: A Historic Structure Report *Schenectady, New York: Union College, 1973. p. 65)*

Flaking and peeling of the zinc coating is a problem with old, hot-dipped galvanized iron sheets. Because of the galvanizing techniques, a thick, brittle coating of zinc was formed. This coating can peel and flake when the iron sheet is deformed—that is, folded and stamped—after the coating has been applied, exposing the iron sheet to corrosion.

Galvanized sheets and sheets of pure zinc are also attacked by a type of corrosion known as "white stain" or "white rust."[42] Closely stacked sheets stored either in a warehouse or unprotected outdoors will be attacked if dampness and extreme temperatures occur. With the absence of oxygen and carbon dioxide between the sheets, the protective layer of zinc hydroxide is formed with resultant loss of metallic zinc. The corrosion then appears as a voluminous white powder. Perforation of the galvanized or zinc sheets can occur rapidly, causing significant damage.

Methods of Preservation and Repair

It is difficult to carry out piecemeal *in situ* repairs to zinc roofs or architectural elements, except under unusual circumstances. Where repairs can be made, solder with a composition of 50% tin and 50% lead or 60% tin and 40% lead (antimony free) is used. A hydrochloric acid flux should be used, but it should be remembered that the flux can dissolve zinc. The excess flux must be rinsed immediately after soldering. Where the zinc is badly eroded, the only practical solution may be to replace the damaged section with a new material.

When used with redwood, cedar, oak, or sweet chestnut, galvanized steel or iron should be protected from the acids in the wood by a bituminous paint applied to the exposed surfaces. Even though galvanized iron and steel can be painted, preliminary surface treatments may be necessary. The metallic surface should be allowed to weather before painting (usually about six months); however, it should not weather until rust appears. The surface is then wiped with a clean cloth and mineral spirits, not hydrochloric acid, muriatic acid, or vinegar (as recommended by some old paint references), and painted with a specially formulated primer for galvanized iron, followed by two finish coats of a compatible oil-based paint.

If an old galvanized roof has begun to rust, it should treated with zinc oxide and flaky aluminum prime coats followed by a finish coat containing flaky aluminum and flaky micaceous iron-ore pigments. Rusting may also be arrested by the application of a zinc-rich paint after the rust has substantially been removed.[43]

In some cases, galvanized sheet metal elements can be removed and repaired in the shop, rather than in the field (figure 141 and 142). Preassembly of large cornices may be cost effective (figure 143).

Where the galvanized coating has been scraped or worn away, it may be necessary to recoat the sheet with zinc. The surface of the iron must be thoroughly cleaned, and one of the galvanizing processes discussed previously must be used. This must be done under controlled conditions in a shop and not *in situ*. Sometimes corrosion is not too severe and the surface can be cleaned and painted in place to prolong the life of the member. All corrosion, rust, and loose paint must be removed before painting. In other cases it may be necessary to reproduce severely deteriorated or lost elements (figure 144). In some situations, often for economic reasons, reinforced polyester, commonly known as fiberglass, has been used for reproduction of missing cornices and other sheet metal details (figure 179).

Direct contact of galvanized iron or steel with plaster and cement must also be avoided. If contact is unavoidable, the galvanized material should be painted as described in this section, so that it is isolated from the alkaline material.

Proper design and installation is very important with galvanized iron or steel roofing and flashing. Special care should be taken to insure that the roof has adequate expansion joints to accommodate thermal expansion and contraction and adequate anchorage to guard against wind damage (figure 123).

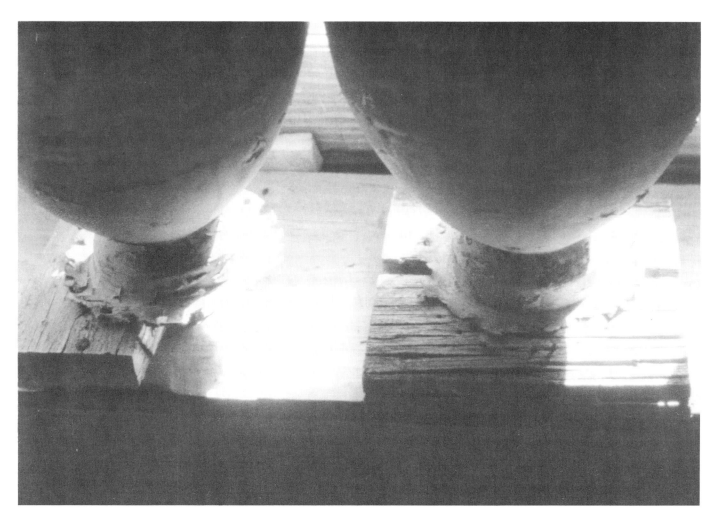

Figure 140. Galvanic Deterioration. *Bases of zinc vases from the roof balustrade of Lorenzo, Casenovia, New York, have deteriorated because of the electrolytic action between the zinc and the machine-cut iron nails used to fasten the vases to the balustrade. The zinc was sacrificed in favor of the iron because the iron is more noble than the zinc. (Douglas Clinton)*

Figure 141. Repair of Galvanized Sheet Metal Capitals. *(a) Fabricated for the 1890 Bullard-Hart House, Columbus, Georgia, these Corinthian capitals were originally assembled from many pieces of pressed sheet metal, which were soldered together to form the acanthus leaves. (b) The capitals were in salvageable condition and were taken to a sheet-metal shop where they were cleaned. Loose pieces were resoldered and caulked; missing pieces were replaced with new stamped pieces; and the completed capitals were repainted. The deteriorated wooden column shafts were repaired and repainted. The restored capitals were refitted onto the shafts and the entire columns were then returned to their original positions. (Thomas Taylor)*

a

Figure 142. Restoration of Galvanized Sheet Iron and Cast-Zinc Cornice. *This is the upper third of a wooden bay window on a Second Empire brick rowhouse in the Logan Circle Historic District of Washington, D.C. (a) From the window down, the bay is wood and glass. The roof of the bay had leaked for years and the wooden roof rafter and projecting supports for the cornice had rotted. The bay window was carefully disassembled and rebuilt replacing all deteriorated lumber. The surviving pieces of galvanized sheet-iron and cast-zinc cornice were taken to a sheet-metal shop. The pieces that were repairable were cleaned; missing portions of brackets on the right were replicated of galvanized sheet iron using the originals as a model. (b) On the opposite side of the bay, all of the brackets and modillions are repaired originals but all of the flat and molded sections are new 26-gauge galvanized steel. The 65-year-old sheet-metal worker on this job said that the only two major advances in metal cornices in his lifetime are the use of pop rivets for fasteners (used also in leatherwork) and the use of autobody putty to patch holes, mold small missing details, and waterproof joints. The putty dries hard and can be sanded. (David W. Look)*

b

Figure 144. Reproduction of Galvanized Sheet-Iron Shingles. *Wind and hail had damaged many of the sheet-iron shingles at St. Edward's University in Austin, Texas (see Figure 122). Mass production of replicas was economically feasible. A die was made with the pattern of the original shingle and new galvanized sheet-steel shingles were stamped. The new, unpainted shingle (right, notice spangled appearance) is a reproduction of the other shingle (left). These shingles are from the private collection of Charles E. Fisher, III. (John Myers)*

Figure 143. Preassembling Cornice. *As illustrated in figure 142, most sheet-metal cornices were supported by wooden support members projecting out from the facade of the building either as an extension of the roof framing or as a cantilever from a parapet wall. In either case, these wooden support members are often found to be rotten and have to be replaced. For large cornices high above the street level, it may be economically unfeasible to use scaffolding for in situ repairs and reconstruction unless the scaffolding is also needed for other work. The entire galvanized sheet-iron cornice of the ZCMI Store in Slat Lake City, Utah, was preassembled on the ground with repaired original parts and some new pieces onto a new support system fabricated on small steel angles. Fifty-foot sections of the preassembled cornice were then hoisted to the top of the facade and bolted onto the building without the need for scaffolding. (Steven T. Baird)*

Chapter 15: Copper and Copper Alloys; Preservation and Repair

Identification

Copper, one of the most corrosion-resistant architectural metals, is ductile, malleable, nonmagnetic, high in electrical and thermal conductivity (second only to silver), and is easily soldered, welded, or brazed. It can be cast, drawn, extruded, hot and cold worked, spun, hammered, or punched.[44] Copper is initially a bright reddish-brown in color, but when exposed to the atmosphere, it acquires a protective patina that turns from brown to black to green over a period that may extend for decades, depending on environmental conditions. The patina is actually a thin, tough layer of corrosion that usually prevents deeper and deeper layers of corrosion (such as rust, which can totally consume iron); therefore, even though copper corrodes, it is corrosion-resistant.

Bronze and Brass are copper alloys that can be combinations (mixtures not compounds) of many elements. "True" bronze is composed of approximately 90% copper and 10% tin[45] and is a rich pink metal seldom seen without an artificial brown patina or a natural green patina. True bronze is particularly suited for casting because of its fluidity in a molten state, its density (not porous), and its ability to retain an impression of even the most intricate mold.

Bronze can also be rolled, extruded, and forged; and in most forms, it is resistant to the wear or abrasion of heavy use. Most bronzes used for architectural purposes today are not true bronzes but rather alloys of copper with silicon, manganese, aluminum, zinc, and other elements—with or without tin. Any copper alloy that contains zinc is termed brass. However, some alloys have both tin and zinc; therefore, there is sometimes little to distinguish between some bronzes and brasses.

To complicate this further, some copper alloys that are definitely brasses are marketed as bronzes. The three types of so-called bronzes most used for architectural purposes are "statuary bronze," "architectural bronze," and "commercial bronze." Of these, only statuary bronze is close in composition to a true bronze, since it is composed of approximately 97% copper, 2% tin, and 1% zinc. Architectural bronze is really a leaded brass composed of 57% copper, 40% zinc, and 3% lead: and commercial bronze is a brass composed of 90% copper and 10% zinc.

Brass is an alloy of copper and zinc with small quantities of other elements. The composition of brass may vary from 95% copper and 5% zinc to 55% copper and 45% zinc.[46]

Brass varies from deep golden-brown to lemon-yellow to silvery-white depending on the amount of surface tarnish (oxidation) and the amount of zinc in the copper mix: 10% zinc for bronze color; 15% zinc for golden color; 20% to 38% zinc for yellow; and above 45% for silvery-white.[47] The color of brasses can also be artificially changed with chemical patinas, especially to achieve a brown statuary bronze color. Brasses are not as hard as steels, but are superior to them in workability and resistance to corrosion.

In modern times, brasses are classified according to color (red, yellow), to zinc content (high, low), to metallographic constituents (Alpha, Beta), and to other metals present such as lead and arsenic.[48] Common brasses include:

Alpha brasses (95% copper and 5% zinc) have a wide range of colors; are ductile and can be cold worked without annealing and hot worked; are corrosion resistant; and have fair electrical and thermal conductivity.

Beta brasses (55-65% copper and 45-35% zinc) have comparatively high tensile strength and hardness, fairly low melting points, and relatively poor corrosion resistance and electrical conductivity. Beta brasses are easily hot worked and may be cold worked without annealing, within limits. Their color range varies and becomes less red as the copper content is reduced. At 58% copper, the color matches that of commercial bronze, and the manufacture by hot extrusion of complicated shapes, which are used with sheets of commercial bronze, is permitted.

Leaded brasses are Alpha and Beta brasses to which lead is added to increase machinability or fluidity during the casting process. Leaded brasses are easily hot worked and may be cold worked within limits; however, they are not as strong, hard, or corrosion resistant as Alpha and Beta brasses.

Causes of Deterioration

Copper is highly resistant to corrosion caused by the atmosphere or salt water. It combines with hydrogen sulfide and oxygen or sulfur dioxide to form a protective copper carbonate or copper sulfate patina[49] which resists further corrosion and generally does not change further in appearance. However, copper is attacked by alkalis, ammonia, and various sulfur compounds that can combine with water to form sulfuric acid. Some bituminous roofing cements, containing sulfur compounds, will attack copper, as will sulfate-reducing bacteria, which act as a catalyst for corrosion. Copper is also corroded by rainwater that has become acidic through contact with moss, lichen, algae, or wood shingles.

Copper is not very active galvanically and therefore is not usually subject to galvanic corrosion unless in contact with more noble metals, such as gold, and, under the right conditions, some stainless steels. However, if an electrolyte is present, the copper will act as a cathode and corrode other, more active, metals such as iron or steel (figure 145 and 146).

Sheet copper roofing is vulnerable to mechanical breakdown of the individual metal units caused by insufficient provisions for thermal expansion and contraction (figure 121), inadequate sheet thickness, excessively large sheet size, improper fastenings, insufficient substructure, and erosion caused by particle abrasion or the velocity effect of aerated water. Excessive thermal stressing causes the copper and its protective patina to become friable; eventually the metal may fatigue, resulting in bulges and cracks. Once fatigue cracks or splits occur, the roof or sheathing has failed as a weather-tight membrane (figure 147a).

The failure of copper members can be accelerated by a number of factors. The use of rough and noncontinuous sheathing boards (figure 147b) or the use of bituminous or asphaltic building papers and patching compounds can damage a copper roof (figure 148). Any architectural element can fail from using the wrong temper or gauge of copper or by using fastenings that restrict free movement.

Because of its softness, copper is easily eroded by abrasive agents (figure 150). This is an especially acute problem in roof flashing or valley areas where the copper can be worn so thin that it fails. It is also vulnerable to impact damage such as hail, and to fatigue and "inelastic deformation" as the result of wind damage (figure 146).

Bronze and Brass, like copper, are corroded by exposure to moisture, acidity caused by polluted air or newly-cut wood, chlorides, acetates, and ammonia.[50] Excrement from birds or other animals is acidic and can also damage bronze, brass, or copper (figure 151).

Bronze and brass oxidize to form a patina that first turns brown, then, black, in color. This coating, consisting of copper sulfide, blackens further with an intermingling of dirt, soot, and dust.[51] This copper sulfide can oxidize to green-blue copper sulfate if the coating is regularly washed with urban rainwater. Some of the sulfate will dissolve and form a green stain on stone or wood beneath the bronze or brass elements.

Salt used to melt snow in the winter can be splashed up on doors, leaving unsightly corrosion, which is also damaging to the bronze (figure 152). Improper cleaning of doors is also frequently a problem (figure 153). Although "bronze disease" is a problem with bronze artifacts that were once buried in the earth, it is seldom a problem with outdoor bronze sculpture or architectural elements.[52]

A kind of corrosion peculiar to brass or bronze with a composition of more than 15% zinc is dezincification.[53] This occurs where acids and other strongly conducting

Figure 145. Galvanic Deterioration. *An electrolytic reaction between the copper roof and the cast-iron roof finial and monitor window frames on the former Temple Beth Emeth, Albany, New York, built in 1887, is causing extensive deterioration of the iron. The corrosion products are staining and streaking the copper. Another area where deterioration is occurring is the valley, which has been coated with an aluminumized asphalt roofing compound. Electrolysis is occurring between the copper and aluminum (causing the less noble aluminum to corrode) and between the aluminum and cast iron of the monitor window frames (causing the less noble aluminum to corrode). (John G. Waite)*

solutions are present. The copper-zinc alloy is dissolved; the copper is redeposited electrochemically; and the zinc either remains in solution or its compounds form a scale. Dezincification may leave the metal pitted, porous, and/or weak depending on the extent and severity of the corrosion.

For many years, the natural corrosion patina on outdoor bronzes, which varies in color from green to black, was thought to provide protection against further corrosion. However, this is not always true. It depends upon (1) how the patina is formed and (2) whether it is soluble in its localized environment. If the patina is formed uniformly and adheres tightly to the surface of the bronze, forming an impervious coating, the patina usually will protect the metal from further corrosion. For various reasons, some corrosion products are porous and allow corrosion to continue deeper and deeper. Factors that probably influence how the patina is formed are wind patterns, rain, surface dirt and soot, industrial pollution, bird droppings, and so forth. In addition, if the patina is soluble in rain contaminated with dissolved chemicals, the patina will offer little protection. When the patina washes away, fresh metal is exposed; it corrodes, is dissolved, and washes away again. If this cycle is repeated many times, a significant loss of material can result. To complicate matters, the porosity and solubility of the patina may vary from spot to spot on one piece of bronze.

Severe pitting and obvious loss of material from corrosion are good indications that the patina is not protective. There are no simple tests to confirm this condition. A bronze conservator should be retained to diagnose the situation and prescribe a conservation treatment.

Bronze is a very durable material. It has always been expensive, which has usually limited its use to well-maintained, monumental buildings, such as banks. However, occasionally bronze architectural elements are vandalized or damaged, as when an automobile damages a street lamp (figure 154) or when graffiti covers a bronze door.

Figure 146. Loose and Damaged Copper Cladding and Deteriorated Steel Fire Escapes. *The corner bay of the Hotel Margaret (1889) in Brooklyn Heights, New York, was clad in ornamental panels of pressed sheet copper. Anchors have deteriorated and the wind has lifted the corners. Galvanic action between the noble copper and the baser steel (in the fire escape) has caused the steel to deteriorate. (David W. Look)*

a

Figure 147. Fatigue Failure. *Fatigue failure occurred on the cooper roof installed during the 1920s on the Senate House in Kingston, New York. (a) Failure was caused by cyclical expansion and contraction of the copper without adequate provisions for it. Additionally, the copper sheet was too thin and not rigid enough to resist buckling and sagging between the too-widely-spaced roof sheathing. The use of bituminous roofing paper between the copper and sheathing also contributed to the failure; when the paper was heated by the sun, it adhered to the copper, further restricting its movement (see figure 117). (b) The drawing shows the actual roof installation and the correct procedure, which allows for expansion and contraction. (John G. Waite)*

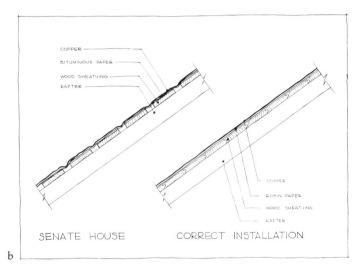

b

Figure 148. Inappropriate Patching Compounds. *Corrosion of a copper roof ridge on the Dakota Apartments (1884), New York City, was caused by the use of an asphalt roofing compound for temporary patches over nailheads and joints between ridge sections. (John G. Waite)*

Figure 149. Resistance to Corrosion. *Little damage had occurred to the copper at The Statue of Liberty. Galvanic corrosion, however, occurred where saline rainwater provided the electrolyte between the copper and the iron armature, resulting in considerable loss in the cross-section of the armature. (Robert Baboian)*

Figure 150. Erosion of Copper. *This eaves detail of the 1920s copper roof on the Senate House State Historic Site in Kingston, New York, illustrates erosion of the copper at the edge of the roof caused by continued exposure to rain and snow, which scoured the roof as it flowed to the gutter. Fatigue failure has also occurred at the base of the standing seam, resulting in a tearing of the copper. This failure was caused by the lack of provision for expansion and contraction, as well as the use of bituminous roofing felts, which restricted the movement of the copper. (John G. Waite)*

Figure 151. Bird Droppings. *The 1914 bronze memorial to the writing of the "Star Spangled Banner," which is located in a niche on the porch of the Baltimore City Hall, is a favorite roost for birds. Bird droppings contain acids which are harmful to bronze and should be removed periodically. (David W. Look)*

Figure 152. Snow Salt Damage. *On the Circuit Court of Appeals Building in Washington, D.C., the lower extremities of the exterior-bronze gates are discolored and unsightly from repeated splashing of snow-removal salt. As long as the salt remains on the gates, the bronze will continue to deteriorate and its surface may even become pitted. (David W. Look)*

Figure 153. Improper Cleaning of Bronze. *The bronze doors on the Pennsylvania Avenue side of the National Archives in Washington, D.C., were cleaned improperly. They now vary in color from a golden bronze to green to copper orange and brassy yellow. Some of the original artificial patina applied at the foundry has been removed, leaving a blotchy appearance. Part of the corrosion from the deicing salt remains, and the doors have a streaked, unattractive appearance. At this point, the only feasible treatment would be to clean the doors thoroughly (down to the bright metal), by mild chemicals or soft abrasive cleaning. A new artificial patina could be applied to return the doors to their original appearance. To protect against future damage, the doors should be given a barrier coating of wax which will need to be renewed periodically. The maintenance staff should be notified not to use salt near the doors and not to clean or polish the doors other than washing them down once a year with a nonionic detergent. When washed, the doors should be thoroughly rinsed with distilled water and wiped dry with a clean cloth to prevent water spots and streaks. (David W. Look)*

Methods of Preservation and Repair

Copper is very durable and seldom needs maintenance but it can be painted to prevent erosion. It can be difficult to obtain a good bond between the copper and paint because grease and oil are rolled into the surface pores of the copper during manufacturing. Traditionally, lead-based paints were often used in the first or prime coat to obtain a good paint bond to the metal. The following instructions for cleaning and for obtaining a good paint bond are given in a 1956 edition of Kidder-Parker.[54]

1. The surface must be thoroughly cleaned and roughened using a solution of 4 ounces copper sulfate to ½-gallon lukewarm water with ⅛-ounce nitric acid.
2. The first coat of paint is to consist of 15 pounds red lead to 1-gallon raw linseed oil, with not more than ½-pint oil dryer.
3. The final two coats of paint are to consist of 15 pounds white lead to 1-gallon raw linseed oil and not more than 5% oil dryer and color pigments. (Alkyd resin paints specially formulated for copper

use with the appropriate primer are now usually substituted for the lead-base paint, but alkyd resin paints do not provide as good protection against erosion and the metal must be repainted more often.)

However, red and white lead paint are now considered to be health hazards. For this reason, high-performance coating systems, such as epoxy primer and urethane finish coats, are now used in place of the traditional red lead and linseed oil paint. The water runoff from roofs with copper valleys painted with lead-based paint is just as harmful, if ingested, as water from lead or lead-coated copper roofs. In fact, it is not recommended that water from any roof be consumed by people or animals.

There are some cases where a natural or unpatinated copper color is desirable; hence, a clear coating, is used. After the copper elements are completely cleaned of flux, dirt, and oxide by a recommended process of abrasion, they can be protected by a lacquer or Incralac coating. Incralac contains an acrylic resin, a chelating agent (Benztriazole), and a leveling agent in toluene or butyl acetate. The application of three separate coats should build up an optimal protective coating of more than 0.001 inches in thickness on the surface.[55] If lacquer or Incralac is used to coat copper, the copper will retain its original color for a number of years; the natural protective patina will not form, except where the coating is broken or worn away. In addition to lacquer, wax coatings may also be used to protect the copper.

When copper architectural elements deteriorate, they should be examined by a specialist to determine if they can be salvaged. If this is not possible, the damaged element should be replaced with new copper of the same weight, configuration, and temper or hardness. Fatigue damage should never be repaired using soldered patches or soft solder (a lead-tin alloy) to fill stress cracks; this solder has a different coefficient of expansion than the copper and will eventually break away. Solder is inherently a weak alloy and should be used only to create watertight joints, not where tensile or compressive strength is needed. However, it does provide some strength in connecting sheets of copper in "weights" less than 20 ounces.[56] To connect thicker sheets, over 20 ounces, copper rivets must be used. All solder used for copper, either for repair or new installations, should be composed of 50% pig lead and 50% block tin and should be applied using a noncorrosive rosin flux.[57] Copper can be welded if the sheets are of sufficient thickness.

Where new sheets of copper are used to repair an existing copper architectural component, the maximum length of the sheets should be 8 feet. Adequate provisions should be made for thermal expansion and contraction within the repaired area and all fastenings should utilize copper cleats held with either copper nails or brass screws. Copper roofing sheet should be separated from the wooden sheathing by rosin building paper to allow free movement of the sheets (figure 147b).

Bronze or Brass can be repaired in a variety of ways. If a bronze or brass object is dented, it may be hammered back in place if the backside is accessible and the metal is not too thick. However, if the metal has stretched, it will be difficult to hammer it back to its original configuration. Severely damaged sections can be cut out, recast, and reattached by riveting or brazing, a form of soldering with a bronze or brass filler metal. Likewise, missing pieces can be reproduced (figure 154). Some scratches can be buffed to match the original finish and texture, as can brazed joints.

Before bronze or brass objects can be brazed they must be cleaned to provide good bonding. At other times, cleaning may be necessary to remove salts, bird droppings, or dirt. Sometimes cleaning is done only for cosmetic reasons. All cleaning removes some surface metal and patina; therefore, it should not be done without good reason. Excessive cleaning can remove the texture and finish of the metal. Since the patina can protect the bronze or brass from further corrosion, it should be retained if possible. Heat from brazing or welding will affect the patina, causing a change in color that may be permanent. If the patina is removed when repairs are made, it can be replaced slowly by weathering which takes 8-10 years; however, the resulting blotchiness may not be acceptable. The patina can be replaced rapidly by chemical means to match the rest of the work if necessary; however, repatination may also remove a slight amount of surface metal (see below).

Surface deposits and corrosion products can be partially or totally removed from copper, bronze, and brass by various procedures. These range from gentle washing with deionized water, a non-ionic detergent, and natural bristle brushes; to chemical stripping; to air-abrasive blasting, using a variety of abrasive media such as soft organic blasting media like crushed walnut shells or corn cobs, to much harder media like plastic or glass beads. Chemical compounds such as rottenstone and oil, whiting and ammonia, and precipitated chalk and ammonia, can be used along with very mild abrasive techniques such as rubbing with a clean, soft cloth.[58] Thick crust can be removed by sodium hexametaphosphate and water or dilute sulfuric acid and water prepared and used by persons trained in handling this dangerous acid.[59] Commercial companies that routinely clean and maintain bronzework use a variety of "secret" formulas which are generally based on their experience and conform to the recommendations of the Copper Development Association. It suggests using a 5% oxalic acid and water mixture together with finely ground India pumice powder.[60] This slurry mixture is rubbed on with a clean soft cloth. After thorough rinsing with clean water, the surface is wiped dry with a clean soft cloth to prevent water spotting (figure 155).

Sandblasting, a common method for cleaning cast iron, is particularly damaging to bronze surfaces. In addition, the practice of cleaning bronze surfaces with glass bead peening, common during the 1970s, has fallen out of favor. Moreover, cleaning down to a bright metal surface, by any means, is often inappropriate and unnecessary. In recent years, gentler low-pressure blasting procedures have been developed by conservators of outdoor bronze sculpture. Using softer blasting media, (crushed walnut shells are currently the most popular), these cleaning methods seek to remove grime and superficial corrosion products while leaving intact more

a

b

Figure 154. Damage to Bronze. *In the Court Square Historic District in Springfield, Massachusetts, five of six bronze street lamps were vandalized or accidently damaged by automobiles backing into parking spaces. (a) The one lamp that survived intact was used to make new molds. (b)The missing leg and lamp were recast (not shown) and/or repaired with funds from a matching grant from the National Park Service in 1976. The recast pieces were chemically treated to obtain a green patina that matched the weathered appearance of the original sections of the lamps. A plan was drafted to relocate the lamps 12 inches from their previous position at the curb to prevent any further damage from parking automobiles. (Thomas Taylor)*

Figure 155. Cleaning Bronze. *Recently, the exterior bronzework was cleaned on the Morgan Guaranty Trust Company on the corner of Wall and Board streets in Manhattan. The original finish of the bronze was a statuary brown artificial patina (a chemical process developed in the 19th century) with the bas-relief sculpture highlighted in a lighter pinkish-gold color, probably just the natural color of bronze without artificial or natural patina. The bronzework was cleaned and sealed with a clear coating. Without a coating, a natural patina would form, causing slow color change from pinkish gold to brown to black and eventually to green over an 8-10 year period. The colors are usually uneven and streaked because of the local pattern of wind and rain. The formation of a natural patina would eventually destroy the contrast between the statuary brown and pinkish gold, which was the original intention of the architects, Trowbridge and Livingston, when the bank was built in 1913. (David W. Look)*

firmly adhered corrosion products, as well as the metal substrate below.

Whether or not surface cleaning produces a bright metal surface, surface coloration can be modified through the creation of chemically-induced patinas. The color range of bronze patinas includes red-brown, gold-brown, shades of green or blue-green, and black. Perhaps more important to the visual appearance is the modulation of specified colors to achieve subtle variations that can enhance highlights and shadows.

Once a bronze or brass surface has been cleaned, some type of barrier coating should be applied to prevent or limit future corrosion. These coatings are designed to prevent or minimize contact between the metal and moisture and pollutants. Original foundry-applied wax or shellac coatings usually deteriorate with time, exposure, and lack of maintenance and therefore need to be renewed. The organic coatings most frequently used for maintaining architectural bronze include waxes, which require reapplication at six-month to two-year intervals; lacquers, which require removal and reapplication at three- to five-year intervals; and combinations of lacquers and waxes.

Lacquer is a type of surface coating in which a binder consists of an organic film-forming substance, often dissolved in a solvent. The term lacquer is usually reserved for coatings obtained by physical drying, whereas a varnish contains a drying oil and is thus dried by oxidation. Upon exposure to the atmosphere, the polymers that make up lacquers tend to attach themselves to each other, a chemical process known as cross-linking. Cross-linked materials are difficult to break up by solvents or by application of reasonable amounts of heat, which makes them nearly irreversible. The potential of some lacquers to undergo cross-linking raises concerns regarding their use as protective coating for bronze sculpture.

Wax coatings are widely used in the conservation of outdoor bronze statuary. Waxes are used in various formulations and are applied using a variety of methods. Both natural and synthetic waxes are commonly applied directly to heated or ambient temperature bronze surfaces, or applied cold as a finish coating over lacquer. While the lifespan of waxes is shorter than that of lacquers and varnishes, waxes tend not to cross-link, making removal relatively easy. Further, waxes are a more forgiving type of coating. Small scratches and pinholes tend to "self-heal" as the wax can soften and redistribute itself somewhat at typical outdoor temperatures. Many conservators of outdoor bronzes add sacrificial cold wax coatings to lacquered surfaces.

The useful lives of present organic coatings differ, depending upon their nature and upon the vicissitudes of the surrounding environment. All coatings should be periodically inspected and renewed when needed. In addition, they should be readily removable through means that will not damage the metal substrate.

The cleaning and repair of copper, bronze, and brass should not be considered a "do-it-yourself" project. A qualified metal conservator should assess the condition of the material and design an appropriate treatment that will then be carried out by the conservator, or an experienced and well-supervised staff of technicians.

Chapter 16: Nickel and Nickel Alloys; Preservation and Repair

Identification

Nickel is an inactive, corrosion resistant, metal, silvery or off-white in color, which resembles iron in strength and toughness and copper in its resistance to oxidation and corrosion.[61] Nickel is ferromagnetic and can be hot or cold rolled, forged, bent, extruded, spun, punched, and deep drawn. For architectural purposes, nickel is used in the form of alloys such as nickel silver, Monel, and stainless steel. Nickel has also been used to plate brass and nickel silver.

Coating of nickel and nickel alloys can be applied for decorative or protective reasons to other metals such as aluminum, beryllium-copper, brass, copper, iron, magnesium. Monel and other nickel alloys, lead-base alloys, steel, tin, and zinc.[62] Electroplating is the most common method of applying the coating, although methods using chemical reactions, pressure welding by hot rolling and spraying or vapor-deposition are becoming more common.[63]

Nickel silver, originally called "German silver," is a class of nickel alloys, none of which contain any silver. Rather, it gets its name from its silver-white color and its ability to take a high polish. Its composition is similar to brass with nickel added. There were many companies that made nickel silver, each with a slightly different formula and trademark. The proportions varied from 5 to 30% nickel, 10 to 35% zinc, 50-80% copper, and small quantities of tin and lead when cast.

Nickel silver is ductile, hard, and moderately strong. Some nickel silvers have the strength of mild steel and their structural use is limited only by cost. The metal can be cast, forged, rolled, drawn, extruded, and machined; and nickel silver parts can be hard and soft soldered[64] and spot-, arc-, and fusion-welded.

Monel metal is a registered trademark name for an alloy of approximately two-thirds nickel and one-third copper with small amounts of iron, manganese, silicon, and carbon. It is similar in appearance to nickel and can either take high polish or be left with a matte finish.

Monel is harder to work than iron. It can be forged, cast, welded, annealed, soldered, brazed, spun and drawn,[65] but it cannot be extruded.[66] Monel has a low coefficient of expansion comparable to that of concrete.[67] It thus resists fatigue cracking caused by thermal expansion and contraction. The high rigidity of Monel permits its transfer or movement to expansion joints without buckling the metal.

Nickel is one of the three main ingredients of *chrome-nickel steel*, commonly known as stainless steel. It will be discussed in detail in chapter 17 on iron and steel.

Causes of Deteriorated

Nickel resists corrosion by salt water, strong alkalis, and most acids, except nitric acid.[68] In nickel components, galvanic corrosion can be avoided by using a base metal or alloy close to nickel in the galvanic series (that is, stainless steel) and by insuring that the nickel coating is thick, nonporous, and continuous.[69] Nickel silver resists corrosion, especially outdoors where it acquires a soft brown or greenish patina that protects the metal from further corrosion. Monel metal is attacked by some acids, alkalis, and salts.[70] When Monel oxidizes, it forms a silver-gray to greenish-brown protective patina (figure 156). Nickel silver and Monel used indoors can usually be cleaned with a mild (non-ionic) detergent and a wetting agent. Outdoors, nickel silver and Monel with natural patinas are usually cleaned in the same manner as other copper alloys (see bronze and brass).[71]

It is often difficult to differentiate the "white metals" (see part I, chapter 6), as nickel, nickel silver, Monel, stainless steel, and aluminum were often called. Most buildings containing white metals were built in the 20th century. Building records often exist that will identify the metal and perhaps even the specific nickel content and fabricator. If records do not exist or evidence is conflicting, the physical remains may be the only source of information. The procedures in "Simple Tests Identify White Metals" (see bibliography) may be dangerous because they involve the use of different acids and may damage the building if not performed correctly in an inconspicuous spot. Only a professional, such as a chemist, metallurgist, metal conservator, or corrosion engineer trained in the use of these materials, should perform these tests.[72]

Methods of Preservation and Repair

Nickel can be brazed, soldered, and welded by metallic arc, electric resistance, oxyacetylene, and atomic hydrogen processes. In soldering nickel, acid flux solder should be used. For use with Monel, prepared "cut acid" soldering fluxes consisting of zinc and hydrochloric acid[73] are available. To prevent corrosion, every trace of the flux must be removed after the soldering is completed.

For Monel metal roofing and sheathing, only fastenings and nails of Monel or other nickel alloys should be used to prevent galvanic corrosion.

Where the nickel plating has worn away or been damaged, the only solution is to replate the base metal with a new coating of nickel. To replate an architectural element, it must first be removed from the building and thoroughly cleaned.[74] Care must be taken not to damage the object when disassembling it. After removal, it can be given an electro-coating of copper to clean or smooth out the surface. The element is then immersed in an electrolytic solution of nickel salts where the element acts as the cathode and the nickel in the solution acts as an anode. Nickel is deposited on the element from the electrolyte. The thickness of the nickel coating can be controlled by the strength of the electrolyte and the amount of time the element is immersed in it.

Figure 156. Oxidation of Monel. *These exterior doors on the Headquarters of the United Mine Workers of America in Washington, D.C., have a greenish-brown patina of oxidation and an accumulation of dirt and fingerprints. Although the patina is protective, it is not attractive, and detracts from the overall appearance of the building. The push bars are brass with chrome plating which has worn through. To restore the doors to their original appearance, they should be cleaned and polished; and the push bars should be removed, cleaned, polished, replated, and reinstalled. (David W. Look)*

Chapter 17: Iron and Iron Alloys; Preservation and Repair

Identification

Iron is a gray-white metal, which in its pure form is relatively soft, tough, malleable, ductile, magnetic, and high in tensile strength. It oxidizes rapidly when exposed to a damp atmosphere and is readily attached by most acids. When alloyed with small amounts of carbon to form steel, it can be hardened by heating and *sudden* cooling, or made more workable by heating and *slow* cooling.[75] Historically, iron in a number of alloy forms has been used for architectural purposes. These alloys include cast iron, wrought iron, various types of steels, iron, and steel sheet metals, and stainless steel.

Wrought Iron is defined as a commercial iron consisting of slag (iron silicate) fibers entertained in a ferrite matrix.[76] It is almost pure iron with less than 1 percent (usually 0.02 to 0.03%)[77] carbon. The slag content varies between 1 and 4% (usually about 2.5%). The slag exists in a purely physical association, that is, it is not alloyed;[78] this gives wrought iron its characteristic laminated structure. The fundamental differences between wrought iron and steel are in their compositions and methods of processing. Steel is cast at a white heat into ingot; wrought iron is removed from the furnace at a lower temperature in a semi-molten plastic condition together with slag, then is formed into bars with most of the slag hammered out.[79] The presence of slag in the composition of wrought iron distinguishes it from steel. Wrought iron also contains less carbon and manganese and usually more phosphorus than steel.[80]

Wrought iron is relatively soft, malleable, tough fatigue-resistant, and easily worked by forging, bending, rolling, and drawing. Until steel was available, wrought iron was used structurally for beams and girders as it had strengthen in both tension and compression. During the late 19th and early 20th centuries, it was not unusual to find a mixture of cast-iron columns and wrought iron or steel beams in the same building. Currently very little wrought iron is being produced.

Cast Iron is an alloy with a high carbon content (at least 1.7% and usually 3.0 to 3.7%)[81] that makes it more resistant to corrosion than either wrought iron or steel. In addition to carbon, cast iron contains varying amounts of silicon, sulfur, manganese, and phosphorus.

While molten, cast iron is easily poured into molds, making it possible to create nearly unlimited decorative and structural forms. Unlike wrought iron and steel, cast iron is too hard and brittle to be shaped by hammering, rolling, or pressing.[82] However, because it is more rigid and more resistant to buckling than other forms of iron, it can withstand great compression loads.[83] Cast iron is relatively weak in tension, however, and fails under tensile loading with little prior warning.

The characteristics of various types of cast iron are determined by their composition and the techniques used in melting, casting, and heat treatment. Metallurgical constituents of cast iron that affect its brittleness, toughness, and strength include ferrite, cementite, pearlite, and graphite carbon.[84] Cast iron with flakes of carbon is called gray cast iron. The "gray fracture" associated with cast iron was probably named for the gray, grainy appearance of its broken edge caused by the presence of flakes of free graphite, which account for the brittleness of cast iron. This brittleness is the important distinguishing characteristic between cast iron and mild steel.[85]

Compared with cast iron, wrought iron is relatively soft, malleable, tough, fatigue-resistant, and readily worked by forging, bending, and drawing. It is almost pure iron, with less than 1% (usually 0.02 to 0.03%) carbon. Slag varies between 1% and 4% of its content and exists in a purely physical association, that is, it is not alloyed. This gives wrought iron its characteristic laminated (layered) or fibrous structure.

Wrought iron can be distinguished from cast iron in several ways. Wrought-iron elements generally are simpler in form and less uniform in appearance than cast-iron elements, and contain evidence of rolling or hand working. Cast iron often contains mold lines, flashing, casting flaws, and air holes. Cast-iron elements are very uniform in appearance and are frequently used repetitively. Cast-iron elements are often bolted or screwed together, whereas wrought-iron pieces are either riveted or forge-molded (heat welded) together.

Mild steel is now used to fabricate new hand-worked metal work and to repair old wrought-iron elements. Mild steel is an alloy of iron and is not more than 2% carbon, which is strong but easily worked in block or ingot form. It is not as resistant to corrosion as either wrought iron or cast iron.

Steel is an alloy of iron and carbon that contains not more than 2% carbon, and is malleable in block or ingot form. Steels may include phosphorus, sulfur, oxygen, manganese, silicon, aluminum, copper, titanium, molybdenum, and nickel. The properties of steels vary greatly in relation to their chemical compositions and the types of heat treatment and mechanical working used in their manufacture.[86] Characteristic affected by these differences include strength, hardness, ductility, resistance to abrasion, weldability, machinability, and resistance to corrosion.

The classification of steel is based on its carbon content, as shown in the following comparison:[87]

Low carbon steel—up to 0.2% carbon

Mild steel—up to 0.25% carbon

Medium carbon steel— 0.25 to 0.45% carbon

High carbon steel—0.45 to 2% carbon

In the late 1880s, steel began to overtake wrought iron in structural systems, and became dominant in the 20th century. A grade of medium carbon steel is used for most structural applications today, while high-strength alloy steels are available for specialized installations.

Galvanized Steel consists of sheet steel with a zinc coating, which makes it highly resistant to corrosion.[88] (See chapter 14 on zinc for further information on preservation treatments.)

Stainless Steel is defined as a steel containing sufficient chromium, or chromium and nickel, to render it highly resistant to corrosion. The composition of stainless steel must be over 50% iron and 11.5% chromium, with the remaining constituents including nickel, columbium, molybdenum, phosphorus, selenium, silicon, sulfur, titanium, and zirconium.[89] Stainless steel is malleable, is hardened by cold working, and is resistant to oxidation, corrosion, and heat. It has characteristics of high thermal expansion and low heat conductivity, and can be forged, soldered, brazed, and welded. Chromium-nickel stainless steel (for example 18-8—18% chromium and 8% nickel) is termed austenitic. It non-magnetic, but ferritic chromium stainless steel is magnetic.

Four stainless steel alloys most commonly used in architectural work are AISI Types 302, 304, 316, and 430.[90] The 300 series alloys are austenitic chromium nickel steels. Type 302 is an austenitic alloy containing 18% chromium and 8% nickel. It has been widely used in building exteriors for many years. It is highly resistant to atmospheric corrosion, very strong and hard, available in many forms, and fabricated easily by all standard techniques. Type 304 is a low carbon variation of Type 302 having similar properties but improved weldability. It has largely replaced Type 302 in architectural applications and is the type most readily available in many forms. Type 316 contains more nickel than Types 302 or 304, as well as 2% to 3% molybdenum, added to improve corrosion resistance. It is often used in locations exposed to severe marine environments or the extremely corrosive industrial atmospheres.

Type 430 is a ferritic chromium alloy which is somewhat less resistant to corrosion than the 300 series of austenitic alloys. It has been found suitable for interior applications and for exterior applications which receive frequent maintenance.

Causes of Deterioration

Iron and Steel (when unprotected) oxidize rapidly when exposed to moisture and air, except for some of the corrosion- resistant alloy steels and stainless steels (figure 157). The oxidation of iron and steel is a highly destructive process (figure 158). The product of this oxidation is rust, which initially consists of a mixture of ferrous and ferric hydroxides (FeO), and later becomes a hydrated ferric oxide ($Fe_2(OH)_3$) with some traces of a carbonate.[91] The minimum relative humidity necessary to promote rusting is 65%, but this figure can be lower in the presence of pollutants.[92] When salts are present, they act as electrolytes, accelerating the corrosion of iron and steel and making it more complicated. Once a rust film occurs, its porosity acts as a reservoir for any liquid present,[93] which also tends to accelerate corrosion. If simple oxidation is not arrested, its rate will accelerate until the metal is completely destroyed.

Iron and steel are also corroded by the following: sea water, salt air, acids, soils, gypsum plasters, magnesium oxychloride cements,[94] ashes and clinkers, and some sulfur compounds. Corrosion is accelerated where architectural details provide pockets and crevices to catch and hold these corrosive agents (figure 156).

Galvanic corrosion will occur in varying degrees when iron and steel are exposed to cupro-nickels, aluminum bronzes, gun metals, copper (see figures 145 and 146), brasses, lead, soft solders, stainless steels, and chromium.[95]

Cast Iron develops a kind of protective scale on its surface, thus it is slightly more resistant to corrosion than ordinary steel. However, although it generally has some resistance to corrosion, cast iron should be kept painted to prevent rusting (figure 160).

A form of deterioration that is unfortunately fairly common is caused by inappropriate repairs. These not only disfigure a building (figure 161) but also decrease its architectural integrity.

Graphitization of cast iron, a less common problem, occurs in the presence of acid precipitation or seawater. As the iron corrodes, the porous graphite (soft carbon) corrosion residue is impregnated with insoluble corrosion products. As a result, the cast-iron element retains its appearance and shape but is weaker structurally.[96] Graphitization occurs where cast iron is left unpainted for long periods or where caulked joints have failed and acidic rainwater has corroded pieces from the backside. Testing and identification of graphitization is accomplished by scraping through the surface with a knife to reveal the crumbling of the iron beneath. Where extensive graphitization occurs, usually the only solution is replacement of the damaged element.

Castings may also be fractured or flawed as a result of imperfections in the original manufacturing process, such as air holes, cracks, and cinders (caused by the "freezing" of the surface of the molten iron during casting because of improper or interrupted pouring).[97] Brittleness is another problem occasionally found in old cast-iron elements. It may be a result of excessive phosphorus in the iron, or of chilling during the casting process. A number of nondestructive tests using, for example, fluorescent fluids and ultraviolet lamps, have been developed to detect these potential defects.[98]

Figure 157. Stone Damage from Rust. *In the 1950s the stairs of Library Hall in Philadelphia were reconstructed. Since wrought iron was not available for the railing, steel was substituted. The design of the railing was poorly detailed. The bottoms of the balusters were fitted into stone steps. Not only did the rusting stain the steps, it cracked the stone because of the expansion in volume of the steel during rusting. (Jack E. Boucher)*

Figure 158. Advanced Corrosion of Rolled Iron. *This column base of a New York Central Railroad pedestrian overpass has not been well maintained and has rusted beyond repair. Such exposed ironwork should be painted regularly to keep it from contact with air and moisture. Note the characteristic way that wrought-iron rust exfoliates, or flakes off in layers. (John G. Waite)*

Figure 159. Defective Original Design Detail. *Corrosion of the connection between the girder and the built-up truss members has occurred on the former Delaware and Hudson Railroad Bridge, 1884, over the Hudson River between Troy and Green Island, New York, because the connection served as a pocket to trap rain and snow in an area difficult to maintain and protect. This connection is almost impossible to maintain without modification in the design. The connection should be sandblasted, primed immediately, and painted. Since the bottom of the vertical truss member is boxed in, which prevents painting with a brush, the inside of this member could be spray painted. (John G. Waite)*

Figure 160. Cast-iron Corrosion, Fracture, and Missing Pieces. *(a) The massive newel posts of the stair railings on the entrance of 637 I Street, NW in Washington, D.C., are hollow and are made up of several pieces screwed and bolted together. The newel post to the right side of the stairs is substantially intact. (b) The finial of the left newel post is missing. Note the threaded rod in the center of the newel post used for assembly. Inside the railing, loose rust has collected to a depth of about a half inch. Water seeped into the hollow rail and froze, resulting in the crack. (David W. Look)*

Table II. Galvanic Series in Sea Water.

ACTIVE END **(–)**	Magnesium Magnesium Alloys Zinc Galvanized Steel
	Aluminum 1100
	Aluminum 6053 Alclad
	Cadmium
	Aluminum 2024 (4.5 Cu, 1.5 Mg, 0.6 Mn)
	Mild Steel Wrought Iron Cast Iron
	13% Chromium Stainless Steel Type 410 (Active) 18-8 Stainless Steel Type 304 (Active) 18-12-3 Stainless Steel Type 316 (Active)
	Lead-Tin Solders Lead Tin
	Muntz Metal Manganese Bronze Naval Brass
	Nickel (Active) 76 NI-16 Cr-7 Fe alloy (Active)
	60 Ni-30 Mo-6 Fe-1 Mn
	Yellow Brass Admirality Brass Aluminum Brass Red Brass Copper Silicon Bronze
	70:30 Cupro Nickel G-Bronze M-Brnoze Silver Solder Nickel (Passive) 76 Ni-16 Cr-7 Fe Alloy (Passive) 67 Ni-33 Cu Alloy (Monel)
	13% Chromium Stainless Steel Type 410 (Passive) Titanium
	18-8 Stainless Steel Type 304 (Passive) 18-12-3 Stainless Steel Type 316 (Passive)
(+) **NOBLE or** **PASSIVE END**	Silver Graphite Gold Platinum

Figure 161. Inappropriate Repairs of Cast Iron. *A simple cast-iron pipe railing guards the areaway of the Old Pension Building in Washington, D.C. The collar on the newel post to receive the bottom rail is missing (it probably cracked off from the pressure of expanding rust and/or ice). Unfortunately, a strap was welded to each side instead of repairing or reproducing the collar. (David W. Look)*

Table II. Galvanic Series in Sea Water.

There is always an electrical potential difference between two different metals. Any time there are two dissimilar metals in electrical contact, the metal closer to the top of this table (most active) will act as an *anode* and will eventually be consumed by corrosion. The metal closer to the bottom of the table will act as a *cathode* and will be protected by the galvanic action. At the anode, positively charged atoms, called positive *ions*, separate from the metal and go into solution in the electrolyte such as ionized water. These positive ions travel through the electrolyte and "plate out" (deposit) on the cathode and release H_2 or reduce O_2 thus giving it an excess positive charge. The negatively charged particles, *electrons*, flow through the two metals (or conductors) as an electrical current to the cathode to neutralize the excess positive charge. (From American Society for Testing and Materials. Standard Guide for Development and Use of a Galvanic Series for Predicting Galvanic Corrosion Performance—G82-83.)

Wrought Iron generally rusts more quickly than cast iron, however the corrosion can be more readily measured and the degree of deterioration ascertained.[99] However, wrought iron is resistant to progressive (severe) corrosion, primarily because of the slag content[100] which acts as a barrier to corrosion.

Steel can resist rusting, but this varies from alloy to alloy. Those alloys containing chromium, nickel, or both, are far more resistant to corrosion than other alloys (see stainless steel). Both tests and experience have shown that high-strength low-alloy steels are more resistant to atmospheric corrosion than ordinary mild steel. Unlike cast iron, steel generally has poor resistance to corrosion from fresh water and sea water. The rate of corrosion increases as the temperature of the water surrounding a steel member rises[101] and as the water movement accelerates.

Galvanized Iron and Steel can resist corrosion, but this is dependent on the type and thickness of the protective zinc coating, the type and thickness of additional protective coatings, and the kind of corrosive environment to which it is exposed. Galvanized steel can generally be used in direct contact with most wood, as long as it is not cedar, oak, sweet chestnut, and redwood, all of which produce acids. Just the contact of moist wood (any species) against the metal can cause an O_2 concentration cell. Galvanized iron and steel can be used with concrete, mortar, lead, tin, zinc, and aluminum.[102] Galvanic corrosion occurs, however, when it is in contact with any of the other metals. Like most types of iron and steel, galvanized steel is also corroded by acids and chemical fumes (see chapter 14).

Stainless Steels have a high resistance to heat, oxidation, and corrosion. Chromium and chromium-nickel stainless steels are among the few metals that remain substantially unaltered in appearance after being exposed to the atmosphere.[103] Stainless steels resist corrosion from hydrogen sulfide and sulfur dioxide, and have good resistance to water and to some soils; thus, they often retain their natural finishes.

The high corrosion resistance of stainless steels is dependent on the presence of a thin, complex, protective film.[104] The *passivation* (resistance to rust) of the stainless steel occurs readily in environments containing oxygen. When corrosion does occur, it is usually localized.[105] As with all metals, the presence of chlorides increases the susceptibility of attack; therefore, stainless steel can be lightly corroded by mortar and pitted by a salt environment.[106] Galvanic action can occur when some stainless steel comes in contact with aluminum, aluminum alloys, steel, zinc, and to a lesser extent copper.[107]

Copper-bearing Steels have a copper content of just 0.1% and are markedly more resistant to atmosphere corrosion than ordinary steel.[108] Known as copper-bearing steel, these steels form a protective oxide coating or "skin" of a uniform deep over brown color which can wash down over other building materials leaving a rust stain. "Corten and "Mayari R" are two trade names of copper-bearing steel. Problems with excessive corrosion have been found to occur when copper-bearing steels are used in a saline environment such as near sea water.

Methods of Preservation and Repair

Iron and steel architectural components are most commonly protected from oxidation by paints. Other protective method include electroplating of nearby harmful metals and humidity control. The U.S. Navy has been successful in preventing rust on ships in the mothball fleet by using "sealed zones" and enclosures over steel components where the relative humidity is kept below 30 %.[109] In the future, similar techniques may be used temporarily for architectural applications such as the "mothballing" of large, abandoned industrial sites or of individual metal components (figure 162).

In the repair of historic iron and steel structures, the introduction of details that provide crevices or pockets to catch and hold water should be avoided wherever possible (figure 159). If it is necessary to retain such details for historical reasons, they should be carefully cleaned periodically and protected against oxidation. Structural arrangements that prevent the free circulation of air should be avoided, and hollow sections should be hermetically sealed if at all possible. Sharp corners and edges should be modified and rounded contours used to prevent mechanical damage to the metal and the breakdown of protective coatings. Sheltered surfaces, such as the underside of eaves where evaporation of moisture is inhibited, should receive additional protective coatings.

A number of finishes are commonly used to protect iron and steel architectural components, including plating with another metal, and coating with plastics, concrete, vitreous enamels, and paints. If these coatings have only partially broken down, simple recoating is in order, such as a coating paint. If the paint shows minor flame cleaning and chemical methods. The selection of an appropriate technique depends upon how much paint failure and corrosion has occurred, the fineness of the surface detailing, and the type of new protective coating to be applied. Local environmental regulations may restrict the options for cleaning and paint removal methods, as well as the disposal of materials.

Many of these techniques are *potentially dangerous* and should be carried out only by experienced and qualified workers using proper eye protection, protective clothing, and other workplace safety conditions. Before selecting a process, test panels should be prepared on the iron to be cleaned to determine the relative effectiveness of various techniques. The cleaning process will most likely expose additional coating defects, cracks, and corrosion that have not been obvious before (figure 164).

There are a number of techniques that can be used to remove paint and corrosion from cast iron:

Hand scraping, chipping, and wire brushing are the most common and least expensive methods of removing paint and light rust from cast iron. However, they do not remove all corrosion or paint as effectively as other methods. Experienced craftsmen should carry out the work to reduce the likelihood that surfaces may be scored or fragile detail damaged.

Low-pressure grit blasting (commonly called abrasive cleaning or sandblasting) is often the most effective approach to removing excessive paint build-up or substantial corrosion (figure 163). Grit blasting is fast, thorough, and economical, and it allows the iron to be cleaned in place. The aggregate can be iron slag or sand; copper slag should not be used on iron because of the potential for electrolytic reactions. Some sharpness in the aggregate is beneficial in that it gives the metal surface a "tooth" that will result in better paint adhesion. The use of a very sharp or hard aggregate and/or excessively high pressure (over 100 pounds per square inch) is unnecessary and should be avoided. Adjacent materials, such as brick, stone, wood, and glass, must be protected to prevent damage. Some local building codes and environmental authorities prohibit or limit dry sandblasting because of the problem of airborne dust.

Wet sandblasting is more problematic than dry sandblasting for cleaning cast iron because the water will cause instantaneous surface rusting and will penetrate deep into open joints. Therefore, it is generally not considered an effective technique. Wet sandblasting reduces the amount of airborne dust when removing a heavy paint build-up, but disposal of effluent containing lead or other toxic substances is restricted by environmental regulations in most areas.

Flame Cleaning of rust from metal with a special multi-flame head oxyacetylene torch requires specially skilled operators, and is expensive and potentially dangerous.[110] However, is can be very effective on lightly to moderately corroded iron. Wire brushing is usually necessary to finish the surface after flame cleaning.

Chemical rust removal, by acid pickling, is an effective method of removing rust from iron elements that can be easily removed and taken to a shop for submerging in vats of dilute phosphoric or sulfuric acid. This method does not damage the surface of iron, providing that the iron is neutralized to pH level 7 after cleaning. Other chemical rust removal agents include ammonium citrate, oxalic acid, or hydrochloric acid-based products.[111]

Chemical paint removal using alkaline compounds, such as methylene chloride or potassium hydroxide, can be an effective alternative to abrasive blasting for removal of heavy paint build-up. These agents are often available as slow-acting gels or pastes. Because they cause burns, protective clothing and eye protection must be worn. Chemicals applied to a non-watertight facade can seep through crevices and holes, resulting in damage to the building's interior finishes and corrosion to the backside of the iron components. If not thoroughly neutralized, residual traces of cleaning compounds on the surface of the iron can cause paint failures in the future.[112] For these reasons, field application of alkaline paint removers and acidic cleaners is not generally recommended.

Following any of these methods of cleaning and paint removal, the newly cleaned iron should be painted immediately with a corrosion-inhibiting primer before new rust begins to form. This time period may vary from minutes to hours depending on environmental conditions. If priming is delayed, any surface rust that has developed should be removed with a clean wire brush just before priming, because the rust prevents good bonding

Figure 162. Unpainted Steel. *The Republic Steel Corporation in Troy, New York, could not meet the new environmental quality standards and shut down its 1920s steel blast furnace which was built for the Burden Iron Company. It had never been painted because steel at very high temperatures does not rust. When the heat was turned off, the steal rusted rapidly. (John G. Waite)*

between the primer and the cast-iron surface and prevents the primer from completely filling the pores of the metal.

Painting is the most common treatment for controlling the corrosion of iron and steel components. Before removing paint from historic architectural iron or steel, a microscopic analysis of samples of the historic paint sequencing is recommended. Called paint seriation analysis, this process must be carried out by an experienced architectural conservator. The analysis will identify the historic paint colors, and other conditions, such as whether the paint was matte or gloss, whether sand was added to the paint for texture, and whether the building was polychromed or marbleized. Traditionally many cast-iron elements were painted to resemble other materials, such as limestone or sandstone. Occasionally, features were faux-painted so that the iron appeared to be veined marble.

Thorough surface preparation is necessary for the adhesion of new protective coatings. All loose, flaking, and deteriorated paint must be removed from the iron or steel, as well as dirt and mud, water-soluble salts, oil, and grease. Old paint that is tightly adhered may be left on the surface of the metal if it is compatible with the

Figure 163. Cleaning Cast Iron. *The facade of the Zions Cooperative Mercantile Institute (ZCMI) Store was sandblasted to locate the screws and bolt connections and thereby discover the method of assembly and disassembly. The cast iron should not be heavily sandblasted (down to the bare metal) unless that entire section of the facade is being dismantled. As pieces are being removed, they should be primed immediately to avoid rusting. If the building is not to be dismantled, it is best to remove only the loose paint with a wire brush, being careful not to damage caulked joints and connection holes. Any bare cast iron should be spot primed. (Steven T. Baird, AIA)*

Figure 164. Exposure of Connections and Joints. *After the Wilmington Opera House was sandblasted, screw and bolt holes were visible. A cast-iron bracket such as this one may be made of as many as 10 pieces. (Steven T. Baird, AIA)*

Selection of Paints and Coatings

The types of paints available for protecting iron and steel have changed dramatically in recent years due to federal, state, and local regulations that prohibit or restrict the manufacture and use of products containing toxic substances such as lead and zinc chromate, as well as volatile organic compounds and substances (VOC or VOS). Availability of paint types varies from state to state, and manufacturers continue to change product formulations to comply with new regulations.

Traditionally, red lead had been used as an anti-corrosive pigment for priming iron and steel. Red lead has a strong affinity for linseed oil and forms lead soaps, which become a tough and elastic film impervious to water that is highly effective as a protective coating for iron. At least two slow-drying linseed oil-based finish coats have traditionally been used over a red lead primer, and this combination is effective on old or partially-deteriorated surfaces. Today, in most areas, the use of paints containing lead is prohibited, except for some commercial and industrial purposes, and the trend to eliminate lead-base paints altogether is likely to continue.

Today, alkyd paints are very widely used and have largely replaced lead-containing linseed-oil paints. They dry faster than oil paint, with a thinner film, but they do

proposed coatings. The retention of old paint also preserves the historic paint sequence of the building and avoids the hazards of removal and disposal of old lead paint.

It is advisable to consult manufacturer's specifications or technical representatives to ensure compatibility between the surface conditions, primer and finish coats, and application methods.

For the paint to adhere properly, the metal surfaces must be absolutely dry before painting. Unless the paint selected is specifically designed for exceptional conditions, painting should not take place when the temperature is expected to fall below 50 degrees Fahrenheit within 24 hours or when the relative humidity is above 80%; paint should not be applied when there is fog, mist, or rain in the air. Poorly prepared surfaces will cause the failure of even the best paints, while even moderately priced paints can be effective if applied over well-prepared surfaces.

Table III. Methods for Surface Preparation of Iron and Steel for Painting

Types of Cleaning	How Done	Characteristics of Cleaned Surface	Type of Paints Used With This Cleaning
Flame cleaning	Oxyacetylene flame consisting of a series of small, closely spaced flames that are very hot and projected at high velocity	Reduces ordinary rust to iron oxide and pops off loose mill scale; after flame cleaning the surface should be wire-brushed	Alkyd and phenolic vehicle paints, baked enamels
Iron phosphate	Metal is immersed in an alkali precleaner and then immersed in a patented solution containing ferric phosphate	Surface provides excellent adhesion for paint and retards rusting	Baked enamels
Pickling (phosphoric acid)	Metal is immersed in warmed dilute phosphoric acid with added rust inhibitors; does not need finishing	Removes all dirt, rust, and mill scale and gives the surface a protective film which retards rusting and is a good base for painting	Natural-drying-oil and resin vehicle paints
Pickling (sulfuric acid)	Metal is immersed in warmed dilute sulfuric acid with other chemicals which confine the action largely to rust and scale and is then rinsed	Removes all dirt, rust and mill scale and gives the surface a slight etching which helps adhesion of the paint	Vinyl, alkyd and phenolic vehicle paints, baked enamels
Rust removers	Applied by brush or spraying, the phosphate type forms a film and retards rusting	Generally used in maintenance painting and with on-site painting where slight rusting has occurred	All types of paint used for maintenance and on-site painting
Sand blasting and grit blasting	Sand or steel grit (crushed shot) in a range of No. 10 to No. 45 screen sizes and dry compressed air at 80 to 100 lb. per sq. in.	Removes all dirt, rust, tight mill scale and all other surface impurities; also roughens the surface, thus providing the best condition for adhesion of the paint	Coal-tar enamels and vinyl vehicle paints; baked enamels; also used for alkyd and phenolic vehicle paints
Solvent cleaning	Wiped with turpentine or mineral spirits	Removal of dirt, oil and grease	Oil-base paints
Wire brushing	Wire brushes operated either by hand or mechanically	Removes rust and loose mill scale but will not remove tight scale or rust. Too much wire-brushing gives a polished surface which has poor paint adhesion properties	Natural-drying-oil and resin vehicle paints

Table III. Methods of Surface Preparation of Iron and Steel for Painting

Good surface preparation is essential for good paint adhesion. This table was not custom tailored to historic preservation and includes most methods used by industry and building construction. It is intended as a guide to or listing of the various methods of paint, rust, dirt, and grease removal. Not all of these methods are practical or feasible on metal building components *in situ*, and even if they were, do not produce equal results. Do not select a method without reading the text. Selection of a method is determined by the location of the iron or steel component, the condition of the paint layer (if any), the amount of corrosion, the surrounding materials, type of exposure, convenience and cost of operation. Many of these methods are hazardous or dangerous and should be undertaken only with proper precautions and equipment both of which are not enumerated here because of a lack of space. For example, when sandblasting, care should be taken to protect the surfaces of the surrounding materials and the health and safety of the workers. Physical characteristics of the surface to be cleaned may eliminate certain methods, for example, cast iron and wrought iron can be sandblasted but sheet iron usually cannot. (From *Materials for Architecture: An Encyclopedia Guide* by C. Hornbostel, Copyrighted 1961 by Litten Educational Publishing, Inc. Reprinted by permission of Van Nostrand Reinhold Company, p. 357.)

Table IV. Types of Paint Used for Painting Metal

Type of Paint	Surface Preparation and Pretreatment	Priming Coat *	Intermediate Coat * (Undercoat)	Finish Coat	Major Use on Iron and Steel
Alkyd vehicle	"Commercial" blast cleaning, pickling, flame cleaning, no pretreatment required	Red-lead alkyd varnish primer*	Same as priming coat except tinted with carbon black or lamp black to a contrasting color (in relation to priming coat)*	Aluminum alkyd, black alkyd, white or tinted alkyd paint	For the exterior exposed to severe weather conditions; for the interior where mild chemical exposure, high humidity and infrequent condensation exist
Coal-tar	Blast cleaning to white metal; surface to be cleaned and prime coat immediately applied	Coal-tar enamel primer applied hot	None	Coal-tar enamel applied hot	For the exterior where iron and steel are to be installed underground or in and under water
		Coal-tar enamel	Coal-tar paint	Coal-tar paint	Same as coal-tar enamel except not as good for foundations in and under water
Oil-base vehicle	Solvent cleaning, wire brushing; no pretreatment necessary	Red-lead oil-base primer*	Same as priming coat except tinted with carbon black or lamp black to a contrasting color (in relation to coat)*	Aluminum varnish or black, white or tinted oil-base paint	For the exterior exposed to normal weather conditions; for the interior where moderately corrosive conditions exist
Phenolic vehicle	"Commercial" blast cleaning; pickling, flame cleaning; no pretreatment necessary	Red-lead mixed-pigment phenolic varnish primer *		Aluminum phenolic, black phenolic, white or tinted phenolic paint	For the exterior where iron or steel is immersed in fresh water or exposed to high humidity and condensation; for the interior only where conditions are the same as the exterior
Vinyl vehicle	"Commercial" blast cleaning, pickling; after cleaning surface to be pretreated with basic zinc chromate vinyl butyral washcoat	Vinyl red-lead primer*	Same as priming coat except tinted with lamp black to a contrasting color*	Aluminum vinyl, black vinyl, or vinyl-alkyd paint in white, black, red, yellow or orange	For the exterior where iron or steel is immersed in salt or fresh water or exposed to high humidity and condensation; for the interior where flame resistance, mildew resistance, corrosion resistance and easy maintenance are necessary

Table IV. Types of Paint Used for Painting Metal

The table lists each basic type of paint to be used on metals, the surface preparation, primer, undercoat, finish coat, and major use on iron and steel. It was intended for use on new construction. The preparation and layers of paint may have to be modified to meet existing conditions. The primer, undercoat, and finish coat of paint should be purchased from the same company to insure their compatibility. The intermediate coat can be the same as the finish coat but tinted to a contrasting color, (From *Materials for Architecture: An Encyclopedic Guide* by Hornbostel, Copyrighted 1961 by Litton Educational Publishing, Inc. Reprinted by permission of Van Nostrand Reinhold Company, p. 356)

*Note: Although red lead makes an excellent primer for metals, paints that contain lead are prohibited in most areas of the United States, except for some commercial and industrial purposes. Iron-oxide and zinc rich primers have very good properties for protecting metals and are commonly available for most paint formulations. See text of chapter for a more thorough discussion of paints.

Figure 165. Sequence of Dismantling. *Once the bolts and screws have been located, the parts can be numbered. The numbers on the photograph indicate to the contractor the order of disassembling the cast-iron facade, which is the reverse order of its original erection. (Steven T. Baird, AIA)*

not protect the metal as long.[113] Alkyd rust-inhibitive primers contain pigments such as iron oxide, zinc oxide, and zinc phosphate. These primers are suitable for previously painted surfaces cleaned by hand tools. At least two coats of primer should be applied, followed by alkyd enamel finish coats.

Latex and other water-based paints are not recommended for use as primers on iron or steel because they cause immediate oxidation if applied on bare metal. Vinyl acrylic latex or acrylic latex paints may be used as finish coats over alkyd rust-inhibitive primers, but if the primer coats are imperfectly applied or are damaged, the latex paint will cause oxidation of the iron or steel. Therefore, alkyd finish coats are recommended.

High-performance coatings, such as zinc-rich primers containing zinc dust, and modern epoxy coatings, can be used on iron or steel to provide longer-lasting protection. These coatings typically require highly clean surfaces and special application conditions which can be difficult to achieve in the field on large buildings.

One particularly effective system has been to coat commercially blast-cleaned iron with a zinc-rich primer, followed by an epoxy base coat, and two urethane finish coats. Some epoxy coatings can be used as primers on clean metal, especially those that are zinc rich, or applied to previously painted surfaces in sound condition.

Epoxies are particularly susceptible to degradation under ultraviolet radiation and must be protected by finish coats which are more resistant. There have been problems with epoxy paints which have been shop-applied to iron or steel where the coatings have been nicked prior to installation. Field touching-up of epoxy paints is very difficult, if not impossible. This is a concern since iron exposed by imperfections in the base coat will be more likely to rust and more frequent maintenance will be required.

A key factor to take into account in selection of coatings is the variety of conditions on existing and new materials on a particular building or structure. One primer may be needed for surfaces with existing paint; another required for newly cast, chemically stripped, or blast-cleaned iron or steel; and a third suitable for flashings or substitute materials—each surface primer followed by a compatible finish coat.

Application Methods

Brushing is the traditional and most effective technique for applying paint to cast iron. It provides good contact between the paint and the metal, as well as the effective filling of pits, cracks, and other blemishes in the metal. The use of spray guns to apply paint is economical, but does not always produce adequate and uniform coverage. For best results, airless sprayers should be used by skilled operators. To fully cover fine detailing and reach recesses, spraying of the primer coat, used in conjunction with brushing, may be effective.

Rollers should never be used for primer coat applications on metal, and are effective for subsequent coats only on large, flat areas. The appearance of spray-applied and roller-applied finish coats is not historically appropriate and should be avoided on areas such as storefronts which are viewed at close range.

A number of types of paints used for iron and steel and their recommended uses are indicated in table IV. In addition to these paints, flaky or micaceous iron ore and aluminum provide a satisfactory coating, using an oil vehicle, without a priming coat.[114] Tar and bitumen paints are used for protecting iron and steel installed underground or underwater. However, these paints can break down when exposed to sunlight because they tend to flow in the summer heat and crack from the winter cold. When used, they usually are coated with a flaky aluminum paint.

Oils, greases, and waxes, reapplied at periodic intervals, have been widely used for the preservation of iron and steel in interior locations and in museums. Waxes may be used to protect the surfaces of some interior architectural elements such as chandeliers, cranes, firebacks, stoves, hardware, doors, and elevators. Some industrial ironwork was never painted because heat prevented rust and now need protection (figure 163).

Plating and Glazing is a common protective measure for iron and steel. The most common protective metals used for plating are lead, tin, and terne, zinc, nickel and Monel (see the appropriate sections for detailed information). Chromium aluminum, and cadmium are also used for plating.

Various plastics, applied by either brushing, dipping, spraying, or cladding, have been used recently for protecting steel.[115] Subsequent reduction in corrosion is dependent on the properties of the plastic, its adherence to the metal, and its porosity. Polyvinyl chloride (PVC) and epoxy resins are now applied under factory conditions to sheet steel; extruded PVC may be applied to steel window frames and pipes; and Neoprene (polymerized chloroprene) and Hypalon (a chloro-sulphanated polyethylene) are also used to protect steel architectural components.

Cast or sprayed concrete is another protective coating used on steel architectural components. This kind of protection has very limited use in the restoration of historic structures, but may be necessary to improve the fire rating of iron and steel structural members in rehabilitation of historic buildings. Under certain building codes, plaster on metal lath, sprayed plaster, or fire-rated drywall will also provide the required fire rating.

A continuous, inorganic glaze of vitreous enamel, which is highly resistance to corrosion, can be applied to steel.[116] Corrosion resistance, especially to acids, can be increased by adding silica and titania; however, this type of coating must be applied under controlled, factory conditions. If the coating is chipped, it is no longer effective in protecting the steel. Like the use of concrete, this technique has limited use in the preservation of historic iron and steel structures which previously were not protected by such coatings.

Repair techniques for iron and steel are numerous. The worst enemy of iron and steel is water and the best protection is often caulking and painting. Just as a small chip or scratch in the paint on an automobile will allow rust to form and then progress under the paint, any break in the paint layer has the potential for serious damage. Information on the removal of rust and old paint and the priming and repainting of iron and steel has been given in the previous section.

Figure 166. Damaged Cast Iron. *This cast-iron perforated stoop in the 700 block of I Street, NW, in Washington, D.C., has fractured in several places because of differential settlement. As the right side of the stairs sank into the ground, the weight of the stoop was redistributed and induced shear, tensile, and torsion forces that were too great for the cast iron to resist. Differential settlement can also be caused by the upward and outward growth of a tree adjacent to a stoop and the downward settlement of a dead tree stump as it decays. No patching or repair work will be effective until the problem is corrected. The stoop should be disassembled and a new concrete foundation poured; the stoop can then be reassembled using welded fractured pieces and recast missing pieces. (David W. Look)*

Figure 167. Welding Cast Iron. *Although cast iron is very difficult to weld, it can be done by a skilled welder. This is a detail of a weld on the cast-iron fence at the Gardiner-Pingree House in Salem, Massachusetts. "Ni-Rods" welding electrodes, made with a nickel alloy, have been used to weld cast iron since 1947. This weld should have been ground down after completion. (Lee H. Nelson)*

Most architectural cast iron is made of many small castings assembled by bolts or screws (figure 165). Joints between pieces were caulked to prevent water from seeping in and causing rusting from the inside out. Historically, the seams were often caulked with white lead paste and sometimes backed with cotton or hemp rope; even the bolt and screw heads were caulked to protect them from the elements and to hide them from view. Although old caulking is sometimes found in good condition, it is typically crumbly from weathering, cracked from the structural settlement, or destroyed by mechanical cleaning (figure 164). It is essential to replace deteriorated caulking to prevent water penetration. For good adhesion and performance, an architectural-grade polyurethane sealant is preferred.

Water that penetrates the hollow parts of a cast-iron architectural element causes rust that may streak down over other architectural elements. The water may freeze, causing the ice to crack the cast iron. Cracks reduce the strength of the total cast-iron assembly and provide another point of entry for water. Thus, it is important that cracks be made weathertight by using caulks or fillers, depending on the width of the crack.

Filler compounds containing iron particles in an epoxy resin binder can be used to patch superficial, non-structural cracks and small defects in cast iron. The thermal expansion rate of epoxy resin alone is different from that of iron, requiring the addition of iron particles to ensure compatibility and to control shrinkage. Although the repaired piece of metal does not have the same strength as a homogeneous piece of iron, epoxy-repaired members do have some strength. Polyester-based putties, such as those used on auto bodies, are also acceptable fillers for small holes.[117]

In rare instances, major cracks can be repaired by brazing or welding with special nickel-alloy welding rods (figure 164).[118] Brazing or welding of cast iron is very difficult to carry out in the field and should be undertaken only by very experienced welders.

In some cases, mechanical repairs can be made to cast iron using iron bars and screws or bolts. In extreme cases, deteriorated cast iron can be cut out and new cast iron spliced in place by welding or brazing. However, it is frequently less expensive to replace a deteriorated cast-iron section with a new casting rather than to splice or reinforce it. Cast-iron structural elements that have failed must either be reinforced with iron and steel or replaced entirely.

A wobbly cast-iron balustrade or railing can often be fixed by tightening all bolts and screws. Screws with

Figure 168. Dismantled Cast-Iron Facade. *The Edgar Laing Stores in New York City were erected by James Bogardus in 1849 and had one of the earliest cast-iron facades. The building was demolished in 1971 for an urban renewal project, but its cast-iron facade was carefully dismantled so it could be reerected on another site at a later date. Unfortunately, while the components were in storage, most of them were stolen and apparently sold for scrap. Dismantling of a building should be considered a measure of last resort, to be attempted after all other efforts to save a building in situ have failed. (Jack E. Boucher)*

Figure 169. Wooden Patterns. *These patterns carved from white pine are inspected, and, if approved, sent to the foundry for making sand molds required for the individual castings. The patterns are made proportionally larger to compensate for the shrinkage of the casting. The percentage of shrinkage is different for cast iron, aluminum, fiberglass, et cetera; therefore, the material of the final casting must be determined before the pattern is carved. (Walter Smalling, Jr.)*

Figure 170. Plastic Patterns. *Historically, most patterns for casting iron were carved from wood and pressed into sand to form molds. For the recasting of the iron shutters of the West Virginia Independence Hall, an attempt to use plastic patterns met with only limited success. How the original shutters, with their deeply undercut, beaded molding were cast in one piece is not known. To achieve the same effect in the restoration, the beaded molding of iron had to be cast separately and applied to the replicas. The patterns are mounted on plywood to give them enough rigidity so they may be hammered into the sand to form the molds. (West Virginia Independence Hall Foundation)*

stripped threads and seriously rusted bolts must be replaced. To compensate for corroded metal around the bolt or screw holes, new stainless steel bolts or screws with a larger diameter need to be used. In extreme cases, new holes may need to be tapped.

The internal voids of balusters, newel posts, statuary, and other elements should not be filled with concrete;[119] it is an inappropriate treatment that causes further problems (figure 143). As the concrete cures, it shrinks, leaving a space between the concrete and cast iron. Water penetrating this space does not evaporate quickly, thus promoting further rusting. The corrosion of the iron is further accelerated by the alkaline nature of concrete. Where cast-iron elements have been previously filled with concrete, they need to be taken apart, the concrete and rust removed, and the interior surfaces primed and painted before the elements are reassembled.

Dismantling and Assembly of Architectural Components

It is sometimes necessary to dismantle all or part of a cast-iron structure during restoration, if repairs cannot be successfully carried out in place. Dismantling should be done only under the direction of a preservation architect or architectural conservator who is experienced with historic cast iron. Extreme care must be taken since cast iron is very brittle, especially in cold weather. If this work has to be carried out in the winter, care should be taken to avoid fracturing the cast-iron structural elements by uneven heating of the members.

Dismantling should follow the reverse order of construction and re-erection should occur, as much as possible, in the exact order of original assembly. Each piece should be numbered and keyed to record drawings.

When work must be carried out in cold weather, care needs to be taken to avoid fracturing the iron elements by uneven heating of the members.

Both new castings and reused pieces should be painted with a shop-applied prime coat on all surfaces. All of the components should be laid out and pre-assembled to make sure that the alignment and fit are proper. Many of the original bolts, nuts, and screws may have to be replaced with similar fasteners of stainless steel.

After assembly at the site, joints that were historically caulked should be filled with an architectural-grade polyurethane sealant. Although the traditionally used white lead paste has the advantage of longevity, it is restricted in many areas.

The Laing Stores in New York City (figure 168) were dismantled in a last-ditch preservation effort. The connecting nuts and bolts were corroded and had to be burned off with a torch. If this work has to be carried out in the winter, care should be taken to avoid fracturing the cast-iron structural elements by uneven heating

Figure 172. Casting Iron. *Molten iron is being poured into the sand molds. For open molds, the molten iron is just poured in from the open top. For closed molds, tunnels (called "sprues") are carved out of the wet sand to allow the molten metal to flow in and "risers" allow the air to escape. Once the casting has cooled to room temperature, the sand is removed from around the casting. The sprues and risers are cut off and any remaining irregularities or ragged edges (called "burrs") are ground smooth. (Walter Smalling, Jr.)*

Figure 171. Sand Mold. *The pattern has been pressed or hammered into the sand to form an impression or mold. Special casting flasks or boxes are used to hold the sand. Only one flask or box is required for an open mold which produces a casting with a flat top. To cast a piece with relief on both top and bottom requires two flasks stacked and bolted together. (Steven T. Baird)*

Figure 173. Preassembly of Cast-Iron Components. *Before the cast-iron pieces are shipped from the foundry to the job site, the components are laid out and preassembled to insure proper fit. If the parts do not fit because of burrs, the pieces are machined to remove irregularities. If the parts still do not fit, the rejected parts are recast until all of the castings fit together. Some small ornamental parts may be left together, but most of the larger pieces are disassembled before shipping. All of the castings shown were necessary to produce a Corinthian pilaster. (Walter Smalling, Jr.)*

of the members. The disassembled cast-iron facade was stored in a secure, dry shelter where the pieces could not be stolen or allowed to deteriorate.[120]

Duplication and Replacement

The replacement of cast-iron components is often the only practical solution when such features are missing, severely corroded, or damaged beyond repair, or where repairs would be only marginally useful in extending the functional life of an iron element. Sometimes it is possible to replace small, decorative, non-structural elements using intact sections of the original as a casting pattern. For large sections, new patterns of wood or plastic made slightly larger in size than the original will need to be made in order to compensate for the shrinkage of the iron during casting (cast iron shrinks approximately 1/8 inch per foot as it cools from a liquid to a solid)[121] (figure 169).

Occasionally, a matching replacement can be obtained through the existing catalogs of iron foundries. Small elements can be custom cast in iron at small local foundries, often at a cost comparable to substitute materials. Large elements and complex patterns will usually require the skills and facilities of a large firm that specializes in replication.

The Casting Process

Architectural elements were traditionally cast in sand molds (figure 171). The quality of the special sands used by foundries is extremely important; unlike most sands, they must be moist. Foundries have their own formulas for sand and its admixtures, such as clay, which makes the sand cohesive even when the mold is turned upside down.

A two-part mold (with a top and a bottom, or cope and drag) is used for making a casting with relief on both sides, whereas an open-top mold produces a flat surface on one side. For hollow elements, a third pattern and mold are required for the void. Because of the difficulty of supporting an interior core between the top and bottom sand molds during the casting process, many hollow castings are made of two or more parts that are later bolted, screwed, or welded together.

The molding sand is compacted into flasks, or forms, around the pattern. The cope is then lifted off and the pattern is removed, leaving the imprint of the pattern in the small mold. Molten iron, heated to a temperature of approximately 2700 degrees Fahrenheit, is pouted into the mold and then allowed to cool (figure 172). The molds are then stripped from the casting; the tunnels to the mold (sprues) and risers that allowed release of air are cut off; and ragged edges (called "burrs") on the casting are ground smooth.

The castings are shop-primed to prevent rust, and laid out and preassembled at the foundry to ensure proper alignment and fit (figure 173). When parts do not fit, the pieces are machined to remove irregularities caused by burrs, or are rejected and recast until all of the cast elements fit together properly. Most larger pieces then are taken apart before shipping to the job site, while some small ornamental parts may be left assembled.

Figure 174. Erection of Cast-Iron Facade. *To assemble the Main Street shop facade of the Wilmington Grand Opera House, many assembled sections and individual pieces were shipped to the job site where they were screwed and bolted together in their final positions. (Steven T. Baird)*

Figure 175. Drilling Holes. *Originally, screw and bolt holes were cast into the pieces of iron for new ironwork; however, for the restoration of existing cast-iron facades which may have settled over the years, the holes are sometimes drilled into the replacement parts at the job site to insure correct alignment. (Walter Smalling, Jr.)*

In addition to traditional wooden patterns, cast plastic patterns are now being tried. Like ice, which expands as it freezes, some plastics do not shrink when cast, but actually expand while setting (figure 170). This expansion can be used to compensate for later shrinkage of the cast iron or aluminum, but the amount of expansion plastic must be carefully matched to the amount of shrinkage of the cast metal in order for this to be effective.

At the job site, the components are erected piece by piece (figure 174) and bolted or screwed together through holes cast in the parts. The new elements should be connected in the same manner as the original components. Bolt holes were originally cast into the pieces to aid trial assembly in the shop and final erection at the job site. With a new building most of the bolt holes will line up; however, with an old building that has settled, the bolt holes may not line up and minor adjustments may be necessary. Thus, in recasting missing or damaged pieces, bolt holes are not always cast into the pieces, but are often drilled on the job site to insure proper alignment (figure 175).

Substitute Materials

In recent years, a number of metallic and non-metallic materials have been used as substitutes for cast iron, although they were not used historically with cast iron. The most common have been cast aluminum, epoxies, reinforced polyester (fiberglass), and glass fiber-reinforced concrete (GFRC). Factors to consider in using substitute materials are addressed in the National Park Service's **Preservation Briefs 16, The Use of Substitute Materials on Historic Building Exteriors,** which emphasizes that "every means of repairing deteriorating historic materials or replacing them with identical materials should be examined before turning to substitute materials."

Cast aluminum has been used recently as a substitute for cast iron, particularly for ornately detailed decorative elements (figure 178). Aluminum is lighter in

weight, more resistant to corrosion, and less brittle than cast iron. However, because it is dissimilar from iron, its placement in contact with or near cast iron may result in galvanic corrosion, and thus should be avoided. Special care must be taken in the application of paint coatings, particularly in the field. it is often difficult to achieve a

Figure 177. Reinforced Polyester Replica. *The original cross of St. Agnes Church, Cohoes, New York, was removed from the steeple in the 1890s to serve as a grave marker. The original wrought-iron steeple cross, still intact, was used as a model to cast a new cross of reinforced (fiberglass) polyester. Fiberglass was chosen as a substitute material because of the inaccessible location (top of the steeple) where maintaining wrought iron (painting) would be difficult and expensive and because from the street level no one would be able to detect the substitute materials. (John G. Waite)*

Figure 176. Aluminum Reproduction. *Cast aluminum is less brittle than cast iron and more impact resistant; therefore, it is more capable of resisting vandals or souvenir hunters. On the iron fence around the Treasury Building in Washington, D.C., the missing cast-iron spear tips were replaced with cast aluminum. Unfortunately, the paint adhesion has failed and the bare aluminum is visible. (John Myers)*

durable coating after the original finish has failed. Because aluminum is weaker than iron, careful analysis is required whenever aluminum is being considered as a replacement material for structural cast-iron elements.

Epoxies are two-part, thermo-setting, resinous materials which can be molded into virtually any form. When molded, the epoxy is usually mixed with fillers such as sand, glass balloons, or stone chips. When mixed with sand or stone, it is often termed epoxy concrete or polymer concrete, a misnomer because no cementitious materials are included. Epoxies are particularly effective for replicating small, ornamental sections of cast iron. Since it is not a metal, galvanic corrosion does not occur. Epoxy elements must have a protective coating to shield them form ultraviolet degradation. They are also flammable and cannot be used as substitutes for structural cast-iron elements.

Reinforced polyester, commonly known as **fiberglass,** is often used as a lightweight substitute for historic materials, including cast iron, wood, and stone. In its most common form, fiberglass is a thin, rigid, laminate shell formed by pouring a polyester resin into a mold and then adding fiberglass for reinforcement. Like epoxies, fiberglass is non-corrosive, but is susceptible to ultraviolet degradation. Because of its rather flimsy nature, it cannot be used as substitute for structural elements, cannot be assembled like cast iron, and usually requires a separate anchorage system. It is unsuitable for locations where it is susceptible to damage by impact, and is also flammable.

Glass fiber-reinforced concrete, known as **GFRC,** is similar to fiberglass except that a lightweight concrete is substituted for the resin. GFRC elements are generally fabricated as thin shell panels by spraying concrete into forms. Usually a separate framing and anchorage system is required. GFRC elements are lightweight, inexpensive, and weather resistant. Because GFRC has a low shrinkage co-efficient, molds can be made directly from

Figure 178. Aluminum Replacement of Minor Structural Elements of a Facade. *For minor structural members without great loads, aluminum can be used as a substitute material; however, the capacity of a cast-aluminum column must be designed or checked by a structural engineer and not just assumed to be adequate. When the Grand Opera House in Wilmington, Delaware, was restored, missing cast-iron columns on the first-floor storefronts (flanking center bay entrance, lower center of photograph) were cast in aluminum to match the missing pieces of the original cast iron. (John G. Waite)*

Figure 179. *Use of Both Cast Aluminum and Fiberglass as Substitute Materials. After the Mansard roof and dormers of the Wilmington Grand Opera House were destroyed by fire the top floor was rebuilt, but not according to the original design. During restoration of the facade, photographs showing the original Mansard roof and dormers were found, which enabled the re-creation of the missing parts of the facade. The oval windows were cast in aluminum; but the moldings and trim, which may have originally been sheet iron, were made of reinforced polyester. (Walter Smalling, Jr.)*

historic elements. However, GFRC is very different physically and chemically from iron. If used adjacent to iron, it causes corrosion of the iron and will have a different moisture absorption rate. Also, it is not possible to achieve the crisp detail that is characteristic of cast iron.

There are many other techniques for the selective repair and replacement of iron and steel architectural elements. If all or part of the assembly is structural and there is any doubt as to its load carrying capacity, it can be load tested. The safe load capacity reduced by an appropriate safety factor will give the maximum safe live load. If this is not adequate for the proposed use, the design can be reinforced or the use of the building or space revised. Once a building is partially opened up for restoration or rehabilitation work or inspection, it is usually possible to add plates, angles, channels, columns, and beams to strengthen or stiffen the design. It is not unusual to add wind bracing or other modifications to meet new code requirements such as those for seismic design.

The piercing of old iron and steel structural members with holes for new pipes or ducts should be avoided because such changes reduce the integrity of the elements and can help induce failure. Most mechanical improvements have a limited life expectancy because of deterioration and obsolescence; therefore, changes to accommodate mechanical equipment should be reversible. Because iron and steel produced in the 19th century had little quality control, the metal was seldom homogeneous and frequently contained faults. A hole in a member forces the load to be redistributed around the hole. This may throw the stresses onto a weaker area, which is inadequate to carry the load.

Stainless Steel

To prevent corrosion (figure 180), stainless steel architectural elements should be washed regularly with warm water and a mild detergent to prevent the accumulation of dirt and other pollutants which can cause corrosion through creation of galvanic cells. Any encrustation of grime and dirt or stains can usually be removed with a commercial stainless steel cleaner. Although deterioration of stainless steel is seldom encountered, it may be physically damaged and require repairs, patching or replacement. Care should be taken to match the composition and finish of the original material with the replacement. If cast stainless steel is replaced, patterns must be made larger to allow for shrinkage which is 9/32 inch per foot.

Figure 180. Corrosion and Pitting of Stainless Steel. *Although stainless steel was originally believed to be totally corrosion resistant, some types can corrode under certain conditions where the atmosphere is highly polluted. These stainless steel gates at the Federal Trade Commission in Washington, D.C. (see figure 108), have probably never been washed since they were hung and recessed into the facade of the building to protect them from the washing effect of rain. Under each bump of white corrosion, the surface of the metal is pitted. Dirt on the surface of stainless steel encourages corrosion at that particular location because the dirt holds moisture next to it. These doors should be cleaned with water and a non-ionic detergent and polished with a soft clean cloth and pumice powder. The gates should then be washed annually to remove surface dirt and wiped dry to avoid spotting. Corroded stainless steel may look like aluminum; in fact, these gates were recently described as aluminum in photographs in an exhibition on the Federal Triangle at the National Collection of Fine Arts Museum. Chemical tests were necessary to determine if the gates were indeed stainless steel as stated in the original specifications. (David W. Look)*

Chapter 18: Aluminum; Preservation and Repair

Identification

Aluminum is light in weight—about one-half that of iron, copper, or brass. It is nonmagnetic and highly resistant to most environmentally caused corrosion, and has a melting point of 660°C, a moderately high coefficient of expansion, and a thermal and electrical conductivity surpassed only by silver and copper.[122] Aluminum is easily worked by most metal fabrication methods. In its purest form, it is very soft with a ductility comparable to that of lead.[123]

A number of aluminum alloys have been developed to improve certain properties. Nonheat-treatable alloys, which include 1 1/4% manganese and 2 to 7% magnesium, are of relatively high strength and are used for corrugated roofing and cladding.[124] Heat-treatable alloys contain varying proportions of aluminum, magnesium, silicon, and sometimes copper.[125] They have high strength and are therefore used for fasteners and for light structural members. The increased strength is obtained by a carefully controlled process of heat treatment. Aluminum alloys used for casting usually contain silicon, silicon and copper, or silicon and magnesium.[126]

Aluminum found in historic buildings may have a variety of surface treatments or finishes: nonfinished, anodized, chemical conversion coatings, painted (or lacquered), plated, porcelain enameled, or laminated.

"Nonfinished" is the term used for a bare aluminum surface with only its natural oxide patina which forms almost instantaneously upon exposure to air.[127] This film is thin, transparent, tough, tenacious, and to a great extent protective. Generally this type of bare finish is used on interior or exterior architectural elements where appearance is of no consequence; however, on historic buildings (1920-1950), the nonfinish is the most common type of finish used both indoors and outdoors. Although it is called a nonfinish, bare aluminum may have a variety of textures: it may be smooth, highly polished, or brushed; or it may be in a pattern formed by casting, extruding, or machining.

Anodized finishes are extra-thick (from 0.05 to over 1.5 mils) oxide films produced by electrochemical treatment.[128] This treatment is accomplished in an acid bath by passing an electrical current through the aluminum. The thickness of the anodized coating depends on the current and duration of the treatment. Quality of the anodized coating depends upon the temperature of the acid bath: the higher the temperature of the liquid, the lower the quality of the coating. Since the electric current raises the temperature, the best quality of anodized aluminum is accomplished by refrigerating the liquid. The anodic coating can be transparent or integrally colored by adding pigments or dyes before it is sealed. Red, blue, and green aluminum produced with dyes in the 1950s have faded, often in a nonuniform manner, causing a blotched appearance. The gold, brown, grey, and black pigments used were more stable and have retained their original color. Today colored coatings are produced by varying the alloy content, which results in color on the surface (only) during the anodizing process. Any working of the metal and any texturing of the surface must be applied to the aluminum before anodizing. The anodized coating must be protected during the shipping and fabrication to avoid damage.

Chemical conversion coatings, formed by chemical processes only, are thinner and less abrasion resistant than anodic coatings and are often used as shop preparation before painting. When conversion coatings are the final finish (without paint), they may be clear or colored gold, gray, golden brown, green, or blue-green.[129]

Whether clear (lacquer) or pigmented (paint), various types of organic coatings can be applied in the factory over chemical conversion coatings, in the field over mechanically or chemically roughened surfaces, or over a suitable wash primer. This process was occasionally used in the 1930s on aluminum doors, frames, and radiator cabinets to create a wood grain finish.

Plated aluminum is achieved by electrodepositing a metal onto the aluminum surface. Chrome and nickel are the two most common metals to be plated on architectural aluminum. These platings are needed where heavy abrasion is anticipated, such as on stair railings. An intermediate layer of copper may be necessary to achieve a smoother surface or a mirror finish.

Porcelain or vitreous enameled (inorganic) finishes are baked-on ceramic coatings applied in the factory and seldom found in historic buildings.[130] Likewise, laminated finishes are fabricated by bonding wood, cloth, plastic, and so forth, onto the aluminum. Laminated finishes have been introduced only recently. The *Care of Aluminum*, published by the Aluminum Association, Inc., describes how to identify various coatings on aluminum.[131]

Causes of Deterioration

Aluminum is resistant to most types of corrosion, including attack by sulfur compounds such as hydrogen sulfide and sulfur dioxide. It combines readily and quickly with oxygen to form a transparent, tightly adherent film of oxide which is relatively inert to further chemical action. Aluminum also resists attack by other atmospheric gases (figure 181), moisture, and many kinds of soils.

Corrosive agents that actively attack aluminum include alkalis, hydrochloric acid, lead-based paints, certain wood preservatives, and chlorides (figure 182). Wet lime mortar, Portland cement, plaster, and concrete will cause some surface corrosion of aluminum, but once cured, (and no longer alkaline), they have no further corrosive effect. Aluminum is often corroded where it comes into contact with damp, porous brickwork and stonework.[132] Although dry, seasoned lumber does not affect aluminum, unseasoned, damp oak, cedar, and redwood produce acids which attack the metal. Even water draining off a roof of unweathered wood shingles will corrode aluminum flashing. In addition, any wet wood in direct contact with aluminum will corrode it.

Aluminum is damaged by galvanic action caused by electrical contact with some other metals in a common electrolyte, especially copper; however, it does remain stable in the presence of zinc, cadimum, and magnesium.[133] Even though aluminum is generally compatible with nonmagnetic stainless steel, corrosion of the aluminum is still possible when the two metals come into electrical contact with an electrolyte, a condition that is more common in industrial environments.

The corrosion of aluminum roofs is accelerated by condensation when moisture forms on the underside of the membrane, or when water pools on the roof surface. Corrosion galvanic couples are encouraged by pools of standing water, especially where the rainwater is acidic.[134]

Although aluminum is generally corrosion resistant, aluminum roofing is very susceptible to damage by mechanical breakdown. Of the most commonly used roofing materials, aluminum is second only to copper in having a high coefficient of thermal expansion; aluminum roofing will suffer from fatigue caused by thermal expansion and contraction. Another critical problem

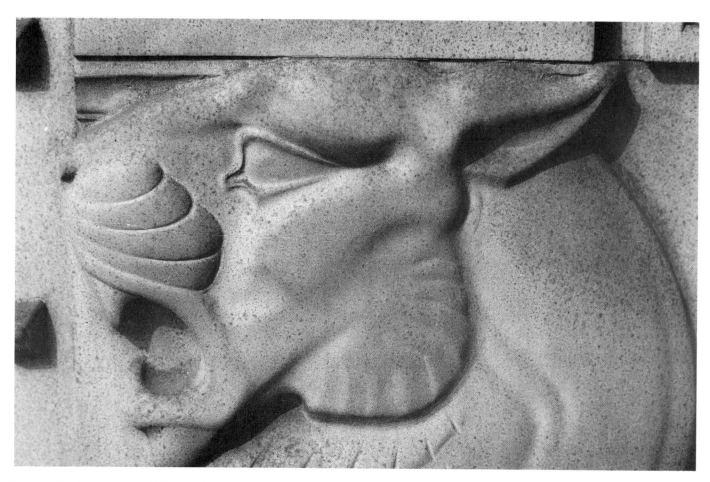

Figure 181. Corrosion and Pitting of Aluminum. *Designed by Carl Paul Jennewein, these cast-aluminum doors on the U.S. Justice Building in Washington, D.C., are pitted (see figure 114). Aluminum corrosion is white; however, surface dirt, grime, and pollution have collected on the corrosion products, forming small dark bumps. The pits are actually beneath the bumps and were formed as surface metal oxidized. Pitting is caused by a difference in potential of two or more points on the surface of the same metal and a local breakdown of the protective oxide film. It is encouraged by foreign particles, such as dirt and chlorides which hold moisture next to the surface. (David W. Look)*

with aluminum is its softness, which results in erosion of the metal as well as the protective patina of aluminum roofs and other exposed elements by abrasive agents.

Human error is another problem in dealing with aluminum. Sometimes the alloy specified for the job is not the best choice for the function or location, or the material used in fabrication is not the alloy specified (figure 183).

Methods of Preservation and Repair

Aluminum architectural elements should be protected by a nonabsorptive, insulative coating to prevent direct contact with corrosive agents. Where aluminum touches masonry, it should be coated with a heavy-bodied bituminous paint, which in turn is covered with two coats of aluminum metal and masonry paint.[135] To protect aluminum from galvanic corrosion caused by contact with other metals, it should be electrolytically insulated by paint, mastics, or other nonconductive materials. To avoid electrolysis, aluminum roofing and flashings should be fastened only with aluminum nails and rivets, and aluminum architectural elements should be pro-

tected from rainwater run-off from copper roofs and gutters. When aluminum is painted for cosmetic reasons and there is no incompatibility with other building materials, it should be primed with zinc chromate and finish coats of compatible paint from the same manufacturer. Aluminum should *not* be painted with copper-containing antifouling paints, because they accelerate corrosion unless at least 4 mils of coating are used under the antifouling paint. This is done frequently on aluminum boats and ships.

Aluminum roofing and wall cladding systems must be carefully designed to accommodate thermal movements and to avoid fatigue damage. If fatigue cracking does occur, there is usually no choice other than to remove the improperly designed section.

Where aluminum elements have been damaged by abrasion or erosion, they can be protected from further damage by coatings of varnish, lacquer, or suitable paint, if the damage is not severe. If the damage is extensive, then the section must be replaced with new metal of a heavier gauge.

The book *Care of Aluminum,* mentioned earlier, discusses five categories of aluminum cleaners: 1) mild

Figure 182. Corrosion and Severe Deterioration of Aluminum. *The corrugated aluminum siding on a commercial building in Green Island, New York, has been severely deteriorated by the splashing of water and snow-melting salts. (John G. Waite)*

soaps and detergents and nonetching cleaners, 2) solvent and emulsion cleaners, 3) abrasive cleaners, 4) etching cleaners, and 5) special heavy-duty cleaners.[136] In cleaning aluminum, the most gentle methods should be tried first. More severe methods should be used only if milder methods are not effective, not just to save time.

Mild soaps and detergents and nonetching cleaners that are gentle enough to be applied with bare hands can be safely used on aluminum without spot testing first. However, some detergents that are too strong to be used with bare hands, such as automatic dishwasher detergents, should always be tested first. Some of these detergents can discolor nonfinished and anodized aluminum and can even bleach painted aluminum.[137]

Nonetching cleaners are acidic or alkaline solutions containing inhibitors that permit the cleaning of the metal without etching. Care should be exercised in their use. All cleaning solutions should be thoroughly rinsed from the surface and wiped dry to avoid water spotting. Although relatively mild, solvent and emulsion cleaners are used for removing dirt and stains that cannot be removed by milder cleaners. They can generally be used on bare, anodized, conversion coatings, and porcelain finished aluminum without spot tests, but product directions should always be followed exactly.[138]

Abrasive cleaners include polishes, cleaners, cleaner-polishes, wax-cleaners, scouring powders, metal brighteners that contain abrasive particles, and may also include water, oil, wax, silicones, soap, acids, or alkali. These cleaners, which depend on vigorous rubbing action along with a chemical reaction, can remove most dirt, stains, and corrosion products from aluminum and will restore most weathered aluminum surfaces.

Care of Aluminum rates abrasive cleaners as moderate and heavy duty. Household cleaners with coarse abrasives should not be used on aluminum, except those with porcelain finishes. Even a very fine abrasive can dull a highly polished aluminum finish. Fine pumice powder and stainless steel wool (grades 0000 to 00) can be used with these cleaners, but regular steel wool may leave rust stains.[139]

Etching cleaners remove metal and can be used only on bare aluminum that is highly corroded or stained. Extreme caution should be used. These strong acid and alkali-based cleaners must be rinsed thoroughly and neutralized if necessary. Fine abrasives such as pumice powder and fine stainless-steel wool may be used with etched cleaners.[140]

Special cleaners are all other cleaners that require special power (other than hand) equipment, such as steam cleaners, rotary wirebrushes, and abrasive blasting.[141]

Decorative aluminum architectural elements (bare, anodized, and conversion coatings) are frequently found with a variety of tooled finishes including an embossed texture, a sandblasted texture, a wirebrushed or satin texture, and a buffed or polished finish. Although the best method of preserving the finish involves the application of a protective coating of varnish or lacquer to prevent dirt and grime from accumulating, it is sometimes necessary to restore the surfaces. For nonfinished or bare aluminum, the sandblasted surface can be restored by a light sandblasting; the wirebrushed surface

Figure 183. Exfoliation Deterioration. *In Washington, D.C., at the Folger Shakespeare Library designed in 1932 by Paul Phillippe Cret, the aluminum alloy balcony railing began to exfoliate in layers, similar to rusting wrought iron. The corrosion product was grayish white and lifted up from the surface as if the metal had exploded. All of the cast ornamental sections were in relatively good condition; only the straight, bar stock was affected. The original specifications stated that the railing was to be an aluminum and chromium alloy. However, a recent laboratory report analyzed a four inch section cut from a sound piece of metal next to a corroded area and indicated that it was high-copper alloy (structural aluminum) fitting into the category of alloy 2017, which is not recommended for exposed outdoor use since it is not corrosion resistant. It is amazing that it lasted 47 years outdoors. All of the straight bar stock of the railing should be replaced with alloy 6063. The cast ornament could be cleaned and reused since they are obviously of more corrosion-resistant alloy and show no signs of deterioration. (David W. Look)*

is restored by hand brushing with a finishing compound of ground pumice and water; and the buffed surface is restored by hand rubbing with pumice.[142] An anodized or conversion coating will be damaged by any of these methods. The repair and refinishing of these and other special finishes can only be done under factory conditions.

Bare finishes, anodized finishes, or conversion coatings should be protected by a coating of varnish or wax because there is usually no inexpensive way to restore a damaged anodized coating other than factory refinishing.[143] However, a portable hand-held anodizer was recently developed for the space program. Anodized aluminum elements should be washed at regular intervals to prevent the accumulation of dirt particles and other pollutants. If allowed to accumulate on the surface, dirt and grime will eventually break down the anodized coating.

Although not recommended for all repairs, the following techniques can be used to join aluminum elements: oxy-gas or acetylene welding, brazing, resistance welding, inert-gas-shielded arc processes, adhesive bonding, bolting, and riveting.[144]

Although welding is not difficult under field conditions, replacement is usually the most practical solution to the problem of a damaged structural architectural element or sheathing. Solder (a lead and tin mixture) should never be used for repairing a damaged aluminum roof because of potential galvanic action between the solder and aluminum. Aluminum roofing should be applied with riveted or other mechanical, nonsoldered and nonwelded connections.

Conclusion

This report, initially published in 1980, is intended to provide updated guidance in the identification, preservation, and maintenance of historic metal building components. The historic preservation movement, begun in the 1960s, has only in recent years seriously utilized scientific conservation technology. As the preservation and reuse of historic buildings increased dramatically in the 1980s and into the last decade of the 20th century, however, some new technologies have become available for treating historic building materials, including metals. In the future, it may be possible to preserve *in situ* even more metal architectural elements that today can be preserved only by treatment in the laboratory. It is still as important as it was in 1980 that, when treating architectural metals, reversible methods be utilized so that the historic components will survive for the future when more effective technology may be available.

Notes

1. Material in this report expands John G. Waite's, "Architectural Metals: Their Deterioration and Stabilization," a lecture for the North American Regional Conference convened by the Rome International Centre Committee for Conservation and the International Centre Committee of the Advisory Council on Historic Preservation in Williamsburg and Philadelphia, September 10-16, 1972, *Preservation and Conservation: Principles and Practices* (Washington, D.C.: Smithsonian Institution Press, and Preservation Press, National Trust for Historic Preservation, 1976) pp. 213-242.

2. Ibid., p. 213.

3. Glenn A. Greathouse and Carl J. Wessel, *Deterioration of Materials: Causes and Preventive Techniques* (New York: Reinhold Publishing Corp., 1954), p. 4.

4. W. D. Hoff; John W. Simpson; and Peter J. Horrobin, eds., *The Weathering and Performance of Building Materials* (New York: Wiley-Interscience, 1970), chapter on "Metals" edited by W. D. Hoff, pp. 186-187. Hereafter cited as "Metals."

5. F. L. LaQue and H. R. Copson, eds., *Corrosion Resistance of Metals and Alloys*, 2d ed. (New York: Reinhold Publishing Corp., 1963), pp. 7-37.

6. *Corrosion in Action* (New York: International Nickel Company, 1977), p. 19, and Jerome Kruger, *Corrosion: Facts for the Consumer* (Washington, D.C.: National Bureau of Standards Consumer Information Series 9, March 1978), p. 1.

7. Ibid., pp. 11-18.

8. American Society for Testing and Materials. *Standard Guide for Development and Use of a Galvanic Series for Predicting Galvanic Corrosion Performance - G82-83* (Philadelphia: ASTM).

9. Corrosion in Action, p. 15.

10. LaQue and Copson, *Corrosion Resistance*, p. 46.

11. W. H. Munse, J. E. Stallmeyer, and F. P. Drew, *Structural Fatigue and Steel Railroad Bridges* (Chicago: American Railway Engineering Association, 1968), p. 2.

12. Greathouse and Wessel, *Deterioration of Materials*, p. 238.

13. Ibid., p. 301.

14. Robert C. McMasters, ed., *Nondestructive Testing Handbook*, Vol. 1 (New York: Ronald Press Co., 1959), sec. 6-8.

15. Greathouse and Wessel, *Deterioration of Materials*, pp. 264-274.

16. Ibid., p. 275.

17. These are other coatings. Ceramic coatings consist of inorganic glasses loaded with refractory or other materials to aid adhesion, decrease brittleness and liability to break off because of differences in temperature coefficients, and to often achieve decorative colors and texture. The use of this kind of corrosion protection for architectural metals which exist *in situ* is not common because the ceramic coating needs to be applied at red heat. See Greathouse and Wessel, *Deterioration of Metals*, pp. 280-286.

18. Ibid., pp. 291-295.

19. Caleb Hornbostel, *Materials for Architecture: An Encyclopedic Guide* (New York: Reinhold Publishing Corp., 1961), p. 287.

20. Lyall Addleson, *Materials for Building*, Vol. 3 (London: Iliffe Books, 1972), p. 69.

21. Hornbostel, *Materials for Architecture*, p. 287.

22. *Lead in Modern Industry: Manufacture, Applications and Properties of Lead, Lead Alloys, and Lead Compounds* (New York: Lead Industries Association, 1952), p. 51.

23. Addleson, *Materials for Building*, p. 69.

24. Ibid., p. 69.

25. Ulick R. Evans, *The Corrosion and Oxidation of Metals: Scientific Principles and Practical Applications* (London: Edward Arnold, Ltd., 1960), p. 518.

26. In the first case the copper nails, the more noble metal, are much smaller than the lead sheets and deterioration of the lead is only slight. In the second case the iron, the baser metal, is much larger than the lead waterproofing and the iron is almost always painted, so the deterioration of the iron is also slight.

27. Jack Bowyer, *History of Building* (London: Crosby Lockwood Staples, 1973), p. 115.

28. Donald W. Insall, *The Care of Old Buildings Today: A Practical Guide* (London: The Architectural Press, 1972), p. 98.

29. Robert M. Organ. "The Corrosion of Tin, Copper, Iron and Steel, and Lead," in *Preservation and Conservation: Principles and Practices* (Washington, D.C.: Smithsonian Institution Press and Preservation Press of the National Trust for Historic Preservation, 1976), p. 254.

30. Hornbostel, *Materials for Architecture*, p. 515.

31. Henry Leidheiser, Jr., *The Corrosion of Copper, Tin, and Their Alloys* (New York: John Wiley and Sons, Inc.), p. 326.

32. Hornbostel, *Materials for Architecture*, p. 515.

33. A formula for the traditional "tinner's red" paint is 10 pounds of Venetian red, 1 pound red lead to 1 gallon of pure linseed oil; Frank E. Kidder and Henry Parker, *Kidder-Parker Architects' and Builders' Handbook*, 18th ed. (New York: John Wiley & Sons, Inc., 1956). p. 2001.

34. Revere Copper and Brass, Inc. *Examination of Corroded Lead Coated Copper Sheet: Austin-Hastings Company Incorporated, Cambridge, Massachusetts* (Rome, New York: Revere Copper and Brass Inc., Research and Development Center, 1964), p. 3.
  "Due to the extremely small solubility of lead in copper, it is difficult to wet a copper surface with molten lead in applying a lead coat. To promote the wetting process, a few percent tin, soluble in both copper and lead, is added to the lead bath. The final product may then be considered as a three-layered composite consisting of the copper substrate, a copper-tin alloy layer, and the lead coat.
  "Pinholes or voids in the coat as produced, dross inclusions in the coat, or abnormal corrosion of the coat all tend to expose the copper-tin alloy layer and the copper substrate to the corrodent. This condition may give rise to a galvanic corrosion all with the copper becoming anodic to the copper-tin alloy, resulting in accelerated pitting of the copper.
  "This particular situation is somewhat aggravated in that the metal is exposed in a horizontal position. This allows rain water and condensed moisture, the electrolytes, to pool in the low spots and remain on the surface for periods much longer than those normally encountered on a pitched roof."

35. Hornbostel, *Materials for Architecture*, p. 592.

36. Ibid.

37. Ibid., p. 596.

38. Ibid.

39. Ian A. Melville and Ian A. Gordon, *The Repair and Maintenance of Houses* (London: The Estates Gazette Limited, 1973), p. 534.

40. Ian A. Melville, Ian A. Gordon, and Peter Scott, *Structural Surveys of Dwelling Houses* (London: The Estate Gazette Limited, 1964), p. 29.

41. Hoff, "Metals," p. 206.

42. The discoloration caused by white storage stain or white rust can be avoided by dipping the sheets in dilute hydrochloric acid (remembering the zinc will dissolve in it), rinsing, and then dipping in a solution of dichromate, after which final rinsing and drying are necessary. Ibid., p. 208; and Hornbostel, *Materials for Architecture*, p. 596.

43. Evans, *The Corrosion and Oxidation of Metals*, pp. 586-587.

44. Hornbostel, *Material for Architecture*, p. 177.

45. Ibid., p. 105. This page contains additional information regarding the various types of brasses and their compositions.

46. Ibid., p. 91.

47. Ibid.

48. Ibid., pp. 91-92. These pages contain additional information regarding the various types of brasses and their compositions.

49. In the past, it was generally believed that the patina was basic copper carbonate but research in the 1930s determined that it was basic copper sulfate. See Donald H. Osburn and John M. Fochlich, "Coloring and Finishing of Copper Metals," *Construction Specifier* (October 1963), pp. 50-55.

50. Organ, "The Corrosion of Tin, Copper, Iron and Steel, and Lead." p. 248. Acetates are salts or esters of acetic acid (found in vinegar and some other organic acids).

51. Ibid., p. 247.

52. H. J. Plenderleith and A. E. A. Werner, *The Conservation of Antiquities and Works of Art: Treatment, Repair, and Restoration,* 2nd ed. (New York: Oxford Press, 1971), pp. 246-250.

53. Hornbostel, *Materials for Architecture*, pp. 91-92.

54. *Kidder-Parker Architects' and Builders' Handbook*, p. 2018.

55. Joseph F. Long, P.E. Manager, Tin Research Institute, Inc., Columbus, Ohio, to John G. Waite, 23 June, 1972.

56. *Copper and Common Sense, Design Principles and Techniques of Sheet Copper Construction*, 6th ed. (New York: Revere Copper and Brass, Inc., 1961), p. 32.

57. *Kidder-Parker Architect's and Builders' Handbook*, p. 2018.

58. Harold L. Peterson, "Conservation of Metals," *History News* 23 (no. 2, Feb. 1968): p. 6.

59. Organ, "The Corrosion of Tin, Copper, Iron and Steel, and Lead," p. 249.

60. *Copper, Brass, Bronze Design Handbook: Architectural Applications* (New York: Copper Development Association, Inc., n.d.), p. 31.

61. Hornbostel, *Materials for Architecture*, p. 330.

62. Ibid., p. 333.

63. Ibid., p. 334.

64. Hard and soft solders are general terms that usually refer to temperature. Soft solders are all soldering alloys that melt below 840°F. and are usually composed of varying proportions of lead and tin. Hard solders are all soldering alloys that melt above 840°F. and are usually silver solders which contain varying percentages of silver, copper, tin, cadmium, nickel, and other metals, but never lead. Hard soldering is the same as brazing. The brazing filler metal (soldering alloy) has a melting point below the melting point of the metal pieces being joined. If the metal pieces being joined, often called the base metal (not to be confused with the baser metal in galvanic corrosion), is melted and fused with the filler metal, the process is welding. In brazing the metal pieces being joined are never melted and the filler metal is drawn into the joint by capillary action. For brazing nickel silver, the filler metal is 10-18 % nickel zinc, and the remainder, copper. *The Brazing Book* (New York: Handy & Harmon, 1977), p. 44.

65. Gerald K. Geerlings, *Metal Crafts in Architecture* (New York: Charles Scribner's Sons, 1929), p. 185.

66. Even at high temperatures, Monel metal is too strong to be extruded. *Practical Design in Monel Metal* (New York: International Nickel Company, Inc., 1931), pp. 9-10, and 25.

67. Hornbostel, *Materials for Architecture*, p. 320

68. Ibid., p. 330.

69. Ibid., p. 333.

70. Geerlings, *Metal Crafts in Architecture*, p. 185.

71. In general, nickel silver and Monel metal can be cleaned using the same methods as cleaning bronze since they all contain copper; however, chemicals should always be spot tested for desired results before general application. *Copper, Brass, Bronze Handbook: Architectural Application*, (New York: Copper Development Association, Inc., n.d.), p. 31; Peterson, "Conservation of Metals," p. 7.

72. "Simple Tests Identify White Metals: Reliable in Result, They Eliminate Guesswork by the Eye and Can be Carried Out With Inexpensive and Readily Available Equipment—Essential in Scrap Recovery, They Also Are Useful for Identification of Materials in Process and Storage," *Inco* 18 (no. 3, 1941): pp. 6-7. (Tests for the identification of nickel, Monel, nickel-silver, steel, cast iron, stainless steel, and Inconel).

73. Hornbostel, *Materials for Architecture*, p. 321.

74. Ibid., p. 334.

75. Ibid., p. 276.

76. LaQue and Copson, *Corrosion Resistance*, p. 305.

77. Addleson, *Materials for Building*, p. 64.

78. Hornbostel, *Materials for Architecture*, p. 285.

79. Addleson, *Materials for Building*, p. 64.

80. Ibid.

81. Geerlings, *Metal Crafts in Architecture*, p. 114.

82. Hornbostel, *Materials for Architecture*, p. 283.

83. Geerlings, *Metal Crafts in Architecture*, p. 45.

84. Hornbostel, *Materials for Architecture*, p. 283.

85. Addleson, *Materials for Building*, p. 64.

86. Hornbostel, *Materials for Architecture*, p. 448.

87. Addleson, *Materials for Building*, p. 64.

88. Ibid., p. 66.

89. LaQue and Copson, *Corrosion Resistance*, p. 375.

90. *Metal Product Outline for Classifying Products Manufactured by NAAMM Member Companies* (Chicago: National Association of Architectural Metal Manufacturers, 1989, second edition), p. 10.

91. Plenderleith and Werner, Conservation of Antiquities and Works of Art, p. 281.

92. Organ, "The Corrosion of Tin, Copper, Iron and Steel, and Lead," p. 251.

93. Ibid.

94. Magnesium oxychloride cements were originally developed in 1867 by French chemist I. M. Sorel, the man who patented the galvanizing process in 1837. Historically, magnesium oxychloride cement was known as Sorel cement, or magnesite cement; today it is known as oxychloride cement. Philip Maslow, *Chemical Materials of Construction* (Farmington, Mich.: Structures Publishing Company, 1974), p. 132.

95. Addleson, *Materials for Building*, p. 63.

96. Ibid., p. 64.

97. LaQue and Copson, *Corrosion Resistance*, p. 367-368.

98. McMasters, *Nondestructive Testing Handbook*, p. 6-1.

99. Hornbostel, *Materials for Architecture*, p. 285.

100. Addleson, *Materials for Building*, p. 64.

101. Ibid., p. 66.

102. Hornbostel, *Materials for Architecture*, p. 461.

103. LaQue and Copson, *Corrosion Resistance*, p. 410.

104. Addleson, *Materials for Building*, p. 67.

105. Ibid.

106. Hornbostel, *Materials for Architecture*, p. 444.

107. Addleson, *Materials for Building*, p. 67.

108. Ibid., p. 65

109. Evans, *Corrosion and Oxidation of Metals*, p. 531.

110. F. Fansutt and J. C. Hudson, *Protective Painting of Structural Steel* (New York: MacMillan Co., 1957), p. 64.

111. Peterson, "Conservation of Metals," p. 4.

112. Organ, "The Corrosion of Tin, Copper, Iron and Steel, and Lead," p. 252.

113. Evans, *Corrosion and Oxidation of Metals*, p. 571.

114. Ibid.

115. Addleson, *Materials for Building*, p. 79.

116. Ibid.

117. Robert Ohlerking, "Cast Iron," *The Old House Journal* 8 (no. 2, Feb. 1980): p. 21.

118. "Ni-rod" welding electrodes used to weld cast iron lamp post. "Inco Echoes," *Inco 17* (no. 2, 1947): p. 20.

119. Ohlerking, "Cast Iron," p. 21.

120. Dismantled Edgar Laing Stores facade components, erected by James Bogardus in 1849, were stolen while in storage; Margot Gayle and Frances Frieder, "Bogardus Building Badly Boosted," *Society of Industrial Archeology Newsletter 3* (No. 4, July 1974): p. 1.

121. J. Scott Howell, "Architectural Cast Iron: Design and Restoration," *Association for Preservation Technology Bulletin* (vol. XIX, number 3, 1987), pp. 51-55.

122. Hornbostel, Materials for Architecture, p. 18-19.

123. Hoff, "Metals," p. 194.

124. Ibid.

125. Ibid., p. 195.

126. Ibid

127. *Care of Aluminum*, 4th ed. (Washington, D.C.: The Aluminum Association, Inc., and the Architectural Aluminum Manufacturers Association, Dec. 1977), p. 1.

128. Ibid.

129. Ibid., p. 2.

130. Hornbostel, *Materials for Architecture*, p. 29, 34-36.

131. *Care of Aluminum*, p. 3.

132. Hoff, "Metals," p. 204.

133. Hornbostel, *Materials for Architecture*, p. 19.

134. Hoff, "Metals," p. 202.

135. Hornbostel, *Materials for Architecture*, p. 19.

136. *Care of Aluminum*, p. 5.

137. Ibid.

138. Ibid.

139. Ibid., pp. 5-6.

140. Ibid., p. 7.

141. Ibid., p. 8.

142. *Aluminum in Architecture* (Pittsburgh, Pa.: Aluminum Company of America, 1932), pp. 159-160.

143. Ibid. p. 160.

144. Hornbostel, *Materials for Architecture*, pp. 26-27.

Bibliography

Metals General

Books

Addleson, Lyell. *Materials for Building.* Vols. 2 and 3. London: Iliffe Books, 1972. cf Metals.

Bakhvalov, G. T. and Turkovskaya, A. V. *Corrosion and Protection of Metals.* Oxford: Pergamon Press, 1965.

Berg, Louis de Coppet. *Safe Buildings.* Boston: Ticknor & Co., 1892. Describes how iron is cast in sand molds made from the impressions of patterns. Gives advantages and disadvantages of a variety of protective coatings from electroplating methods to paint. Describes the process of galvanizing.

Bloxam, Charles Loudon. *Metals: Their Properties and Treatment.* New York: D. Appleton and Co., 1872.

Bowyer, Jack. *History of Building.* London: Crosby Lockwood Staples, 1973.

Britton, S. C. *Anti-Corrosion Manual.* London: Science Surveys, Ltd., 1958.

Burns, R. M., and Bradley, W. W. *Protective Coatings for Metals.* New York: Reinhold Publishing Corporation, 1967.

"Builders' Metals and Hardware." *Industrial Chicago/ The Building Interests.* Vol. 2. Chicago: The Goodspeed Publishing Co., 1891, pp. 384-476.
Covers almost all metals used in architecture.

Cheesman, Frank P. *A Review of Technical Paints for Metal.* Williamsport, Pa.: National Paint Works, 1905.

Condit, Carl W. *American Building Art: The Nineteenth Century.* New York: Oxford University Press, 1960.

_____. *American Building: Materials and Techniques from the First Colonial Settlements to the Present.* Chicago: University of Chicago Press, 1968.

Davey, Norman. *A History of Building Materials.* New York: Brake Publishers Ltd., 1971.

Department of the Environment. *Paint Metalwork: Advisory Leaflet No. 11.* London: Her Majesty's Stationery Office, 1967.

Evans, Ulick R. *The Corrosion and Oxidation of Metals: Scientific Principles and Practical Applications.* London: Edward Arnold Ltd., 1900.

Fitch, James Marston. *American Building I: The Historic Forces That Shaped It.* 2nd ed. revised. Boston: Houghton Mifflin Co., 1966.

Geerlings, Gerald K. *Metal Crafts in Architecture.* New York: Charles Scribner's Sons, 1929.

Gibbons, E. V. *The Corrosion Behavior of the Major Architectural and Structural Metals in Canadian Atmospheres: Summary of Ten-Year Results of Group I.* Technical Paper No. 328. Ottawa: National Research Council of Canada, Division of Building Research, 1970.

Greathouse, Glen A., and Wessel, Carl J. *Deterioration of Materials: Causes and Preventive Techniques.* New York: Reinhold Publishing Corporation, 1954.

Grover, H. J.; Gordon, S. A.; and Jackson, L. R. *Fatigue of Metals and Structures.* Washington, D.C.: Department of the Navy, 1954.

Hamlin, Talbot. *Benjamin Henry Latrobe.* New York: Oxford University Press, 1955.
References to lead roofs in Washington, D.C.; scarcity of tin roofing, and sheet iron roofs at Princeton College.

Harris, J. C. *Metal Cleaning Bibliographical Abstracts, 1842-1951.* Philadelphia: American Society for Testing Materials, 1953.
Exhaustive list of scientific technical publications.

Hedges, Ernest S. *Protective Coatings on Metals.* London: Chapman & Hall Ltd., 1932.

Hudson, Kenneth. *Building Materials.* London: Longman, 1972.

Huff, W. D. "Metals," edited by John Simpson and Peter J. Horrobin. In *The Weathering and Performance of Building Materials.* New York: Wiley-Interscience, 1970.

Innocent, C. F. *The Development of English Building Construction.* Cambridge: Cambridge University Press, 1916.

Insall, Donald W. *The Care of Old Buildings: A Practical Guide for Architects and Owners.* Reprint from *The Architects Journal* for the Society for the Protection of Ancient Buildings, n.d.

_____. *The Care of Old Buildings: Practical Guide.* London: The Architectural Press, 1972.

Jefferson, Theodore Brewster, and Woods, Gorham. *Metals and How to Weld Them.* 2nd ed. Cleveland, Ohio: James F. Lincoln Arc Welding Foundation, 1967.

LaQue, F. L., and Copson, H. R., eds. *Corrosion Resistance of Metals and Alloys.* 2nd ed. New York: Reinhold Publishing Corporation, 1963.

Leidheiser, Henry. *The Corrosion of Copper, Tin and Their Alloys.* New York: Wiley-Interscience, 1971.

Look, David W. *Inventory of Metal Building Component Catalogs in the Library of Congress.* Washington, D.C.: National Park Service, U.S. Department of the Interior, Aug. 1975.

McKay, Robert James, and Worthington, Robert. *Corrosion Resistance of Metals and Alloys.* New York: Reinhold Publishing Corp., 1936.

Melville, Ian A., and Gordon, Ian A. *The Repair and Maintenance of Houses.* London: The Estates Gazette Ltd., 1973.

Metalworking: Yesterday and Tomorrow. New York: American Machinist, 1977.

Munse, W. H., Stallmeyer, J. E., and Drew, F. P. *Structural Fatigue and Steel Railroad Bridges.* Chicago: American Railway Engineering Assoc., 1968.

National Bureau of Standards. *Corrosion and Metal Artifacts: A Dialogue Between Conservators and Archaeologists and Corrosion Scientists.* Washington, D.C.: U.S. Government Printing Office, 1977.

Newman, John. *Metallic Structures: Corrosion and Fouling, and Their Prevention.* London: L. & F. N. Spon, 1896.

Nield, B. J. *Problems in Service—Metallurgical Considerations Avoidance of Failure.* New York: American Elsevier Publishing Co., 1970.

Organ, Robert M. *Design for Scientific Conservation of Antiquities.* Washington, D.C.: Smithsonian Institution Press, 1968.

_____. "The Corrosion of Tin, Copper, Iron and Steel, and Lead." In *Preservation and Conservation: Principles and Practices.* Washington, D.C.: The National Trust for Historic Preservation, The Preservation Press, 1976.

Paints and Protective Coatings. Washington, D.C.: Departments of the Army, the Navy, and the Air Force, 1969.

Plenderleith, H. J., and Organ, R. M. *The Conservation of Antiquities and Works of Art, Treatment, Repair, and Restoration.* London, New York and Toronto: Oxford University Press, 1957.

Plenderleith, H. J., and Werner, A. E. A. *The Conservation of Antiquities and Works of Art.* 2nd ed. London: Oxford University Press, 1971.

Ragsdale, L. A., and Raynham, E. A. *Building Materials Technology.* 2nd ed. London: Edward Arnold Ltd., 1972.

Robinson, Cervin, and Bletter, Rosemarie Haag. *Skyscraper Style: Art Deco New York.* New York: Oxford University Press, 1975.
Has chronological list of buildings and their addresses.

Sabin, A. H. *Painting to Prevent Corrosion.* New York: Edward Smith & Co., 1898.

Salvadori, Mario, and Heller, Robert. *Structure in Architecture.* Englewood Cliffs, N.Y.: Prentice-Hall, Inc., 1964.

Salzman, L. F. *Building in England Down to 1540: A Documentary History.* Oxford: The Clarendon Press, 1952.

Sereda, P. J. *Weather Factors Affecting the Corrosion of Metals: Research Paper 613.* Ottawa, Canada: National Research Council of Canada, Division of Building Research, 1974. Reprinted in the American Society for Testing and Materials: *Special Technical Publication No. 558,* 1974, pp. 7-22.

Sexton, A. Humbolt. *The Corrosion and Protection of Metals.* Manchester, England: The Scientific Publishing Co., 1906.

Simpson, Bruce Liston. *Development of the Metal Castings Industry.* Chicago: American Foundrymen's Assoc., 1948.

Speller, Frank N. *Corrosion: Causes and Prevention.* New York: Edward Smith & Co., 1898. Reprinted. New York: McGraw Hill Book Co., Inc., 1951.

Tylecote, R. F. *A History of Metallurgy.* London: The Metals Society, 1976.

U.S. Department of the Interior, Bureau of Reclamation. *Paint Manual: A Water Resources Technical Publication.* 3rd ed. Washington, D.C.: U.S. Government Printing Office, 1976.

Vlack, Don. *Art Deco Architecture in New York: 1920-1940.* New York: Harper & Row, Publishers, 1974.

Waite, Diana S., ed. *Architectural Elements: The Technological Revolution.* Princeton: The Pyne Press, 1973. Unpaged.

_____. "Roofing for Early America." Chapter 8 in *Building Early America: Contributions toward the History of a Great Industry.* Edited by Charles E. Peterson. Radnor, Pa.: Chinton Book Co., 1976.

Waite, John G. "Architectural Metals: Their Deterioration and Stabilization." In *Preservation and Conservation: Principles and Practices.* Washington, D.C.: The National Trust for Historic Preservation, The Preservation Press, 1976.

Periodicals

Clute, Eugene. "Drafting for Metal Work. A Study of Current Practice with Special Reference to Collaboration on the Part of Architect, Sculptor and Craftsman." *Metal Arts.* Part 1: Vol. 1 (no. 1, Nov. 1928): 12-19. Part 2: Vol. 1 (no. 2, Dec. 1928): 109-114. Part 3: Vol. 2 (no. 1, Jan. 1929): 11-14. Part 4: Vol. 2 (no. 2, Feb. 1929): 69-72. Part 5: Vol. 2 (no. 3, Apr. 1929): 161-168. Part 6: Vol. 2 (no. 5, June 1929): 235-238. Part 7: Vol. 2 (no. 6, July 1929): 297-314. Part 8: Vol. 2 (no. 9, Oct. 1929): 449, 486.

_____. "Metals and Methods." *Metal Arts*. Part 1: Vol. 1 (no. 1, Nov. 1928): 47-51. Part 2: Vol. 2 (no. 1, Jan. 1929): 15-40. Part 3: Vol. 2 (no. 2, Feb. 1929): 73-98. Part 4: Vol. 2 (no. 3, Apr. 1929): 135-139. Part 5: Vol. 2 (no. 4, May 1929): 215-221. Part 6: Vol. 2 (no. 5, June 1929): 243-246. Part 7: Vol. 2 (no. 6, July 1929): 289-296. Part 8: Vol. 2 (no. 9, Oct. 1929): 245-248. Part 9: Vol. 3 (no. 2, Feb. 1930): 85-86, 94.

"Etched Metal Panels Grow in Popularity." *Metalcraft* 6 (no. 6, Jan. 1931): 49.

Fistere, John Cushman. "Use of White Metals." *Architectural Forum* 55 (Aug. 1931): 232-240.

Gibson, B. M. "The Use of the Airbrasive Process for Cleaning Ethnological Materials." *Studies in Conservation* 14 (no. 4, 1969): 155-164.

"Hotel New Yorker Typifies the Modern Use of Metals, The." *Metalcraft* 4 (no. 2, Feb. 1930): 346-353. Cast iron marque, bronzework, Monel kitchen, and nickel-silver doors on Manufacturers Hanover Trust.

Lynes, Wilson. "Some Historical Developments in Regard to Corrosion." *Journal of the Electrochemical Society* 98 (no. 1, Jan. 1951): 3C-10C.

Malmstrom, L. L. "This Trend to White Metals. Is it Merely a Flash of Popularity which will Subside . . . or does it Portend even Greater Use in the Future?" *Metalcraft* 8 (no. 3, Mar. 1932): 128-133.

McGill, Henry J. "The Metal Craftsman and the Architect." *Metal Arts* 1 (Dec. 1928): 69-70, 118.

McKay, R., and Searle, H. E. "Corrosion. The Tendency of All Metals to Return to Their Ores." *Inco* 5 (no. 4, 1925): 9, 20-21.

Parkhurst, Clif. "Maintenance of Architectural Ornamental Metal." *Metalcraft* 5 (no. 3, Sept. 1930): 127-129.

Parlett, Samuel. "A Bibliography of Ornamental Metal Work." *Metal Arts*. Part 1: Vol. 1 (no. 1, Nov. 1928): 57-59. Part 2: Vol. 1 (no. 2, Dec. 1928): 115-117. Part 3: Vol. 2 (no. 1, Jan. 1929): 49-51, 57. Part 4: Vol. 2 (no. 2, Feb. 1929): 114-118. Part 5: Vol. 2 (no. 3, Apr. 1929): 174-177. Part 6: Vol. 2 (no. 6, June 1929): 269, 276. Part 7: Vol. 2 (no. 7, July 1929): 369, 381. Part 8: Vol. 2 (no. 10, Nov. 1929): 523, 537.

Peterson, Harold L. "Conservation of Metals." *History News* 23 (no. 2, Feb. 1968). Reprint.

Roberts, C. A. Llewelyn. "The Use and Abuse of Metalwork." *Metalcraft* 3 (no. 3, Sept. 1929): 115-118, 150. Covers casting, hammering, chasing, pressing, and stamping metals.

Roskill, O. W. "Occurrence and History of the Metals used in Architecture." *Architectural Review* 82 (June 1937): 253-300.

Rudram, A. T., and Warner, L. M. "Corrosion-Inhibitive Paints." *Metallurgical Reviews* 9 (1964): 179-200.

"Simple Tests Identify White Metals: Reliable in Result, They Eliminate Guesswork by the Eye and can be Carried Out With Inexpensive and Readily Available Equipment—Essential in Scrap Recovery, They Also Are Useful for Identification of Materials in Process and Storage." *Inco* 18 (no. 3, 1941): 6-7.

Lead

Books

Department of the Environment. *Leadburning:* Advisory Leaflet No. 46. London: Her Majesty's Stationery Office, 1977.

Hofman, Heinrick Oscar. *Metallurgy of Lead.* New York: McGraw Hill Book Co., Inc., 1918.

Hope's Leadwork, Architectural Leadwork Suitable for Modern Buildings. New York: Henry Hope & Sons, 1928.

Lanciano, Claude O. *Rosewell: Garland of Virginia.* Glouchester, Va.: Glouchester Historical Committee, 1978.

Lead Industries, New York: Lead Industries Association, 1931.

Lethaby, William R. *Leadwork, Old and Ornamental, for the Most Parts English.* New York: Macmillan & Co., 1893.

Whiffen, Marcus. *The Public Buildings of Williamsburg.* Williamsburg, Va.: Colonial Williamsburg, Inc., 1958.

Wilson, H. Weber. *Your Residential Stained Glass: A Practical Guide to Repair & Maintenance.* Chambersburg, Pa.: Architectural Ecology, 1979.

Wilson, Kenneth M. "Window Glass in America." Chapter 9 in *Building Early America: Contributions toward the History of a Great Industry.* Edited by Charles E. Peterson. Radnor, Pa.: Chinton Book Co., 1976.

Periodicals

Cluss, Adolf. "The Effects of Lead Plates in Masonry." *American Architect and Building News* 24 (Sept. 8, 1888): 115-116.

Clute, Eugene. "Lead and Glass in Silhouette." *Architecture* 65 (Jan. 1932): 13-20.

"Eight Pages of Lead Details." *American Architect* 137 (Jan. 1930): 50-57. Photos of many gutters, leader heads, and straps; ornament; garden statues, and boxes.

"Hardlead in Architecture: Practical Points on the Varied Uses of This Material." *Metal Arts* 3 (no. 3, Mar. 1930): 106-110, 142. Roof of National Cathedral, Washington, D.C.

"Old Roofing Tin [sic]" *Carpentry and Building* 11 (Aug. 1889): 164. First terneplates were made by Jos. Truman in New York City in 1825.

Weaver, Martin E. "A Short Note on an early Sash Window Found at East Hampton, Long Island." *Bulletin of the Association for Preservation Technology* 10 (no. 1, 1978): 55-62.

Tin

Books

American Sheet and Tin Plate Company Reference Book. Pittsburgh, Pa.: American Sheet and Tin Plate Company, 1923.

Britton, Sidney Charles. *The Corrosion Resistance of Tin and Tin Alloys.* Greenford, Middlesex: Tin Research Institute, 1952.

Burgess, George Kimball, and Woodward, R. W. *Conservation of Tin in Bearing Metals, Bronzes, and Solders.* Washington, D.C.: Government Printing Office, 1919.

Dunbar, Donald Earl. *The Tin-Plate Industry: A Comparative Study of Its Growth in the United States and in Wales.* New York: Houghton Mifflin Co., 1915.

Mantell, Charles Letnam. *Tin: Its Mining, Production, Technology, and Application.* New York: Reinhold Publishing Corporation, 1949.

Polansky, V. S. *Tin-Plate Manufacture: A Bibliography.* Pittsburgh: Carnegie Library of Pittsburgh, 1941.

Vosburgh, H. K. *The Tinsmith's Helper and Pattern Book with Useful Rules, Diagrams, and Tables.* New York: Williams Company, 1879.

Waite, Diana S. *19th Century Tin Roofing and Its Use at Hyde Hall.* Albany, N.Y.: New York State Historic Trust, 1971.

William, Hall V. *The New Tinsmith's Helper and Pattern Book.* New York: U. P. C. Company, 1917.
Also covers sheet copper.

Periodicals

"American Tin-plates." *American Architect and Building News* 37 (Sept. 24, 1892): 191-194.
Discusses extent of American production, compares quality of foreign verus domestic production, and debates duties on tin-plate.

"Finishing the Edges of Tin Roofs." *Carpentry and Building* 4 (Apr. 1882): 76.

"Finishing Tin Roofs at the Eaves and Flashing Around Chimneys." *Carpentry and Building* 3 (Feb. 1881): 36.

"How to Lay Tin Roofs." *Carpentry and Building* 11 (Apr. 1889): 68-69.

"Manufacture of Tin Plates." *Scientific American* 65 (Oct. 3, 1891): 213

"Paint for Tin Roofs." *Carpentry and Building.* Vol. 1 (June 1879): 118, (July 1879): 139; vol. 4 (Dec. 1882): 235-236; vol. 9 (Apr. 1887): 78; vol. 25 (June 1903): 163.

"Painting Tin Roofs." *Carpentry and Building.* Vol. 5 (May 1883): 97-99; vol. 6 (May 1884): 101-102; vol. 7 (Dec. 1885): 234.

Plenderleith, H. J., and Organ, R. M. "The Decay and Conservation of Museum Objects of Tin." *Studies in Conservation* 1 (no. 2, June 1953): 63-72.

"Should Roofing Tin Be Painted on the Underside?" *Carpentry and Building* 26 (Dec. 1904): 350; vol. 27 (Feb. 1905): 44.

"Specifications for Tin Roof in Montana." *Carpentry and Building* 26 (Aug. 1924): 224.

"Tin for Valleys." *Carpentry and Building* 4 (July 1882): 16; vol. 4 (Oct. 1882): 191.

Zinc

Books

Catalogue of Ornamental Designs in Zinc. Chicago: Zinc Roofing & Ornamenting Co., 1871.

Lones, Thomas East. *Zinc and Its Alloys.* New York: I. Pitman & Sons, Ltd., 1919?

Morgan, S. *Zinc and Its Alloys.* Plymouth, England: MacDonald and Evans, 1977.

Schikorr, Gerhard Oskar Emil. *Atmospheric Corrosion Resistance of Zinc.* New York: American Zinc Institute, 1965

Slunder, C. *Zinc—Its Corrosion Resistance.* London: Zinc Development Association, 1971.

Zinc and Its Corrosion Resistance. New York: American Zinc Institute, 1928.

Periodicals

"Architects Specifications for Sheet-Metal Work." *Sheet-Metal Builder* 2 (July 15, 1879): 68-69.
Covers straight and curved moldings, miters, friezes, trusses and stop blocks, brackets and modillions, window caps, dormers, hanging gutters, conductors, spun-zinc work, and tinwork.

Downs, Arthur Channing Jr. "Zinc for Paint and Architectural Use in the 19th Century." *Bulletin of the Association for Preservation Technology* 8 (no. 4, 1976): 80-100.

"Galvanized-Iron." *Sheet-Metal Builder* 1 (Sept. 1874): 87.
As early as 1829, Dr. John W. Reverse of New York experimented with zinc coating on iron.

"Galvanized-Iron Front." *Carpentry and Building* 11 (Nov. 1889): 229.

"Galvanized Iron vs. Tin for Roofing." *Carpentry and Building* 1 (Apr. 1879): 78-79.

"Galvanized Sheet-Iron; Its Great Utility, with a Glance at Some of the Objectionable Features Pertaining to It." *Sheet-Metal Builder* 1 (Jan. 1875): 162.

Liggett, T. "Sherardizing Process: Galvanizing by the Formation of Zinc-Iron Alloy." *Engineering Magazine* 43 (May 1912): 277-279.

"Pressed Zinc Ornament." *Sheet-Metal Builder* 2 (Dec. 15, 1875): 130.

"Putting Up a Galvanized-Iron Cornice." *Sheet-Metal Builder* 1 (July 1874): 56-57.

"Sheet-Metal Crown-Mouldings." *Sheet-Metal Builder* 2 (Oct. 15, 1875): 107

"Sheet-Metal Foot-Mouldings." *Sheet-Metal Builder* 2 (Oct. 15, 1875): 118.

"Sheet-Metal Gutters." *Sheet-Metal Builder* 2 (Jan. 15, 1875): 143.

"Specifications of Workmanship, Materials and Construction, As Applied to Sheet-Metal Architectural Work." *Sheet-Metal Builder* 1 (Sept. 1874): 86.
For galvanized moldings, brackets, modillions, dentils, friezes, window and door caps, dormers, and gutters.

Trood, S. "Sherardizing Process." *Engineering Magazine* 48 (Oct. 1914): 117-120.

Copper

Books

Brewer, William J. *The History of Copper.* New York: St. Paul Printing and Publishing Co., 1902.

Copper and Common Sense, Design Principles and Techniques of Sheet Copper Construction. 6th ed. New York: Revere Copper and Brass, Inc., 1961.

Copper Flashings: A Handbook of Data on the Use of Copper as a Flashing Material with Standard Details of Construction & Specifications for Sheet-Copper Work. New York: The Copper and Brass Research Assoc., 1924.

Dawson, R. J. C. *Fusion Welding and Brazing of Copper and Copper Alloys.* London: Newnes—Butterworth, 1973.

Flinn, Richard Aloysius. *Copper, Brass and Bronze Castings; Their Structures, Properties, and Application.* Evanston, Ill.: Non-Ferrous Founders Society, 1961.

Fuller, John. *Art of Coppersmithing: A Practical Treatise on Working Sheet Copper into All Forms.* New York: David Williams Co., 1904.

Revere Copper and Brass, Inc. *Examination of Corroded Lead Coated Copper Sheet: Austin-Hastings Company, Incorporated. Cambridge, Massachusetts.* Technical report (Project No. RS-13), prepared May 7, 1964. Unpublished.

Welding, Brazing, and Soldering of Copper and Its Alloys. Radlett, Herts., Great Britain: Copper Development Assoc., 1951.

Periodicals

Angelucci, S.; Fiorentino, P.; Kosinkova, J.; and Marabelli, M. "Pitting Corrosion in Copper and Copper Alloys: Comparative Treatment Tests." *Studies in Conservation* 23 (1978): 147-156.

Beij, Karl Hilding. "Corrosion of Open-Valley Flashing." *U.S. Bureau of Standards Journal of Research* 3 (no. 6, Dec. 1929): 937-952.

_____. "Seams for Copper Roofs." *U.S. Bureau of Standards Journal of Research* 5 (no. 3, Sept. 1930): 585-608.

Darling, J. C. "Electroplating with Copper." *Scientific American* 69 (Sept. 9, 1893): 168.

Osburn, Donald H., and Foehl, John M. "Coloring and Finishing of Copper Metals." *Construction Specifier* (Oct. 1963): 50-55. Reprint.

Robertson, W. D., et al. "An Investigation of Chemical Variables Affecting the Corrosion of Copper." *Journal of the Electrochemical Society* 105 (1958): 569-573.

Sweetser, Sarah. "A Surviving Eighteenth Century Copper Roof." *Bulletin of the Association of Preservation Technology* 9 (no. 2, 1977): 10-15.

Vernon, W. H. J., and Whitby, L. "The Open-Air Corrosion of Copper. Part II. The Mineralogical Relationships of Corrosion Products." *Journal of the Institute of Metals* 44 (1930): 389-396.

Bronze

Books

Architectural Bronze. Bronze Lighting Fixtures. New York and Providence: Gorham Co., 1916.

Berman, Harold. *Bronzes; Sculptors and Founders, 1800-1930.* Chicago: Abage, 1974.

Jackson, Harry. *Lost Wax Bronze Casting; A Photographic Essay on this Antique and Venerable Art.* Flagstaff, Ariz: Northland Press, 1972.

Kilburn, W. L. *Copper & Bronze Welding of Tube and Sheet Copper for Piping and Roof-Work.* London: The British Oxygen Co., Ltd., 1936.

Ornamental Iron and Bronze. Chicago: Winslow Brothers Co., 1910.

Periodicals

"Bronze Doors for the Congressional Library at Washington." *Carpentry and Building* 19 (Jan. 1897): 2.

"Bronze Doors of Old Designs." *Carpentry and Building* 27 (Dec. 1905): 344.

"Bronze Doors; Stock Exchange Building, Los Angeles, Calif.; Samuel E. Lunden, Arch." *Metalcraft* 7 (no. 5, Nov. 1931): 186-187.

Degan, Eugene B. "Building with Bronze." *Buildings: The Construction and Building Management Journal.* (Jan. 1966). Reprint.

Drexler, Arthur. "Seagram Building; Mies van der Rohe and P. Johnson, Archs." *Architectural Record* 124 (July 1958): 139-147.
Description of bronzework and how it was made.

"Handsome Bronze Doors for Boston Public Library." *Carpentry and Building* 26 (Oct. 1904): 298.

"Lost-Wax Process of Bronze Casting, The.: A Detailed Description of the Present-day Practice of an Age-Old Art." *Metal Arts* 3 (no. 3, Mar. 1930): 111-112, 136, 138.

"Model Specification for Architectural Bronze, A" *Metalcraft* 4 (no. 5, May 1930): 512-514.

Morris, Kenneth, and Krueger, Jay W. "The use of Wet Peening in the Conservation of Outdoor Bronze Sculpture." *Studies in Conservation* 24 (1979): 40-43.

"New York Life Building: Cass Gilbert, Arch., Awarded First Place." *Metalcraft* 3 (no. 3, Mar. 1929): 122-128, 148-149.

"Statue that . . . , The." *Carpentry and Building* 10 (Apr. 1888): 71.
Bronze statue of William Penn to top Philadelphia City Hall.

Sturgis, Russell, "Bronze Doors of the Boston Public Library." *Scribner's Magazine* 36 (1904): 765-768.

"Symbolic Designs in Modern Style Distinguish The Chanin Building." *Metalcraft* 2 (no. 3, Mar. 1929): 104, 108-109.

Weil, Phoebe Dent. "A Review of the History and Practice of Patination." Proceedings of a Seminar, *Corrosion and Metal Artifacts—A Dialogue Between Conservators, Archaeologists, and Corrosion Scientists.* March 17 and 18, 1976. Gaithersburg, Md.: National Bureau of Standards, Special Publication No. 479, July 1977.

_____. "Conservation of Outdoor Bronze Sculpture." *National Sculpture Review* 25 (no. 23, Fall 1976): 26-30.

_____. "Problems of Preservation of Outdoor Bronze Sculpture: Examination and Treatment of 'The Meeting of the Waters' in St. Louis, Missouri." *American Institute of Conservation Bulletin* 14 (no. 2, 1974): 84-92.

_____. "The Approximate Two-Year Lifetime of Incralac on Outdoor Bronze Sculpture." *ICOM Committee for Conservation, 4th Triennial Meeting, Venice 1975.* Reprint No. 75/22/2.

_____. "The Use of Glass Bead Peening to Clean Large-Scale Out-Door Bronze Sculpture." *The Bulletin of the American Institute for Conservation of Historic and Artistic Works* 15 (no. 1, 1974): 51-58.

Brass

Books

Anaconda Architectural Drawn Shapes. Waterbury, Conn.: The American Brass Co., 1931.
Architraves; moldings; column, cornice, division bar, door framing, glass framing, handrail, pilaster, sash framing, sill, soffit, stop, and transom bar sections; and structural shapes.

Brown, William Norman. *The Principles and Practice of Dipping, Burnishing, Lacquering and Bronzing Brass Ware.* London: Scott, Greenwood & Sons, 1912.

Day, Joan. *Bristol Brass, a History of the Industry.* Newton Abbot, Great Britain: David and Charles Industry History, 1973.

Gates, Philip. *The Brass Founders' and Finishers' Manual.* London: C. Lockwood & Son, 1926.

Gillett, Horace Wadsworth. *Brass-Furnace Practice in the United States.* Washington, D.C.: U.S. Government Printing Office, 1916.

St. John, Harry Mark. *Brass and Bronze Foundry Practice.* Cleveland: Penton Publishing Co., 1958.

Periodicals

"Brass Casting." *Scientific American* 73 (Sept. 14, 1895): 165.

"It is said that King Street is richer in old brass knockers. . . ." *Carpentry and Building* 16 (Aug. 1894): 172.

"Origin, Manufacture, and Uses of Brass, The." *Sheet-Metal Builder* 1 (Dec. 1874): 132.

Nickel

Books

Howard-White, Frank Butler. *Nickel, an Historical Review.* Princeton, N.J.: Van Nostrand, 1963.

Nickel and Its Alloys. Circular no. 100. Washington, D.C.: National Bureau of Standards, 1924.

Romance of Nickel, The. New York: International Nickel Co., Inc., 1950.

Periodicals

"Electro-Plating of Metals; Methods of Nickel Plating." *Scientific American Supplement* 70 (Dec. 24, 1910): 405-406.

"An Iron Store-Front on Broadway, New York; Mr. R. M. Hunt, Architect." *American Architects and Builders News* 1 (Oct. 1876): 228.

"Nickel-Plated Screws." *Sheet-Metal Builder* 2 (Jan. 15, 1875): 140.

Wadhams, A. J. "The Nickel Industry." *Metal Progress* 19 (Mar. 1931): 92-98.

"Welding Nickel." *Scientific American Supplement* 76 (Oct. 18, 1913): 256.

Nickel Silver

Books

May, Earl Chapin. *Century of Silver, 1847-1947: Connecticut Yankees and a Noble Metal.* New York: R. M. McBridge & Co., 1947.

Nickel Silver in Architecture. New York: International Nickel Co., Inc., 1935.

Periodicals

"Canadian Doors Swing for World Freedom: Gift to United Nations Building Reflects Country's Natural Resources as Well as Workmanship of Its Craftsmen." *Inco* 26 (no. 2, 1953): 4-5.

"Inco Echoes." *Inco* 13 (no. 3, 1935-1936): 22-23.
The fireplace screen of the historic Pringle House, in Charleston, S.C., was bought in 1730 and made of Paktong (nickel silver), imported from China.

Lee, Anne. "Chicago Daily News Building." *Architectural Forum* 52 (Jan. 1930): 21-59.
Nickel silver used for elevator doors, radiator grilles, trim, and railings.

"Metal in the Hotel New Yorker and the Manufacturers Trust Company's West Side Branch." *Metal Arts* 3 (no. 1, Jan. 1930): 4-10.

"Nickel Silver Lends its Beauty to the National Bank of Commerce, Houston, Texas; Alfred C. Finn, Kenneth and J. E. R. Carpenter, Associated Arch." *Metal Arts* 2 (no. 10, Nov. 1929): 502-506, 537.

"Palmolive Building, Chicago; Henry J. B. Hoskins." *Architectural Forum* 52 (May 1930): 655-666.

Parkhurst, Clif. "The Well Balanced Use of Modern Alloys Contributes to the Architectural Success of the New Waldorf-Astoria; Schultz and Weaver, Archs." *Metalcraft* 7 (no. 5, Nov. 1931): 170-174, 179.

"White Metal Inside and Outside City Bank Farmers Trust Company, New York City; Cross and Cross, Architects." *Metalcraft* 6 (no. 4, Apr. 1931): 160, 164-169, 177-179, 194-195.

Monel Metal

Books

Crawford, C. A. "Nickel and Monel Metal with Especial Reference to Annealing." *American Institute of Mining and Metallurgical Engineering. Technical Publication.* No. 35. New York: International Nickel Co., Inc., 1927.

Monel Metal and Nickel Alloys. New York: International Nickel Co., Inc., 1932.

Practical Design in Monel Metal for Architectural and Decorative Purposes. New York: International Nickel Co., Inc., 1931.

Wheeler, Edwin S. *Monel Metal and Nickel Foundry Practice.* New York: American Institute of Mining and Metallurgical Engineers, Inc., 1939.

Technical Information, Monel, Nickel and Nickel Alloys. New York: International Nickel Co., Inc., Aug. 1936-Sept. 1938.

Periodicals

"American Sheet & Tin Plate Company . . . is offering a new product known as Monel Metal, to be used in lieu of Copper Sheets." *Carpentry and Building* 31 (Feb. 1909): 60.

"Anchoring a Ceramic Building Facade: First Installation Using Alloy Wire to Secure Fired Clay Sheathing Completed." *Inco* 23 (no 4, 1949): 19, 29-30.

"Anchoring a Building's Bricks: They Secure Masonry to Frame Work and Overcome Vibrations Caused by Street Traffic." *Inco* 23 (no. 2, 1949): 8.

"Architectural and Memorial Metal Work." *Inco* 11 (no. 2, 1932): 2.
Cast Monel entrance gates, carry official seal of the City of Pittsburgh, at the bank room of the Federal Reserve Bank of Pittsburgh, weighs 4,000 pounds. Bank has over 10,000 pounds of Monel castings and 5,000 pounds of sheet and wrought Monel.

"Color Dominant in Design of the Union Trust Building; Smith, Hinchman, and Grylls, Archs." *Architects and Engineers* 136 (Nov. 1929): 32-39.

Cret, Paul Phillippe. "Metal Work of the Integrity Trust Company's Main Office." *Metal Arts* 2 (no. 8, Sept. 1929): 392-401.

"Drafting for Metal Work, Part VI. Working Drawings and Shop Drawings of Elevator Doors of Monel Metal in the Union Trust Company Building, Detroit, Michigan." *Metal Arts* 2 (June 1929): 234-237.

"Georgia's Capitol Dome Restored with Corrosion-Resistant Monel; Over 42,000 Pounds Required for Job." *Inco* 27 (no. 7, 1959): 22-24.

Hanson, A. E. "Breaking Away From Traditions in Ornamental Metal Work: Design, Distinctive in its Use of Monel Metal, Characterizes the Main Entrance and Banking Sections of the Union Trust Building." *Inco* 9 (no. 1, 1929): 7-9.

"Inco Echoes." *Inco* 14 (no. 2, 1936): 22-23.
Brooklyn Museum has been reroofed with Monel by Cooperative Sheet Metal Works, Bronx, N.Y.

"Laboratory Measures the Life of a Roof, The." *Inco* 11 (no. 3, 1932): 21.

Merica, P. D.; Waltenberg, R. G.; and McCabe, A. S. "Some Mechanical Properties of Hot-Rolled Monel Metal." *Proceedings of the American Society for Testing of Materials* 21 (1921): 922.

"Metals Contribute to Pleasing Departure from Classic Forms; Federal Reserve Bank, Pittsburgh, Walker and Weeks, Archs." *Metalcraft* 8 (no. 2, Feb. 1932): 72-75, 86.

"Modern Diners." *Inco* 8 (no. 2, 1928): 26.

"Molding and Casting of Architectural Decorations; The Foundry Practice in Producing the Decorative Castings for the Federal Reserve Bank of Pittsburgh." *Inco* 11 (no. 2, 1932): 18-21.

"Monel Metal in Hospital Service." *Inco* 3 (no. 4, 1922): 13.

"New York Answers a Roofing Problem: New Covering for Public Library and Repairs to Pennsylvania Railroad Terminal Indicate that Ordinarily Good Roofing Materials Won't Always Meet Requirements." *Inco* 13 (no. 4, 1936): 18-19, 31.

"Notable Achievements in Metal Give Distinction to Building of Modern Design; Modern Type of Architecture is Effectively Used in New Banking Quarters of Integrity Trust Company." *Metalcraft* 3 (no. 2, Aug. 1929): 79-83.

"Roofed for the Years . . . Monumental and Other Structures Designed for Long Life Given Permanent Coverings." *Inco* 24 (no. 3, 1950): 12-13, 30.
Monel flashing on roofs of Pentagon, Washington, D.C.; Metropolitan Museum of Art in New York City (whole roof also); National Cathedral, Washington, D.C.; Sunbury Station of the Pennsylvania Power and Light Co.; Hospital for Chronic Diseases on New York's Welfare Island.

Williams, Hugh R. "Monel Metal; Points of Superiority of This New Natural Alloy in All Fields for Non-Corroding Steel." *Scientific American* 88 (Aug. 16, 1919): 98-99.

Iron (General)

Books

Andes, Louis Edgar. *Iron Corrosion: Anti-Fouling and Anti-Corrosive Paints.* London: Scott, Greenwood & Co., 1900.

French, Benjamin Franklin. *The History of the Rise and Progress of Iron Trade.* New York: Wiley and Halsted, 1858.

Fryer, William John, Jr. *Architectural Iron Work.* New York: John Wiley & Sons, 1876.

Bibliography

Periodicals

Bannister, Turpin C. "First Iron Framed Buildings." *Architectural Review* 107 (Apr. 1950): 231-246.

Barff, F. S. "The Treatment of Iron for the Prevention of Corrosion." *Van Nostrand's Eclectic Engineering Magazine* 16 (Apr. 1877): 300-302.
From the *Journal of the Society of Arts* 20 (May 1879): 438-443.

Barnes, Sisley. "George Ferris' Wheel: The Great Attraction of Midway Plaisance." *Chicago History* 6 (no. 3, Fall 1977): 177-182.

Burnham, Alan. "Last Look at a Structural Landmark." *Architectural Record* 20 (Sept. 1956): 273-279.

Cornell, John B. "Men Who Have Assisted in the Development of Architectural Resources—No. 1." *Architectural Record* 1 (Dec. 31, 1891): 244-247.

Hawkes, Nathan M. "First Iron Works in America, Lynn, Mass., 1642." *Magazine of American History* 22 (Nov. 1889): 404-410.

"100 Years of Metalworking: 1855-1955." *Iron Age Magazine* 175 (no. 27, June 1955): cf "Casting,": B2-B3; "Iron and Steel,": D2-D6; "Metal Finishing,": G2-G3; "Nonferrous Metals,": H2-H5. "Welding, Brazing, Joining,": L2-L3.

"Specifications for Building the Custom-House at Wheeling, Virginia, Including Accommodations for a Post Office and United States Court Room." *Bulletin of the Association for Preservation Technology* 5 (no. 1, 1973): 76-91. Reprinted from Office of the Construction of Buildings, Treasury Department, March 5, 1856.

"Specifications on Architectural Iron Drawn Up by New York Building Congress." *Metalcraft* 5 (no. 3, Sept. 1930): 142-146.
Covers shop drawings, samples, materials, workmanship, stairs, stringers and facias, treads, platforms, risers, newels, balustrades, soffits, spiral stairs, pipe rails and standards, fire escapes, ladders, window frames, door frames, bucks, saddles, sills, elevator door sills, elevator shaft facias, elevator shaft aprons, doors, and frames.

"Three Documents on Ironworks in Canada and The Northeastern United States at The Beginning of the Nineteenth Century." *Bulletin of the Association for Preservation Technology* 5 (no. 3, 1973): 5-33.

Vernon, W. H. J. "The Role of the Corrosion Product in the Atmospheric Corrosion of Iron." *Transactions of the Electrochemical Society* 64 (1933): 31-41.

Wells, James S. C. "Rustless Iron." *Popular Science Monthly* 29 (1886): 393-397.
Bower-Barff Method.

Wood, M. P. "The Protection of Ferric Structures from Corrosion." *Engineering News* 46 (Sept. 26, 1901): 213-216.

Cast Iron

Books

Bicknell, A. J. *Street, Store and Bank Fronts.* New York A. J. Kicknell & Co., 1876.

Christovich, Mary Louise, et al. *New Orleans Architecture: The American Sector.* Vol. 2. Gretna, La.: Pelican Publishing Co., 1973.

Fairbairn, Sir William. *On the Application of Cast and Wrought Iron to Building Purposes.* London: Robson, Levy, Franklin, 1854, and London: John Weale, 1857-1858.

Gayle, Margot, and Gillon, Edmund V., Jr. *Cast-Iron Architecture in New York: A Photographic Survey.* New York: Dover Publications, Inc., 1974.

Hitchcock, Henry-Russell. *Architecture in the 19th and 20th Centuries.* Baltimore, Md.: Penguin Books, 1967.

Illustrations of Iron Architecture, made by The Architectural Iron Works of the City of New York. New York: Baker & Godwin, Printers, 1865.

Kidder, Frank Eugene. *The Architect and Builders Pocketbook.* New York: John Wiley & Sons, 1904. Reprint, 1921.

Kowsky, Frank. *Iron for Art's Sake: Bartholdi's Centennial Fountain 1876.* New York: Friends of Cast-Iron Architecture, Aug. 1977.

Lee, Antoinette Josephine. *The Rise of Cast Iron District in Philadelphia.* Ph. D. dissertation. George Washington University, 1975.

Southworth, Susan, and Southworth, Michael. *Ornamental Ironwork: an Illustrated Guide to Its Design, History, and Use in American Architecture.* David R. Godine, 1978.

Victorian Ironwork: A Catalogue by J. B. Wickersham. With a new Introduction by Margot Gayle. Reprint of the Wickersham Catalogue of 1857. Philadelphia: Athenaeum Library of Nineteenth Century America, 1977.

Waite, John G. *Iron Architecture in New York City: The Edgar Laing Stores and The Cooper Union.* Albany, N.Y.: New York State Historic Trust, 1972.

Walter, Thomas U., and Smith, J. Jay. *A Guide to Workers in Metal and Stone.* Philadelphia: Carey and Hart, City & Publisher, 1846.

Wickersham, John B. *A New Phase in Iron Manufacture.* New York: Fowler & Wells, Printers, 1855.

Wright, David G. *Baltimore City Cast Iron; Architectural Glimpse: Past and Future.* New York: Friends of Cast-Iron Architecture, Feb. 1978.

Periodicals

"America's Cast Iron Age." *Architectural Forum* 120 (Apr. 1964): 111-113.

". . . Announcing a New Engineering Material: Ductile Cast Iron." *Inco* 23 (no. 1, 1949): 3.
Produced by incorporating a nickel-magnesium alloy in the molten iron.

Bannister, Turpin C. "The Genealogy of the Dome of the United States Capitol." *Journal of the Society of Architectural Historians* 7 (Jan. 1948): 1-32.

_____. "Bogardus Revisited." *Journal of the Society of Architectural Historians.* In 2 parts: "The Iron Fronts," vol. 15 (Dec. 1956): 12-22; and "The Iron Towers," vol. 16 (Mar. 1957): 11-19.

_____. "Some Early Iron Buildings in New York." *New York History* 24 (Oct. 1943): 518-524.

"Big Iron Facade Building being Restored." *American Institute of Architects Journal* 65 (Aug. 1976): 12.

Davis, Frohman Paul. "Early Metal Space Frame Investigated: First Structural Repairs of U.S. Capitol Dome Made in 100 Years." *Progressive Architecture* (Dec. 1960): 164-171.

Gayle, Margot. "A Heritage Forgotten: Chicago's First Cast Iron Buildings." *Chicago History* 7 (no. 2, Summer 1978): 98-108.

_____. "Cast Iron Architecture U.S.A." *Historic Preservation* 27 (no. 1, Jan.-Mar. 1975): 14-19.

Gayle, Margot, Frieder, and Frances. "Bogardus Building Badly Boosted." *Society for Industrial Archeology Newsletter* 3 (no. 4, July 1974): 1.

Gold, Michael W. "Bogardus Cast Iron: Designed to be Dismantled and Rebuilt." *Historic Preservation* 23 (no. 3, July-Sept. 1971): 12-19.

Hamilton, Stanley B. "Old Cast-Iron Structures." *The Structural Engineer* 27 (Apr. 1949): 173-191.

Higgs, Malcolm. "Contributions of Cast Iron." *Journal of the Society of Architectural Historians* 33 (no. 3, Oct. 1974): 227-228.

_____. "The Exported Iron Building of Andrew Handyside & Company of Derby." *Journal of the Society of Architectural Historians* 29 (no. 2, May 1970): 175-180.

Hitchcock, Henry-Russell. "Early Cast Iron Facades." *Architectural Review* 109 (Feb. 1951): 113-116.

Huxtable, Ada Louise. "Harper & Brothers' Building— 1854." *Progressive Architecture* 38 (Feb. 1957): 153-154.

_____. "Store for E.V. Haughwout & Company— 1857." *Progressive Architecture* 39 (no. 2, Feb. 1957): 133-136.

"Inco Echoes." *Inco* 17 (no. 2, 1947): 20. Ni-Rod welding electrodes used to weld cast-iron lamp post.

"Iron and Silk in a Notable Alliance." *Metalcraft* 1 (no. 5, Nov. 1928): 224, 244-246.

Kahn, David. "Bogardus Fire and Iron Tower." *Journal of the Society of Architectural Historians* 35 (no. 3, Oct. 1976): 186-203.

Laughlin, Clarence. "Louisiana Fantasy." *Architectural Review* 141 (May 1967): 330.

Lee, Antoinette J. "James Bogardus in Philadelphia." *Nineteenth Century* 2 (no. 1, Spring 1976): 33-36. The production of iron in America was aided by the discovery of anthracite, or hard coal, in Pennsylvania in the 1840s.

MacKay, Robert. "Cast-iron Architecture on Beacon Hill in Boston." *Antiques* 107 (no. 6, June 1975): 116-121.

McKee, Harley J. "Cellar Window Grilles in Philadelphia." *Bulletin of the Association for Preservation Technology* 5 (no. 2, 1973): 38-53.

Muthesius, Stefan. "Iron Problems in the 1850's." *Architectural History* 13 (1970): 58-63.

O'Gorman, James. "Bogardus Original." *Architectural Review* 147 (Feb. 1970): 150-156.

Peterson, Charles E. "The Penn Mutual Building. Philadelphia, 1850-1851." *Journal of the Society of Architectural Historians* 9 (Dec. 1950): 24-25.

"Richmond Will Restore Tour Buildings Behind 1865 'Ironfront' Facade." *Architectural Record* 158 (July 1975): 35.

Rix, Michael. "Industrial Archeology and the Church." *Industrial Archeology* 4 (no. 1, Feb. 1967): 44-50.

Robinson, Cervin. "Architectural Iron Work." *Architectural Forum* 126 (no. 4, May 1970): 63-70.

_____. "Late Cast Iron." *Architectural Forum* 135 (no. 2, Sept. 1971): 46-49.

_____. "Late Cast Iron in New York". *Journal of the Society of Architectural Historians* 30 (no. 2, May 1971): 164-169.

Seward, H. "Stanley Mill." *Journal of the Society of Architectural Historians* 15 (May 1956): 24-26.

"Shrinkage of Iron." *Scientific American* 75 (July 4, 1896): 6.

Sturges, W. Knight. "Cast Iron in New York." *Architectural Review* 114 (Oct. 1953): 233-237.

Taylor, J. "Charles Fowler." *Architectural History* 11 (1968): 57-74.

Weisman, Winston. "Commercial Palaces of New York." *Art Bulletin* 36 (no. 4, Dec. 1954): 285-302.

Weisman, Winston R. "The Anatomy and Significance of the Laing Stores by James Bogardus." *Journal of the Society of Architectural Historians* 31 (no. 3, Oct. 1972): 221-222.

_____. "Mid 19th Century Commercial Building by James Bogardus." *Monumentum* 9 (1973): 63-75.

Wrought Iron (and Sheet iron)

Books

Hoever, Otto. *An Encyclopedia of Ironwork; Examples of Hand Wrought Ironwork from the Middle Ages to the end of the 18th Century.* New York: Weyhe, 1929.

Illustrated Catalogue of Artistic Wrought Iron for House Work: Grills, Transoms, and Guards. New York: J. W. Fiske, 1891.

Sonn, Albert H. *Early American Wrought Iron.* 3 vols. New York: Charles Scribner's Sons, 1928.

Wallace, Philip B. *Colonial Ironwork in Old Philadelphia.* New York: Architectural Book Publishing Co., Inc., 1930.

Periodicals

"Best Paint for Iron Roofs, The." *Carpentry and Building* 6 (Nov. 1884): 206.

Castle, Sidney E. "Ironwork—As an Art." *Metalcraft* 3 (no. 1, July 1929): 31-35.

Davis, Myra Tolmach. "Samuel Yellin's Sketches in Iron." *Historic Preservation* 23 (no. 4, Oct.-Dec. 1971): 4-13.

"Early Iron Building Construction." *Engineering News* 50 (Sept. 10, 1903): 214-215.
Gives description of construction condition of iron of the Bank of the State of New York erected in mid 1850s in Manhattan. Illustrated with photographs and drawings of details of rolled wrought iron beams.

"18th Century English Ironwork." *Metalcraft* 8 (no. 4, Apr. 1932): 158-159.

"Enameled Iron Ceiling, An." *Sheet-Metal Builder* 2 (Sept. 15, 1875): 91.

"Finish of Wrought-Iron Work." *Carpentry and Building* 14 (May 1892): 120.

"Iron Architecture." *Sheet-Metal Builder* 1 (Apr. 1874): 7.

"Iron Ceiling Over Plaster." *Carpentry and Building* 10 (Dec. 1888): 257-258.

"Iron Cut Nails." *Carpentry and Building* 17 (Oct. 1895): 256.

"Iron Doors Under Fire." *The Architect: A Journal of Art, Civil Engineering and Building* 11 (Feb. 28, 1874): 126.

"Iron Roof Sweats." *Carpentry and Building* 19 (Dec. 1897): 299.

Jackson, P. H. "Iron and Concrete Construction." *American Architect and Building News* 16 (Oct. 4, 1884): 163-166.

Jewett, Robert. "Solving the Puzzle of the First American Rail-Beam." *Technology and Culture* 10 (July 1969): 375.

Mapes, John G. "Modern Blacksmithing: The Art of Making Ornamental Iron." *Metal Progress* 20 (Dec. 1931): 84-88.

"Metal Lath in Perfect Condition After 37 [sic] Years." *Metalcraft* 6 (no. 1, July 1930): 48. Sic: Title is incorrect; it should read "After 67 Years."

"1905 Catalogue of Iron Store Fronts: George L. Mesker & Co." *Bulletin of the Association for Preservation Technology* 9 (no. 4, 1977):

"Painting Structural Iron." *Carpentry and Building* 24 (Dec. 1902): 305.

"Painting the Brooklyn Bridge." *Engineering News* 9 (Sept. 16, 1882): 327.

Peterson, Charles E. "Iron in Early American Roofs." *The Smithsonian Journal of History* 3 (no. 3, 1968): 41-76.

"Preservation of Iron in Concrete." *American Architect and Building News* 81 (July 11, 1903): 13-14.

"Production of Wrought Iron: A Brief Non-Technical Description of the Prevailing Practice." *Metal Arts* 5 (May 1930): 199-200, 220.

"Some Precautions to Observe in Specifying Wrought Iron." *Metalcraft* 6 (no. 1, Jan. 1931): 69, 72.

Skempton, A. W., and Johnson, H. R. "The First Iron Frames." *Architectural Review* 131 (Mar. 1962): 175-186.

Steel (and Some Iron)

Books

Birkmire, William Harvey. *Skeleton Construction in Buildings.* New York: John Wiley & Sons, 1893.

Cushman, Allerton S., and Gardner, Henry A. *The Corrosion and Preservation of Iron and Steel.* New York: McGraw Hill Book Co., Inc., 1910.

Ericsson, Henry. *60 Years a Builder by Ericsson.* Chicago: A. Kroch & Son, 1942.
Written in collaboration with Lewis E. Meyer. Excellent. Essential reading for understanding the development of the skeletal construction of skyscraper construction.

Fancutt, F., and Hudson, J. C. *Protection Painting of Structural Steel.* New York: The Macmillan Co., 1957.

Ferris, Herbert W., ed. *AISC Iron and Steel Beams 1873-1952.* New York: American Institute of Steel Construction, 1957.

_____. *Historical Record, Dimensions and Properties: Rolled Shapes, Steel and Wrought Iron Beams & Columns As Rolled in U.S.A., Period 1873 to 1952 with Sources as Noted.* New York: Institute of Steel Construction, 1953.

Freitag, Joseph K. *Fireproofing of Steel Building.* New York: John Wiley & Sons, 1899.

Gale, W.K.V. *Iron and Steel.* Telford, Salop, England: Ironbridge Gorge Museum Trust, Museum Booklet No. 20.04, 1979.

Hall, Albert M. *Nickel in Iron and Steel.* New York: Engineering Foundation, 1954.

Loomis, W. H. *Twenty-five Years Experience Testing, Experimenting, and Manufacturing Protective Coverings for Iron and Steel Structural Work.* Williamsport, Pa.: National Paint Works, 1901.

Nickel Alloy Steels. 2nd ed. New York: International Nickel Co., Inc., 1949.

Lowe, Houston, *Hints on Painting Structural Steel and Notes on Prominent Paint Materials.* Dayton, Ohio: Lowe Brothers Co., 1905.

Randall, Frank A. *History of Development of the Building Construction in Chicago.* Urbana, Ill. University of Illinois Press, 1949.

Temin, Peter. *Iron and Steel in the Nineteenth Century.* Cambridge, Mass.: M.I.T. Press, 1964.

Periodicals

Barff, F. S. "Explanation of a Method of Preventing Corrosion of Iron and Steel, As Applied to Naval and Military Purposes." *Van Nostrand's Eclectic Engineering Magazine* 18 (Apr. 1878): 350-354.

Darling, J. D. "Electroplating with Copper." *Scientific American* 69 (Sept. 9, 1893): 168.

Fleming, Robins. "A Half Century of the Skyscraper; Tracing the Expansion and Refinement of a Brilliant American Achievement." *Civil Engineering* 4 (no. 12, 1934): 634-638.

_____. "Whence the Skyscraper? Many Men and Numerous Concepts Preceded the Construction of the Home Insurance Building in 1884." *Civil Engineering* 4 (1934): 505-509.

Fryer, William J., Jr. "Skeleton Construction. The New Method of Constructing High Buildings." *Architectural Record* 1 (Dec. 31, 1891): 228-235.

Gruner, M. L. "Corrosion of Iron and Steel." *Van Nostrand's Eclectic Engineering Magazine.* In 2 parts: Part 1, vol. 29 (Sept. 1883): 210-216; part 2, vol. 29 (Oct. 1883): 306-310.
Translated from *Annales des Mines.*

Penn, Henry. "Wrecking Home Insurance Building Reveals Excellence of Old Metals." *Engineering News-Record* 108 (Feb. 18, 1932): 247-248.

Sanderson, J. C.; Connell, J. L.; and Thielbar, F. J. "The Home Insurance Building." *Western Society of Engineers* 37 (no. 1, Feb. 1932): 1-2.

Sarton, R. H. "Selecting and Specifying an Appropriate Type of Steel Window." *Metalcraft* 6 (no. 1, Jan. 1931): 43-48, 64.

Sloan, Maurice M. "Specifications of Iron and Steel in Buildings." *American Architect and Building News* 68 (June 30, 1900): 101-103.

"Statue of Liberty, New York, The." *Scientific American Architects and Builders Edition* 2 (Nov. 1886): 101-103.

"Wrecking a Chicago Landmark." *Engineering News-Record* 124 (part 2, May 9, 1940): 648-651.

Stainless Steel

Books

Architectural and Domestic Uses of Stainless Steel, The. New York: Electro-Metallurigal Co., 1937.

Fabricators of Stainless Steel: What and Where Stainless Steel Shapes, Hardware and Equipment Are Available for Architectural and Domestic Applications. New York: Electro-Metallurgical Co., 1937.

Stainless Steel for Architectural Use. ASTM Special Technical Publication 454. Philadelphia: American Society for Testing and Materials, 1968.
Papers from Symposium on Stainless Steel for Architecture, San Francisco, 1968.

Van Alen, William. "Architectural Uses." In *The Book of Corrosion Resisting and Heat Resisting Chromium Alloys.* Cleveland, Ohio: The American Society of Steel Treating, 1933.

Periodicals

Cooper, H. A. "Cast Stainless Steel . . . For Architectural Ornamentation." *Metalcraft* 6 (no. 5, May 1931): 218-220.

"Fine Craftsmanship in Steel in the Foyer of the Chrysler Building: William Van Alen, Architect." *Metal Arts* 3 (no. 6, June 1930): 238-240, 266.

Gruen, Victor, FAIA. "Cities and Urban Growth." *Inco* 28 (no. 5, 1962): 35-40.

"Metal Everywhere Greets the Eye . . . Earl Carroll Theater, New York: The Metal Playhouse; George Keister, Architect." *Metalcraft* 7 (no. 4, Oct. 1931): 130-135, 161.

"Metal Work of the Empire State Building, New York City: Shreve, Lamb & Harmon, Archs." *Metal Arts* 3 (no. 7, July-Aug. 1930): 278-280, 308.

"Metal Being Used Effectively on Empire State Building to Secure Vertical Lines." *Metalcraft* 5 (no. 2, Aug. 1930): 94-96.

Murchison, Kenneth M. "The Chrysler Building: As I See It." *American Architect* 138 (Summer 1930): 24-33.

"Philadelphia Savings Fund Society Building, Philadelphia, Pa.; Howe and Lescaze, Archs." *Metalcraft* 9 (no. 1, July 1932): 10-11.

Van Alen, William. "Striking Uses of Metal Are Made in Chrysler Building." *Metalcraft* 4 (June 1930): 532-540.

_____. "The Structure and Metal Work of the Chrysler Building." *Architectural Forum* 53 (no. 4, Oct. 1930): 493-498.

Van Dyke, Dr. George. "The Architectural Use of Stainless Steel." *Metalcraft* 8 (no. 1, Jan. 1932): 11-16.

Whitmer, V. W. "Soldering the Stainless Steels." *Metalcraft* 8 (no. 4, Apr. 1932): 172-173.

Aluminum

Books

Alcoa Aluminum Extruded Shapes. Pittsburgh, Pa.: Aluminum Co. of America, 1933.

Aluminum Brazing Handbook. Edited by the American Welding Society. New York: Aluminum Association, 1971.

Aluminum Construction Manual. New York: Aluminum Association, 1959.

Aluminum in Architecture. Pittsburgh: Aluminum Co. of America, 1932.

Aluminum Paint: Thin Flat Flakes of Aluminum that Overlap like Falling Leaves. Pittsburgh, Pa.: Aluminum Co. of America, 1936.

Finishes for Aluminum. Pittsburgh, Pa.: Aluminum Co. of America, 1940.

Handbook of Aluminum. Quebec: Aluminum Co. of Canada, 1961.

Bibliography

Hobbs, Douglas Brown. *Aluminum, Its History, Metallurgy, and Uses.* Milwaukee: The Bruce Publishing Co., 1938.

_____. *Working with Aluminum.* Milwaukee: The Bruce Publishing Co., 1947.

Platt, William H. H. *Aluminum Repair.* London: C. Lockwood & Son, 1922.

Richards, Joseph William. *Aluminum: Its History, Occurrence, Properties, Metallurgy, and Applications.* Philadelphia: H. C. Baird & Co., 1890.

Riveting Alcoa Aluminum. Pittsburgh, Pa.: Aluminum Co. of America, 1948.

Sinclair, Ronald, Associates. *Forming Aluminum.* 5 vols. Sydney, Australia: Aluminum Development Council of Australia, 1971.

Structural Aluminum Design. Richmond, Va.: Reynolds Metals Co., 1960.

Welding and Brazing Alcoa Aluminum. Pittsburgh, Pa.: Aluminum Co. of America, 1947.

Periodicals

"Aluminum Gargoyles Proclaim the Unusual Character of Metal Appointments in Ohio Savings Bank and Trust Company Building, Toledo, Ohio; Halsy, McCormack and Helmer, Architects." *Metalcraft* 6 (no. 2, Feb. 1931): 84-89.

"Aluminum in Building: New Alcoa Administration Building at the Davenport Plant; Harrison and Abramovitz, Architects." *Architectural Forum* 90 (June 1949): 76-80.

"Aluminum-leaf Coating." *Architecture* 61 (Apr. 1930): 255.

"Aluminum Siding for Residential Construction Has Baked Paint Coat." *Architectural Forum* 92 (Mar. 1950): 210.

Bolton, James. "An All-Metal Office Building in Richmond." *Architectural Record* 71 (Feb. 1932): 121-122.

"Bucky Fuller Finds a Client; Young Henry Ford Translates the Geodesic Dome into Aluminum and Plastic." *Architectural Forum* 98 (May 1953): 108-111.

"Corrosion of Aluminum." *Scientific American Supplement* 71 (June 10, 1911): 362.

"Cracking of Aluminum Castings." *Scientific American Supplement* 64 (Nov. 23, 1907): 328.

Emerson, J. E. "Aluminum Air Ships of the Future." *Scientific American* 65 (Oct. 31, 1891): 277.

"Empire State; Chrome-Nickel Steel and Aluminum in the World's Tallest Building." *Metalcraft* 6 (no. 6, June 1931): 247-251, 269.

"Fine Craftsmanship in Steel in the Foyer of the Chrysler Building: William Van Alen, Architect." *Metal Arts* 3 (no. 6, June 1930): 238-240, 266.

"Finishes of Architectural Aluminum." *Metal Arts* 2 (Oct. 1929): 453-456, 486.

Hobbs, Douglas B. "Aluminum Details in the Cincinnati Union Terminal; Fellheimer and Wagner, Archs." *Architectural Record* 74 (Sept. 1933): 227-236.

Jenks, I. H. "Aluminumin Contact with Common Building Materials." *Royal Architects Institute of Canada Journal* 28 (Aug. 1951): 236-238.

"New Offices with Facade of Aluminum for Aluminum Company of America." *Architectural Record* 99 (June 1946): 16, 18.

"Setting of the Cap-Stone." *Harpers Weekly* 28 (no. 1461, Dec. 20, 1884): 839, 844-845.

"Specifications for Architectural Aluminum Work." *Metalcraft* 8 (no. 4, Apr. 1932): 168-170. Covers materials, temper, workmanship, design, finish and color, waterproof joints, provisions for caulking, expansion, cutting and fitting, bolts and anchors, glass and glazing, protection, painting.

Van Alen, William. "Metal in Modern Architecture." *Metal Arts* 2 (no. 4, May 1929): 183, 227.

"Washington's New Folger Library of Shakesperiana . . ." *Metalcraft* 8 (no. 5, May 1932): 194-195.